REFLECTED GLORY

1. Defunct telephone line
2. Overlooking hill (in the South)
3. Command wire to logpile
4. Logpile (concealed bomb)
5. OP position
6. Russian grenade
7. Improvised explosive device (sack)
8. Improvised explosive device (stones)

Operation Roulade

The single blade of grass that is straight, metallic, different.

Frontispiece by Steve Warwick-Fleming

Reflected Glory

by

Carney Lake

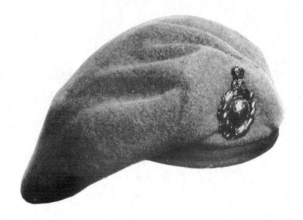

LONDON   NEW YORK   SYDNEY   TORONTO

This edition published 1994
By BCA by arrangement with
LEO COOPER
an imprint of
Pen & Sword Books Limited

Copyright © Carney Lake 1990, 1994.

CN 1972

Typeset by:
South West Typesetting, Sidmouth, Devon.

Printed in Great Britain by:
Redwood Books Ltd., Trowbridge, Wilts.

To the riflemen and recce-troopers, corporals, troop sergeants and officers of Her Majesty's Royal Marines Commandos, whose honourable profession I had the privilege to follow for six years, this book is dedicated with respect and affection.

Contents

Acknowledgements

With thanks to St. Anne's Music Ltd. for kind permission to quote words from:

'Rubber Bullets' (Creme, Godley, Gouldman)
recorded by 10cc
released by Phonogram Ltd.

Ⓟ 1973

And with special thanks to the Ministry of Defence, the Army Legal Corps and the Royal Air Force for their kind assistance and co-operation.

I am also grateful to Steve Warwick-Fleming who drew the frontispiece.

Author's Note

Security considerations alone compel this account to be a novel. In order to preserve their identity and the privacy to which they are entitled, the names of the characters have been changed. In all other respects, the book is based firmly upon fact. Indeed, to capture something of the events, the characters and their morale was the author's sole purpose.

Barrack-Room Language

Field-Marshal Lord Wavell once observed that the songs of the British soldier do not look well in print. This, of course, because they are liberally spiced with expletives.

Away from songs, servicemen swear in particular circumstances. In humour—sometimes; in anger—frequently; under stress—invariably. Most commonly favoured is the normal four-lettered epithet. This, together with its present participle and variations of region and rank, is therefore reproduced where its omission would be strictly inaccurate or otherwise unfaithful to the context.

Preface

At the end of three of the physically hardest weeks we remembered, we had earned the unshakeable satisfaction of knowing we had achieved exactly what we set out to do. We had summited five of the dominating peaks of the Swiss Bernese Oberland; the Tieralplistock, the Diechterhorn, the Jungfrau, the Mönch and the Eiger. We had done this in similar manner to much of our soldiering; with forethought and imagination and without casualties. Who could ever take this away from us now? Who indeed? It was a *very* tired troop who descended one last time to Lauterbrunnen, but the following night we celebrated hugely.

To ourselves, savouring the return to civilisation, we were serving servicemen who had recently spent hard days above the snow-line in successful endeavour. To the British residents who had crowned their life's work by retiring to Switzerland, we were ambassadors. We represented the youth and hope of the Old Country. We exuded vitality and purpose. We were, after all, extremely fit. Thus we found ourselves plied first with invitations, then with drinks and questions. Where were we from? Where had we been? What had we been doing before? Would we come back to Switzerland to climb again next year? And so on.

On the verandah of one memorable chalet, gazing down at picture-green pasture browsed by cows with gently clanking bells round their necks, I was somewhat bemused to hear a former desert campaign battery commander remark—more, I now believe, in sorrow than anger—"Not enough reflected glory from the Army these days." Bemused because, breathing deeply the pure air of personal achievement, I was aware of no such collective shortcoming at the time.

Strictly speaking, the Royal Marines are a part of the naval service and have been so since their inception in 1664. But my host had a point. The fight against terrorism had all but removed the Armed Forces from the public eye. In a bid to deprive the terrorist of the oxygen of publicity, we say nothing of ourselves and so stand to lose vital public support. There is a tale or two on our side of the fence that could yet be told with advantage.

Here is one. I hope the retired English gentleman on the Swiss verandah will get to read it. He certainly inspired it.

CL
The Grosvenor Hotel
London
26 10 90

Foreword

I am sure that everyone who reads this book will be impressed by the immense detail that the author has so painstakingly and devotedly acquired and so vividly arranged. It is not an academic study of military history, tactics or drill; but rather a brilliantly etched picture of life in the Royal Marines as seen through the eyes of the author and other men. All have undergone extraordinary physical discomforts in training to achieve the coveted Green Beret. All are widely different, real-life characters coming from a range of backgrounds. It is written with an engaging blend of humour, character insight and professional pride.

It is a book that will lead the reader to ask himself why these men endure and overcome the agonies and extremes of endurance. Why do these men, trained to the highest standard of martial proficiency, so willingly offer their lives to the requirements of their country? It is certainly not for the pay, nor to learn a trade for later civilian life, nor even for family security. It is, I believe, because they think differently from the masses and have accepted a challenge to their pride, to be much more than the normal run of men. Once fully fledged Bootnecks, they feel and fully appreciate the stimulus of an *esprit de corps* which exerts an ever stronger hold on their pride and stature as their experience is widened and their mettle further tested over the years.

I first met Royal Marine Commandos when I was a young guerrilla leader in the Arakan, Burma. Just after their heavily opposed landing at Myebon, I had a requirement to blow up a crucial Japanese installation and I asked, successfully, for a little extra muscle. I was lent a troop of Royal Marines under a mature, pipe-smoking, West Country Sergeant. During our successful foray, I was most impressed by the professionalism and 'oneness' of his troop. The well-oiled team-work and the imperturbable keenness of every individual was an eye-opener. I well remember the Sergeant's reply to my effusive thanks and praise—"That's alright Sir, you see we are Royal Marines!" I knew then that I had glimpsed the inner spirit of a unique Corps.

Since those wartime days, I have had inspiring dealings with the Corps in many parts of the world and always they were 'men apart'. In more recent years the whole nation has been full of pride and admiration at their magnificent achievements in the Falklands Campaign.

In this book we follow these men through the trials and pitfalls of training; through their first experience of the vicious IRA terror-tactics in Ulster; and through peace-keeping operations in Cyprus where courage, tenderness and compassion walk hand in hand. Finally in the 'trip-wire sewn countryside of South Armagh', the author is chillingly explicit in describing a section's night task of making safe a large rural area of mines and improvised explosive devices. One can feel the incredible tensions and almost smell the sour sweat of fear.

Read this book and take pride that Britain breeds such men. A Corps of this calibre, with the impetus of three and a quarter centuries' continuous service behind it, is neither to be neglected nor lightly cast aside.

John Salmon MC TD
Major, Royal Artillery, 'V' Force and 22 SAS Regiment.

CHAPTER 1

The Forge

Along the Kent coast clattered a train on its way from Charing Cross to Folkestone. It had just left Sandwich; next stop—Deal. On board a number of ordinary-looking young men began to stir, anticipating its slowing. Signal posts flipped past and an air of apprehensive expectancy pervaded the smoke-filled interior. Brakeblocks tugged at wheels, carriages jerked. Slowing, it screeched to a halt at the platform before disgorging its passengers. Southern Region doors slammed. Briefly the train rested. Then it rolled on, clicking and humming as it gathered speed in the gloom. Afternoon drizzle fell.

Only youth did they all have in common. Some of them carried a suitcase or a grip. Some wore a raincoat or a jerkin. The hair of some was long; of others it was cropped short in anticipation. Not one of them spoke, but several ran forwards over the footbridge and down the other side in apparent eagerness, surrendering their ticket as they passed through the station building. Outside waited a four-ton truck, dark green and black, gaunt and silent, its huge knobbly tyres somehow menacingly symbolic of their first real brush with the military, an encounter that, one way or another, they knew or sensed would change them for ever. Some sauntered casually towards it whilst others approached uneasily, viewing the yawning jaws of its canvas-topped rear with scepticism, even outright suspicion. One man carried a case on which were biroed the initials 'K.E.N.S.' Between the last two letters was the merest hint of an apostrophe. He walked the last hundred paces of civilian life unhurriedly and without care. He was in no rush to surrender his integrity, inviolability and perhaps even his sanity, even to the Royal Marines.

1

They were not yet a recruit squad; but within the hour they would be. Just another fortnightly squad, ages ranging between eighteen and twenty-eight, butchers, bakers and candle-stick makers. Some had never left home before, others had already crossed continents and travelled the world. Some were mere schoolboys setting out on their chosen careers, 'juniors' as young as sixteen, put with the more worldly recruits for administrative convenience. Others were turning their back upon a recognised job in industry or commerce or on a career in another Service. Some had had one job, others thirty-one. Of the most popularly conceived reason for enlisting—unemployment—there was not one, the shocks and stresses of military life holding out no appeal to those without a modicum of self-reliance. Neither was there sign of the Service being used as a bolt-hole by men with a criminal record, Recruiting Offices demanding unblemished character in exchange for the privilege of being killed or maimed in peacetime. Most were seeking something. Seeking to find out what was inside themselves, seeking to make a break for themselves, seeking to make something of themselves or seeking simply a bit of adventure, a chance to see a bit of life, a chance to escape from the crashing boredom of washing powder ads and bingo, Mum 'n' Dad and commuter trains and 'You haven't lived if you haven't watched Tranmere Rovers'; from a life where the only hope of escape from a dead-end job was the football pools or two weeks a year on the Costa; a life ratio of five days dead-from-the-neck-up to two of cheap shirts and booze, London Weekend and late-night sex with girls who swooned over pop stars followed by empty Sundays sleeping it off in the armchair before starting all over again on Monday. A life tailor-made for the simple blandishment of 'Some of the toughest training a man can face' to act as a lifeline to anyone thinking 'There's gotta be more to it all than this ...'

From cities and suburbia and the Outer Hebrides they came and queued to clamber aboard the four-tonner with consummate difficulty. In about two days they would be doing it with such ease they all might well have lived aboard a Bedford since birth.

YORK

Outside, a sign on the wall depicted an elegant black swan. Over the door was the licensee's name. In the saloon a waist-coated barman leant against the bar reading a newspaper, whilst above the fireplace a pendulum clock showed a few minutes past eleven. Just gone opening time. The doors were already open.

"Ken Smith?" said a large man entering. ('He's reet quick ont draw lad, so mek sure thar gits t'bugger first.')

The barman looked up... (A heavy. Fists like pistons...)

"'Oo wants ter know?" he said, his accent Cockney, his eyes instinctively appraising the other. (A slack, weak jaw.)

The newcomer drew back a punch that would have sent the barman through the wall. Barely had it started on its journey forward, however, when his own jaw was broken. He slumped between stools. The barman walked round the public side, raked four inches of cuban heel across his face and left him out the back, bleeding and unconscious. People wanted to fight all the time in Yorkshire. 'Such an uncivilised carry on, Sidney.' He picked up the paper, walked through and read it in the lounge bar. Presently someone came in. He served.

He was twenty-three, from Shoreditch, London, the eldest of five and he had two ambitions. To be a millionaire and to see the world. In pursuing these aims so far he had had more jobs than he was years of age; on docks and construction sites from Wapping and Whitechapel to Philadelphia USA he'd been a hod-carrier, unskilled labourer, chippy's mate, chain-man; in shirt-sleeves he'd worked the stalls of Petticoat Lane and for two years, wearing three piece whistle 'n' flute, he'd worked for a merchant bank in the City. He had managed a lousy pop group, sold ladies' underwear door to door, gone up north and managed a bar. Up here they took him for the flash Cockney he was and tried to put him down. Without success. He was tired of doing battle with life's peons though. Over financial deals, card games, women ... They wasted your energy. What a man like him needed was an edge, an aura, something to keep the riff-raff at bay ...

He stood on York station, awaiting a train to the capital. The suitcase by his side bore the biroed initials 'K.E.N.S.'. He had an idea.

★ ★ ★

SOMERSET

Their sweat mingled. She was velvet, pure velvet... Good, so bloody good! God Almighty! Luscious, fertile... like... like... (he groaned)... like... (she wrapped her legs around him, her hair damp

with exertion)... like the golden cornfields of Wessex swaying in the
breeze...

"Phil... oh Phil... PHIL! OH!" she squealed, clawing at his hair
and back, locking him between her thighs. Her milky breasts jerked
involuntarily up and down faster and faster... she felt his warmth,
his supple strength... Oh God... God! Cream... hot cream!
Delicious... exquisitely delicious, marvellously sensuous hot cream
on a warm summer's day... naughty, lascivious, wanton,
forbidden... but ohhh...!

She stroked his body, listening to the slowing of his heartbeat. He
cradled her head in the crook of his arm, roaming in her mouth with
his tongue, covering her face with kisses and with his free hand
feeling down there...

A lot of people reckoned West Country folk did nothing but make
love in haystacks when the sun shone. Those who did had obviously
never tried it, thought Phil Haythorne, delving behind him to pull a
sharp straw out of the crack of his backside...

Ever since the sprouting of hair and the first furtive gropings of
adolescence behind the cricket nets, they had been classmates and
lovers. Son of the saddler, daughter of the postmistress, their
entwined careers in classroom and on the playing fields seemed to
stretch ahead forever. He tall and athletic, she lithe and lissom,
together they were a fixture, permanent, a local institution...

"Phil," she said. "You are staying on in school next year to take
'A' level aren't you?" She took it for granted he was.

"What for?" **Another** year? That would make him eighteen when
he left. He shuddered... Eighteen and knowing nothing.

"Well, you are going to be a teacher aren't you? We can go to
teacher training college together..."

"No," he said slowly, "I got other plans."

"Like what?" she said crossly, sitting up and pulling stalks out of
her hair indignantly.

He worked on a farm instead. And when he was old enough for
adult entry he received an envelope. And the afternoon he walked
down the wet platform at Deal he knew his real life had begun.

LONDON

In Fleet Street there was traffic chaos. At the foot of a building
fronted by scaffolding stood the skip which was causing it. At
intervals, masonry and broken tiles shot down a chute into it.

Builders were renovating a roof.

A young man with the sort of pale skin that goes with red hair walked up to the skip and threw a folder of papers and some books into it. The papers revealed pages of computations and one of the books a name, 'N M Taverner.' Seconds later, with a thundering crash, they were buried. The young man raised an arm in salute to the builders.

"Neil! What on earth are you doing?"

He turned. It was the senior partner's buxom and inviting thirty-six year old secretary. She did things for his imagination. Like taking off her shoes at her desk which faced the door and crossing and uncrossing her legs. Frequently he found himself standing there talking to her with a full-blown ill-concealed erection practically staring her in the face. Rumour had it she was married to a jealous Army captain in MoD. Nevertheless Phyllis had more or less promised him that when he qualified ...

He was twenty-two. Behind him lay five mind-shrinking years manacled to a firm of actuaries. Years that had just been buried a second time by a fresh fall of slate and rotted timber.

"Your things ...!" she said, amazed and pointing to the skip.

"Don't need 'em any longer," he said. "I've quit."

"Quit?? Neil! You can't do that!"

"I just have," he said airily. "So long, Phyl ..."

He put an arm around her and gave her a long and longing kiss, feeling the luscious curves beneath her dress. In his mind he saw again her superb rounded thighs and tan stockings and he saw himself slowly rolling them down her legs in the privacy of a little hotel nearby which he had mentally earmarked as the place their affair should begin. Behind them, brick-ends and more masonry thundered down the chute. Pin-striped brief-case owners waved at the dust with copies of a pink newspaper.

Soon afterwards he waited on the Kent station of Whitstable. Not on the Charing Cross side, however. This time to catch a train going in the other direction.

Somewhere in the recesses of their minds, all of them nurtured the same daydream. To live rather than to exist, to do rather than to watch; to avoid the straitjacket, the endless hours of mindless talk, the squalid streets filled with faceless people, careers that were ruts. Each one saw himself slipping away to where the air was clean, to where there were trees and the smell of earth. In their mind's eye, there was always only a handful of them, four or five or six maybe. The trees swayed and shook droplets onto them and there was silence except for the minute sounds of woods around them. There was solitude and peace of mind and the eyes of the others were as clear as spring-water, not dogged and troubled and trammelled by everyday civilisation. There was always more, much more to their daydreams. Things they could only sense, not grasp. Because they had not yet experienced them. But each one knew that now was the time to do something if ever they were going to.

★   ★   ★

Short, bunchy and muscular and with the remains of a black eye, a Colour-Sergeant in Lovat uniform with gold-on-green badges of rank, sat behind a simple desk, a trestle table covered by a grey Ministry of Defence blanket. In front of him a nominal. He looked up. As though addressing morons, he began to speak.

"Right, we're gonna play the numbers game. I'm gonna give you **two** numbers; one's your **official** number; the other's your **bed** number. The reason we give you a **bed** number, is so that we don't get two men to a bed and fings like that. Right, who've we got 'ere? Adams?"

A man stepped forward and unthinkingly placed both hands on the desk.

"**Don't** lean on the *desk*!" rapped the Colour-Sergeant. The man withdrew his hands in a frenzy of desire not to offend.

He worked his way through the list, ticking off each name on the nominal. As each man stepped forward the Colour-Sergeant read out two numbers, once only. Some sweated with the strain of having to remember a number they would retain for the rest of their career, possibly their life. Others sweated with fear because in trying to remember their official number they had barely walked a dozen paces before they had forgotten their bed number.

"MacVicker ..."

"Yes, Colours."

The Colour-Sergeant read out two numbers to him; then looked at him twice.

"You got a father in the Corps, MacVicker?"

"Two, actually, Colours."

"We make the jokes, MacVicker. WO2?"

"Yes, Colours."

"You chewing gum, MacVicker?"

"Yes, Colours."

"Get rid of it, then. Mazzi ..."

"Yes."

"That's 'Yes Colour-Sergeant' Mazzi ..."

In the tiered rows of a lecture room they sat, digesting their first government meal. A few had broken the ice but most remained tense and withdrawn. An officer entered, resplendent in Lovat uniform, gleaming Sam Browne, brown leather gloves, Green Beret on his head and medal ribbons on his chest. Smith KEN nudged the man next to him and made a coolly appreciative gesture. He knew a real guv'nor when he saw one. Haythorne counted the pips on each shoulder, added them up, divided by two and concluded the officer was a Captain. On the morrow he would collect twenty press-ups for calling an officer's stars 'pips'.

Avid for new experience, later that night Taverner scribbled in the pages of a notebook: 'The Depot, Deal. After supper a Captain addressed us. Something like ... "You people are by no means in a position strange to myself. Twelve years ago I was sitting where you are now. Twelve years ago in fact, almost to the very day. However, in order to make sure that we get only those of you who are one hundred percent sure you want to become a Royal Marine, it is our practice to give you five minutes to yourselves whilst you think the proposition over. Anyone who is not absolutely one hundred percent sure, do not hesitate to leave the room; we will pay your fare home again, or give you a bed for the night if you live so far away that you cannot travel overnight. I will say this — it is better you leave us now, you can always apply to join us again later. Once you have joined us you cannot easily leave us."

'He leaves the room and all other military personnel go with him including the Colour-Sergeant whom we have noticed in particular because of his black eye. One bloke gets up and shuffles along the row and disappears through the door. I can see the Sergeant and Corporals all gathered outside the doors at the rear of the lecture room. The rest of us either want to become Royal Marines or are too embarrassed to run the gauntlet of eyes we would have to if we moved.

'Silence. We gaze at the flags and the Corps memorable dates behind the dais. The Captain comes back in:

'"Okay then. I take it that all of you still here have made up your mind once and for all now." He pauses, waiting for the murmur of assent which doesn't come.

'"In a few moments then you will all sign your Certificate of Attestation. Then you will be in. It is a hard and uncompromising life but one which I can assure you, you will find worthwhile and

rewarding. If you want promotion it's there for the taking. Keep
your eyes and ears open, take an interest in the world, start reading
newspapers — and I don't just mean the Daily Trash — and be alive to
what's going on. It only remains for me to tell you to work hard and
to wish you good luck. Work hard and good luck!"

'We then took the oath and signed. Doing this felt like signing up
for Siberia, and that, it may yet turn out, is exactly what we have
done. Some signed for three years, most of us for nine; but
whichever it was none of us have got a hope of getting out now.
We're well and truly in and that's that.

'After this sombre business, however, the Colour-Sergeant with
the black eye lifted us with a tremendous performance that was,
although brief, almost a parody of himself. He has a voice — the only
way I can describe it is to say that he must eat gravel for breakfast,
and this combined with a sort of London-military accent and a thick
vein of humorous sarcasm makes his delivery superb. I look forward
to him addressing us as often as possible. It is pure entertainment.

'He stood out front and what he said was, "TER-MORRER-"
(looking around to see if anybody wasn't absolutely riveted on him)
"You are all going to see ver BAR-BAH!" (He said the word 'barber'
with tremendous emphasis, and then he added as though to make
sure we all understood the significance of this pronouncement):
"Nah, 'e cuts 'AIAH ..." (The staggering simplicity of this
explanation nearly curled us up and even the man himself smiled
slightly.) "So TER-NOIGHT you will all wash your OWN 'aiah ..."
(Our *own*, nobody else's) "... 'cause we get coal miners and all 'ere,
and vey blunt 'is SCISS-ERS."

'We were then introduced collectively to the training team; a
Lieutenant, a Sergeant, and four Corporals. They looked a rather
formidable lot yet curiously they were quite relaxed and not at all
the shouting stamping bullying type of little Hitler one expects.
Perhaps they don't go in for all that in the Marines. Each one gave
us a short run down on himself; when he joined, what he's been
doing, where he's been, what his specialist qualifications are and so
on. These people make TV notions of toughness seem ludicrous.
They have an air of quiet confidence and quite unlike John Wayne
and co. they laugh but you can see from their eyes and
weatherbeaten skin they're in a different class to self-styled 'hardmen.'

'Later the team leader, the Sergeant, gave us a demonstration of
how to wash your socks and underwear through each night, and the
reasons for doing it, etc., etc. The Marines take nothing for granted
about your existing standards of hygiene whilst theirs is of a very

high order. I enjoy these demonstrations immensely; whoever is telling us something raises his voice and slows his speech down so the words come out distinctly, as though addressing a bunch of half-wits; which we are, of course, in their eyes.

'Some blokes were watching this sock-washing demo with rather non-plussed looks on their faces. I'm sure it's not the hardest thing we're going to have to master so God help them. Anyhow there was one—I noticed him on the train on the way down—who was watching and listening to all this very intently with a look of sheer enjoyment on his face as though he found it as entertaining as I do. Later I got talking to him. When I asked him his name he said, "Which one d'ya wanna know? I got four. Kenneth Eric Norman Smith. My ole lady had acute attack o' verbal diarrhoea the day she named me." He's got a very ready smile and seems to be taking to all this like a duck to water. Which is not surprising since he comes from the East End.

'It's ten-o-clock (No. 2200). The bloke in the next bed hasn't unwound at all. He spent half an hour fussing with his clothes on his chair and seems terrified because so far no-one has shouted at us. He told me in a prophet-of-doom voice that we ain't seen 'fuck-all' yet and it'll all start tomorrow morning and the cunning bastards propose to sort us out by getting us to relax then catching us off guard by coming in screaming and shouting at us in the middle of the night etc., etc. He had a mate who joined so he knows exactly what's in store and so on. I think it's his first time away from home. He's certainly very suspicious of everyone. But as a prophet of gloom he began to get on a lot of people's nerves so I told him to get into bed and shut up.

'Well, it's the first night of our new careers, feeling awkward and foolish in a strange world surrounded by strangers. In the years to come we'll look back and laugh at all this, even those of us who don't make it. I wonder how many of us here now are going to make it. I suppose everyone's thinking the same at the moment, looking at everyone else and...'

The lights went out. Taverner capped his pen. Smith lay on his pillow wondering. Haythorne snuggled down with a memory.

There was an unpleasant thud followed by a crash, then groaning.

"Uuuuurrrggh... uuuurrrggh...!"

In the dark, commotion. Voices kept asking what was happening. One voice close to panic kept saying over and over again, "Get the Sergeant! Get the Sergeant! For Chrissake get the Sergeant!"

The lights went back on and the Team Leader reappeared, look of bland impatience upon his face.

In between two racks of double-tiered beds, a man lay on the floor, groaning, blood pouring down his face. A mere signature away from still being civilians, some of the occupants of the surrounding beds looked pale and shocked, ready to faint or cry at the sight of it.

The man on the floor, sitting on someone else's bed when the lights went out, decided to jump from it to his own — both of them top ones — in the dark. In so doing he split his head open against a barrack-room girder supporting the ceiling, catching the edge of it in mid-flight clean across his forehead just above the nose. Swathed in first-field dressings, he was stretchered off to sick-bay.

The Sergeant thought the incident highly amusing and boded well for the future.

"I know you're keen, lads, but get your heads down tonight, right? We'll teach you all that commando stuff in the morning."

★   ★   ★

At the end of the squad's first full day, Haythorne wrote a postcard home saying that they had run everywhere they went, drawing clothing and boots and kit and having haircuts and being photographed and getting their dog-tags stamped and tonight they all agreed it seemed like six months since joining. Smith 'phoned the Queen of Shoreditch, his mother, saying more or less the same thing and adding that he was okay and there was no need for her to come down and rescue him. His mother had been bitterly opposed to the idea of her boy joining 'that rough lot.'

Taverner wrote, 'The Drill Sergeant, the one they call 'Timber', is a character, (but I don't suppose there is such a thing as a drill instructor who isn't.) When handing back our freshly stamped dog-tags, which we all promptly put on in order to feel more soldier-like, he explained how to knot the string so the discs — bearing our name, rank, number, religion and blood group — hang separately. As people slipped them over their heads there was a certain amount of heroic posturing. Timber immediately squashed this feeling with the brutal announcement, "You are now Government Property. Which means you're expendable."

'He paused whilst the impact of this went right home. Then he continued. "The great, good and honourable British Government will clothe you, feed you and pay you for the rest of your time in the Service, just so it can have the right to terminate your life any time it chooses, if it thinks it's in the nation's interest to do so. So start getting used to the idea. It's part and parcel of being a professional soldier. We in the Royal Marines, however, place a different value on your lives. Dead, you can't do your job, so we train you to stay *alive*, wherever you are, whatever you're doing. Nevertheless, just remember what I said. You're Government Property, you're owned. So if you *do* die ... wherever and whenever it is that you finally keel over ... if that's *you*, croaked, (grinning maliciously) finito, endex, gone to the big parade ground in the sky, get your oppo to cut off the red one ... (yanking the dog-tags round someone's neck) and bring it *back*. Somebody wants to account for you. Leave the green one where it is so the burial party know who they're burying ... they might not be able to recognise your face when they chuck the soil in on ya." Then, looking at the shocked faces, he said, "There isn't a war on at the moment so don't worry about it."

'Someone immediately said, "Sar'nt, I read a newspaper report about a bunch of Paras buying themselves out the Army 'cos they didn't want to serve in Ulster again." Timber simply looked at him and said, "That's the Paras. This is the Marines."'

Day two.

"Touchyatoes! STANNUP! Siddown! STANNUP! Touchyatoes! STANNUP! Roun'attree'nbackagain — GOpe!"

"Runnin' roun' me inacircle — GOpe!"

"Jummonthebacko'themaninfronto'ya — GOpe!"

"Round'attree'nbackagain — GOpe!"

"And Steady! Half circle in front o' me — GOpe!"

Inhumanly compelling and effortlessly delivered, the commands came from a small, dark-skinned, dapper figure with an air of demonic energy, a solid knot of gristle upon which people choke in their stew. Muscles of stark definition burst from every conceivable quarter. His clothes, pressed into finger-cutting creases by a team of experts and worn as a python would its skin, bulged with the contours of his anatomy. On his feet were laced sparkling white gym shoes. The calves of a sprinter, thighs of a weight-lifter and trunk of a swimmer reposed beneath knife-edge navy blue gymnast's trousers. Out of a white PT vest thrust the sculptured torso of a body-builder. Through its truncated, red-trimmed neck and sleeves there poked plates of pectoral, dishes of deltoid, biceps, triceps and forearms like the well-greased piston rods of a steam locomotive about to haul a record-breaking express. Either side of his head

between neck and collar bone protruded a bunch of such developed
trapezius that he appeared to be wearing a pair of rolled socks on
each shoulder underneath his singlet. Midway between lip and nose
was a moustache the thickness of a razor blade. Loose negroid curls
adorned his head, cut short and brushed back in the manner of a
Teddy boy. The eyes were intense, the face impassive, the
demeanour intolerant, the stance arrogant. On one bicep, barely
visible against his dusky skin, was a tattoo, a kukri cut by three
scrolls bearing the words 'Borneo', 'Sarawak' and 'Sabah' and below
which was the date, 1964. In the centre of his chest, in red worked
on white, was his badge of office, the crossed Indian clubs and stars
of the Physical Training Wing.

He surveyed the squad, eyes resting fleetingly and critically upon
their heaving chests, noting the flab, the scrawn, the shapeless
brawn, the blotchy skin mottled pink and red after but a few
minutes' exertion. Attired in sports shirt, white shorts, gym shoes
and socks-navy-long, the squad stood still. Suddenly, without the
frippery of civilian clothes, the men underneath seemed painfully,
pitifully, fraudulently exposed.

Mercilessly the dark eyes roamed over them, expressionless, yet
registering minute approval, amusement, contempt... taking in
emergent muscles, the odd deep chest, the occasional burgeoning
pair of shoulders, the big, the small, the long, the short and the tall.
Finally, in an accent that originated somewhere between Bermuda
and South America, he began to speak; in terse, pithy, laconic
phrases, spitting out words like a mopping-up operation, in bursts of
three to five rounds, punctuated by the occasional single shot,
looking constantly about him, addressing every man, his eyes
riveting, his voice urgent, his unusual emphasis fascinating, his
clipped speech spellbinding.

"Awright. First off. I wanna have. A few words *wid* you. Come
closer. All of *you*...

"Okay. Dat's *bettah*. Good. Stand there. Leave yourself a-lone.
Listen in. Don't fidget. Pay 'tention *to me* . Can you hear me on the
left? Can you hear me on the right? Okay.

"Right. The honeymoon is over, gents. Now we gonna start. First.
A liddle warm-up. Get the blood flowin'. Start you thinkin'. Not too
early is it? *Is it*? Oh dear. Oh deary me. Well. There's more to come.
Don't fidget. I oughta introduce myself. My name's. Corporal
Ricardo. I'm your Squad. Physical Treaynin'. Instructor. I'm from
Guiana. By the way. 'Case you wondered. I'm a *Wog*. A liddle
Spanish. But mainly *Wog*. I came six thousand miles. To make you
white men *sweat*. And that's exactly what I gonna do. I gotta few

weeks. To get you fit. To go to Lymp-stone. To start commando treaynin'. Someuvyou will be goin'. Others won't. It's up to *you*. Lemme say dis now. It's gonna be hard. I gonna make you cry. I gonna make you nearly *die*. I gonna break your liddle heart in *two*. It's menna be hard. Those of you who can't take it. Ain't gonna make it. You gonna go right back where you came. And you know what de basic lesson of life *is*? *Never* go back where you *came*. Remember that. Go forward. Be positive. Hit hard. Never go back.

"It's all in the mind, men. You gonna love *me*. You gonna *hate* me. Sometimes you're gonna want to kill me! (I don't mind.) But work *with* me. Never against *me*. And always remember. When you goin' through it. When you get to the King's Squad. There ain't no-one in the world better than *you*. And the day you go down the Quartermaster's Store. And trade your noddy hat. For the Green Beret. You're gonna *know* it. And *then*. It'll be worth it. And you'll buy me a *beer*. WHATCHA GONNA DO?"

"BUY YOU A BEER, CORPORAL!"

"Fuckin' right you will. YOU ALL GONNA MAKE IT?"

"YES, CORPORAL!"

"EV'RY ONE O' YOU?"

"YES, CORPORAL!"

"WHO'S GONNA BE THE BEST SQUAD EVER?"

"WE ARE, CORPORAL!"

"Good. That's what I wanna hear. A bit o' *spirit*. By the way. There's a dance in the Naafi. On Saturday. You all seen the posters? Well, forget it. You won't be goin'. You'll be too tired. Why? 'Cos I got you. Saturday mornin'. An' de girls. Don't want a kid. Who's half a-sleep.

"Someuvyou played sports in civvy street. All the better. For those that did. But basically. You did nothing. You neglected your body. That's why you joined. 'Cos you wanna be strong. And fit. And use the *gift*. That God *gave* you. Your body. And your brain. Mens sana. In corpore sano. You know what that means? A healthy mind. Is in a healthy body.

"We give you a basic. Physical fitness test. Then we start you. On Swedish PT. Teach you posture. Co-ordination. Et cetera. Take you on runs. And speed-marches. There's a lot of them. We take you in the gym. For vaulting. Rope-climbing. And so on. And down the pool. Teach you to swim. You must be able to swim in full battle *kit*. Before you leave here. It's a commando *skill*. You! STANNUP STREAIGHT! YOU DISGUSTIN' CREATURE …

"That's what I mean. Posture! Stand up *streaight*. The natural way. CHEST OUT. GUT IN. Before you leave here. You'll learn to take

charge of your body. So you don't walk a-round. Wid your gut
hangin' over your *belt*. And your arse *fallin'* out your trousers. Like
some disgustin' civvy.

"You can't quit. But we can get rid of *you*. Just dig out. Never put
less than your best. Into anything. That's all you gotta do. We're not
joinin' you. You're joinin' us. Remember that. If you get to Lymp-
stone. You gotta week. To buy your ticket. We only want those who
wanna stay. And those that do. You might. Just. Make it. Do I
sound hopeful? I hope I do. All you gotta do is work. WORK! This
ain't civvy street! This is the ROYAL MARINES! HERE—YOU WORK!
TOUCHTHEGYMWALLAN'BACKAGAINTOME—GOpe! C'MON! C'MON!
LET'S GO-GO-GO-GO-GO! C'MON YOU FUGGIN' TURKEY—MY TWO
YEAR OLD DAUGHTER CAN RUN FASTER THAN THAT! EV'RYBODY
NOW—CRAWL! GET ON YOUR BELLY AND CRAWL! **CRAWL**, YOU
GUTLESS CREEPS! IF YOUR GIRLFRIEND PISSED ALL OVER YOU NOW,
YOU COULDN'T DO A THING ABOUT IT, COULD YOU?? **C R A W L** ...!!!
YOU FUGGIN' CROTONS...!!"

Faces in the dirt, they didn't notice the expression on his face.

"The beret," said Timber, "is worn like this. Badge over the left
eye, and pulled down to the right, beret-band parallel to the deck.
You wear the blue beret on parade until you've earned the green
one—those of you who get that far. And in the field, you wear the
cap-comforter, or noddy hat. 'Noddy hat' because that's what you
are. Noddies.

"These here are ear-defenders. You wear 'em on the range. They
go inside your ears and they come in three sizes—large, medium and
small. If you've got big ears, don't choose small ones. 'Cos if it
disappears down your lug'ole, you have to go to sick-bay. And if they
can't get it out with tweezers, they'll send you back to me, and I'll
dig it out with a bayonet.

"Now I don't care what they do in the Yank army or the Chogi
navy or the Gyppo air force or anything else, for that matter; but in
the Royal Marines you address a sergeant as 'Sergeant', or possibly
'Sar'nt'. Just as you address a corporal as 'Corporal', not 'Corp.'
Anybody calling me 'Sarge' gets the sharp end of my pacestick up his
nostrils.

"Before you go on the range you'll see a film about range conduct.
Now some of these films are made by out-of-work actors; like,
between Oscars, they make training films for the Army. Never mind

their ponciness—just pay attention to what's said. But be prepared for some differences when you get onto the range—the most obvious one of which is that we don't have their bedside manner.

"One other thing. You don't wear a white T-shirt underneath your shirt. Why? Because it makes a bloody great white aiming mark right in the centre of the chest, that's why. Half the Yanks who came back in a box from Vietnam were wearing white T-shirts."

('Dear Mrs. Schicklegruber,

Your Johnny got his when a gook spotted his nice white T-shirt and put one through him from five hundred metres. It hurt like hell.

Johnny was a fine kid, Mrs. Schicklegruber, but I want you to know that the US will not be intimidated in this way by a lousy bunch of no good slant-eyes. The white T-shirt is therefore still on issue. The Chairman of the Uniforms Committee, a close friend who also happens to be president of the company that makes them, has re-assured me on this point personally.

Sincerely,

Harvey Headbanger, US General.')

"Any questions?" said Timber.

"I think I've hurt my leg, Sergeant, in that PT..."

"Excuse me," interrupted Timber, "Is that a question? Is it? I asked for any questions and you tell me you've hurt your leg. Is that a question? Is it? No it isn't, is it, it's a statement, isn't it? You've hurt your leg—that is not a question, that is a statement, isn't it?"

"Yes, Sergeant."

"You've hurt your leg. Well, I'm sorry. Deeply, truly, terribly sorry. Which leg is it? The left? Are you sure? Alright. I'll tell you what I'll do. Go down the Quartermaster's Store, knock on the door, tell him I sent you and ask him to change it one-for-one. Okay? Any—questions?"

"Yeah, when do we get to go on the range, Sarge?"

"Sarge? Sarge?? You dozy siphilitic pee-brained pinhead, what did I just say? Come out here, you ..."

★   ★   ★

LYMPSTONE

Up the bleak Exe estuary a Siberian wind whistles, turning men's faces raw and rippling the waters of a raised brick pond-like structure. Round its edges there clings a veneer of ice. Men stand in line, hugging themselves against the piercing wintriness. On a rope stretched high over the pond a man crawls, pulling himself from one side to the other. In the centre he stops and swings down, holding on only by his hands. The rope bounces with his weight. He cocks a leg back over it, straightens an arm, beats with the other leg and succeeds in regaining the topside of the rope. Quickly he crawls to the other side, jumps down dry and makes off to the relative sanctity of the leeward side of a hut.

A second man pulls himself out over the water. He too swings down. Unlike the first he cannot regain the topside. His grunting spasms of endeavour betray rising panic. Hanging listlessly, he eyes the water and desperately tries again. His efforts grow weaker ...

"Off", says a physical training instructor with the face and expression of an executioner.

The man lets go and falls. Gasping with shock, he surfaces and swims for the side, hauling himself out and taking his place at the back of the queue. There are between twenty and thirty in front of him. He shivers. Soon he is crying with cold. The wind whistles up the Exe estuary. It is a grey afternoon.

In the dark warmth of a classroom an instructional film plays upon a screen. Nodding heads are frantically jerked into attentiveness. One man's droops too far ...

A rigid hand scythes down onto his shoulder. His own flies to his shoulder in pain and anguish.

"Stay awake, son, or I'll massage the other one for ya ..." says a voice, gentle but oozing malice.

Up hill and down dale the squad scramble; through gorse and stony winding underground tunnels from which all light is excluded they crawl; chest-deep in marsh they wade; through blind water-filled tunnels they float; up ropes and along aerial networks of wires and ladders they climb. Round country tracks and lanes they run. In silence, except for the chomp-chomp-chomp-chomp of rubber-soled boots and the monotonous incantations of an NCO:

"Close up in the rear! Open your legs in front!"

For mile after mile they watch the spreading stain of sweat on the man in front. They stare at the web straps of his fighting order, alternately slacking and tautening with each stride; at the mesmeric lifting and pounding of his boots and at the gravel of the road below. Compassion is eradicated in the desire to succeed; a mother falling would be trampled underfoot by her sons. Each body-chafing, foot-pounding, lung-busting run ends in the excruciation of the infamous Heartbreak Lane where, with mocking encouragement, a sign on a tree reads '500 metres to go. It's only PAIN ...'

"STAND STILL!"

Heaving and gasping they halt, passionately ignoring the desire to collapse. Motionless and erect, vision blurred by stinging sweat, they listen for the verdict;

"Good. Fifteen seconds to spare."

It is the only reward they seek. When they have learned to run without stopping for thirty miles in full battle kit they can consider the beret somewhere within reach.

Living with an intensity utterly foreign to their old lives, they find themselves doing in a day what previously they never would have considered doing in a month. Of events that carry such momentous personal significance many harbour a desire to record something. But beyond the writing up of lecture notes and the scribbling of a few lines home, few put pen to paper. There is always something else to be done first. It is a camp not a campus. No leisurely academic year or two is allocated for the writing and presentation of a thesis. No pens are capped and feet put up for lack of inspiration. A rifle barrel must shine, a gas-plug gleam and toe-caps glitter by twenty-minutes-past-seven in the morning. PT kit must be starched a spotless white and be pressed and dry for the period after that. And knowledge assimilated from small spiral-bound notebooks sold in the Naafi for the period after that.

'The 84mm Carl Gustav is a shoulder-controlled spring-and-percussion operated anti-tank weapon weighing 36lb and firing ...'

'The difference between hypothermia and hyperthermia is ...'

'In treating abdominal wounds NEVER attempt to put back into the body any protruding internal organs. Lie the patient on his back, draw up his knees ...'

They learn to respond to pressure. Huge meals are bolted in minutes flat so as to snatch an extra five minutes with duster and Brasso, four-by-two and pull-through, notebook and aide-memoire.

'A contour is an imaginary line joining all points of equal ...'

'Things are seen because of their ...'

'Aids to judging distance are ...'

Each day, each man reaches down inside himself for a little more. Fatigue versus failure; motivation versus the desire to quit; the **guts** to go on versus the ever-lurking question 'What the shit am I doing this for?' Battle fitness, Tarzan course, Judo battles in the Commandokwai. Tests, timings, trials. And when motivation wears thin, they learn to cope with the practical consequences of failure ...

Bearing a suspicion of rust near the foresight, Mazzi's rifle is described as a "lousy shitty corroding mass of fucking mangled scrap-iron." For this heinous crime, he is awarded two extra parades in the evening at a time when the rest of the squad is 'free' to wash, scrub, press, oil and polish in preparation for the next day. With dwindling reserves of daily energy, that alone normally takes him to near midnight. At not yet seventeen, the youngest member of an adult squad and the most in need of precious sleep, tonight it will take him into the small hours. And tomorrow begins at 0600 just the same.

Haythorne sits on his bed and slits open a letter from home. As he reads of things he had long forgotten a lump enters his throat, prompted by the homely normality of everything his parents write. The words begin to blur. Tears of nostalgia and self-pity prick the back of his eyes. They know nothing of all *this*. Turning his head away in search of privacy, he vows they never will.

Like a sad dog the stocky Koupparis sits on his bed opposite and looks away in silent sympathy. There is nothing he can do so he merely continues bulling a boot. His nose, blood-clotted and blocked, gruels him constantly. It was broken during a bout in the ring. Haythorne was his opponent.

In a lavatory cubicle a door bangs. Inside, Smith D. — Dave Smith — turns and kneels down in front of the pedestal. He lifts the seat, sprinkles cleansing powder around the bowl and starts to scrub. Some do the room, others the hand-basins and showers. There are rounds in the morning. The company commander's.

In another room Gilbrook watches Taverner gingerly peel off his socks and sitting on the end of his bed, bathe open and suppurating sores on the tops of his toes with cotton wool and iodine. It is a nightly ritual. All of them have sores on their feet which constant usage and wet boots prevent healing. As he tips iodine from the bottle and wipes the pad of cotton wool over his toes, Gilbrook watches his pale, haggard face remain impassive whilst his eyes go from simple agony through Christ-on-the-cross to those of a man being branded with a hot iron.

By shaving last thing at night, Gilbrook himself thought he had found a way to save time and nausea in the crowded heads each morning. One night he forgot. Tired out, he threw his kit into his locker and got his head down. Now he shaves in the river each morning, a nauseous and time-consuming process, particularly if the tide is out.

The component parts of Smith KEN's rifle lie on his coverlet. His hands are swollen, painful, thorn-ridden, cracked and festering from gorse, earth, rifle oil and wet. That is not all that is troubling him. His face bears a hunted expression. In unguarded moments he has seen the same look on the faces of others. Some are openly talking about taking the soft option back to Civvy Street. Why not? Why not him too? What stupid misplaced foolish pride could possibly prevent him? Where did all this... *lunacy* fit in with his old dreams?

He sniffs and wearily pulling on a pair of housewife's washing-up gloves, picks up the gas-plug of the rifle and begins to clean it, spitting on the little knob of metal, working a match-head over and over its surfaces, grinding the hardened black gas fouling into a paste and wiping it off with four-by-two; repeating the process again and again, using more matches and spit and four-by-two, until finally it starts to gleam. A vestige of fouling on the centre channel means press-ups in puddles, it means crawling through gorse during a smoke break, it means...

Glancing up as he works he stares at a picture of an old flame on his locker door. A dolly bird, leaning on the bonnet of a sports car. He lets out a sigh between his teeth. It might have been taken on the far side of the moon for all the relevance it has to this crap.

Dog-tired from two hours of extra drilling, Mazzi drags himself up the stairwell, opens the door and flops onto his bed which is surrounded by a mountain of kit awaiting his attention. After a while he leans up on an elbow and watches Smith assemble his rifle with a final metallic 'co-cock-click-snap' as he eases its spring and applies the safety catch.

"What's it all about, Ken?" asks Mazzi, desperately seeking motivation.

"Search me, mate," says Smith blankly. He rises prior to going to help his namesake fish dog-ends out of the urinals.

"I s'pose," he sighs, "If you don't beat it, it'll beat you, that's all."

The days pass into weeks and the weeks into months. Their memory of them becomes a blur of being never less than hammered, of being hounded from dawn to dusk and far into the night. They remember only the gruesome discipline of standing to attention for hours at a time on an icy windswept parade ground whilst an inspection takes place; of taking lessons in map reading and navigation sitting on frozen soil; of pulling on wet clothes in the morning; of removing cloying black camouflage cream with the aid of a mess-tin of soap and water and an o.g. towel; of shaving faces, red and swollen from windburn, with excruciating bristle-tugging skin-ripping strokes, then re-applying the pore-clogging cream, all the time exposed to a knifing Dartmoor wind...

Sleeplessness, blisters, sore-skin, raw wind. The training team lean on them to see if they are up to it. Those whose morale the regime destroys say goodbye to the Royal Marines and to their hopes of becoming one of them. From those who cannot eradicate ingrained sloppiness, who cannot make the adjustment from welfare state-bred habits to the harsh functional reality and realism of the military, the team get their answers. Of the 61 who arrive from Deal, four are back-trooped through sickness or injury. At the end of a week in which it is open to the remainder to 'opt-out', 31 choose to return to civilian life. Some the training team encourage to buy their ticket, others leave despite exhortations to stay. The remaining 26 amalgamate with the squad ahead, down to 14 after its opt-out week. The squad's prophet of doom is among the 31 who go; no-one is sorry to see the back of him. But one of the 26 who remain is the recruit who at Deal, nearly wrote himself off after only six hours in the Corps, a record. In the years to come, he will go on to create other records, with skis and rifle in the biathlon.

They change and know that they are changing. And are interested to make some observation or record of the changes. Their humour changes with them. They see themselves as blackguards, culprits, anti-heroes, the butt of everything. They learn what they had long suspected; that power is the idol of those who don't have it and the aphrodisiac of those who do. The simple action of having put themselves at the disposal of other men is always good for a laugh. Jokes told against the teller, with the moral of 'sucker', are always the most hilarious. All gentleness, compassion, mystery, virtue and innocence disappear from their vocabulary, possibly for ever. Their humour becomes black, blatant, blunt, brutal, chauvinist, cynical, reaching the height of spontaneity, plumbing the depths of anarchy, always sexual, often racial, frequently morbid, never mawkish, sick but not sham, self-reliant never self-righteous, catalytic, cathartic, chaotic.

They learn the pricelessness of a life that has death as its natural, logical, simple and inescapable conclusion; and as often as not, its only reward. Cheerfully, they regard it as a joke with a sick punch-line that can be brutally and unexpectedly delivered at any time, the imminence of which merely accentuates the joke. Merciless in their mickey-taking of others, at themselves they laugh openly, grimly, uproariously. That the honest lives of practical men should be at risk whilst altruists, egotists, bigots, racists, intelligensia, self-seekers and tearers-down of democracy sleep warm and safe in bed at night, that they should sweat and shiver and suffer whilst their elected representatives and their Oxbridge educated sidekicks quietly go about selling the country's secrets in pursuit of privately-held ideals, is to them enormously, hilariously, excruciatingly funny. That they stand to be spent on the idealism and causes of such people, or for no cause at all, is the one premise, the one huge joke, against which all other humour pales.

Publicly, in places such as Exmouth railway station, and privately in notebooks and files—but never as graffiti on spotless toilets and lockers—the soldier-poets record their lyric sentiments for posterity:

> *'Join the Navy and see the world; join the Marines and yomp the fucker.'*

> *'Death to Corporal Ricardo; the bastard's made me die enough times.'*

> *'There's a camp dance in the Naafi but I'm too shagged out to go;*
> *But Bert and Al and Taffy are ashore with Mick in tow;*
> *Think I'll get me 'ead dahn—s'nice and quiet in bed;*
> *Might increase the chances of getting the Green Hat on me head.'*

> *'I loved her more than life itself.*
> *In return she gave me VD;*
> *I didn't know she'd been with someone else;*
> *So now I'm off PT.'*

To which had been added, *"Dream on, boys."*

Mazzi, during this time, made a note of himself; 'I have changed my ways completely. My swearing has got completely out of hand, and when I go to dances, I am drinking a lot more. I have progressed from my half-a-pint of shandy, and can now take five pints of lager and lime without any trouble. However, it begins to get a bit expensive, especially when I go with the lads. I am glad I got out of that rut I was in in school. I have learned a lot being in a squad with Ken and Neil and Phil. I think I proffed being put in an adult squad.'

Haythorne had the makings of a damn good Marine, ripe for the King's Badge for best all-round recruit. But about the time of opt-out week, he hit a bad patch. With a blue fountain pen, he confided the inner struggle to the pages of an indexed notebook:

> *'Why do they have to keep telling me, "You must, you must, you must." One day I'll turn around and say "No." They'll*

say, "You must learn to obey." I must, I must, I must.
'Written under great pressure in Room 24, B Block
by someone who should never have passed his 'O'
levels.   Phil Haythorne.'

Gradually the crisis subsided as he began to see he wasn't being
told to do things just for the hell of it.

Smith wrote: 'Time was when a word was soft and meaningful.
Not spilling spite and aggro and demanding instant obedience like
these bastards. And once upon a time, as I remember it, telegraph
poles stood upright and didn't have to be lugged everywhere. And
someone else fished dogends out the karzi. The world changed. Or
mine did. And not for the better neither. The wind is harry taters
each morning and the sky is sodden with rain and fog off that
stinking river. But like the lunatics we are we pretend it's still
summer and parade in PT shorts. Then go running in the river.
Fucks me, I'm gonna crack. I can't take much more of this
madness.'

On the last day of opt-out week, Smith decided to buy his ticket,
but Taverner heard and talked him out of it. For days afterwards,
Smith harboured a grudge against Taverner.

Steadily, through the phenomenon of shared hardship and
experience, their loyalty grows exclusively to themselves and to each
other and to that larger extension of themselves, the Corps,
diminishing and replacing old loyalties. For those who are left, a
significant psychological hurdle has been reached and surmounted
with the closing of 'opt-out.' Coming together for the first time, the
new squad takes a deep breath, straightens its back and sets its eye
on the distant end.

★ ★ ★

DARTMOOR

Tired legs, aching shoulders and smarting faces take them across
the moor, criss-crossing it day and night with the aid of map and
compass. Orientate the map, calculate the magnetic variation, take
three bearings, find the back bearings, mag to grid rid, make a
resection and find your position on a drab, featureless landscape
where the weather is always provided by Lympstone. Advance to
contact, day recce, night compass march, live firing, digging in,
cam and concealment, tactical withdrawal, section attacks ... In all
weathers and at all hours they yomp the moor, seeking the next grid
reference, the next position, the next set of orders; a deserted
farmhouse, a track-stream junction, a helicopter rendezvous, a

checkpoint that is no more than the antenna of an instructor's radio set poking up from behind some rocks.

Lying hour after hour in ambush position at night, the eyes of a weary recruit begin to droop ... and shut, though the ground is too cold and wet to entertain thoughts of sleep. Soundlessly, with the guile of a poacher, an instructor approaches. For a second he watches ... then buries the toe of his boot in the man's backside. In shock and pain the recruit whips round ... and sees a finger wordlessly pointed at him in silent accusation. Guiltily, he turns back to his front and contemplates propping his chin up on the point of his bayonet sooner than be caught asleep again.

Dawn pales into grey snow-laden skies. A bitter wind sweeps the tors. Clusters of rocks and boulders poke up grimly. Cloud smudges everything. Heather twitches.

Lashed by squalls of sleet that cannot decide whether to be snow or rain, men tumble out of the rocks, stripping their sodden clothes to the waist. In a ragged line they stand shoulder to shoulder along a sheep track, huddled together, each trying to hide behind the other for warmth, nipples like matchsticks, ribs like washboards, skin goosepimpled and blue-going-red. Early morning PT.

Squelching through sodden elephant grass in boots and denims, a bare-chested Ricardo strides towards them, gleefully rubbing his hands together, relishing their perished countenances.

"MORNIN' MEN ...!"

Smith eyes him.

"You're a country boy, Corporal, d'ya like all this stuff?" he enquires, indicating their desolate surroundings.

"Shuddup Smith. TEN-SHON! Widda jump—LEFT TURNAH!"

"Just think," says the Cockney as they double off up and down the track, "but for a lucky accident, London could'a bin built 'ere...".

The car of Juggernaut rolled onwards, gathering momentum. Now there was no height they could not scale, no distance they could not run, no demand to which they were not equal. By dint of competition, rivalry, inspiration, example and instinct they spurred themselves and each other on. Only strength, effort and emergent skill had any place in their lives. They discovered new depths to themselves and a new respect shone in their eyes for themselves and each other. They learned the priceless value of willpower in overcoming their limitations and they saw how their abilities were extended far beyond their former selves, through portals marked Endurance, where Sleep was spurned and Fatigue repelled, into a new and vital territory called Achievement. Individually they were

automata, machines, tightly coiled springs incapable of any thought
or action not directed solely and exclusively to one end. The
attainment of the Green Beret, the symbol of their warrior
manhood, the supreme accolade upon their coming of age, the
ultimate acknowledgement of their worth.

The thing moved from the comparative to the superlative. It was
not enough to be better. They had to be the best, the fastest, the
hardest, the most skilled, the highest scorer. Hardness they
discovered was no mere matter of size or fists. It was an attitude of
mind, the quality inside a man that drove him on, that permitted
him never to give up, that 'forced his heart and nerve and sinew to
serve his purpose long after they were gone.' It meant little Douglas
was as hard as big Hill. It enabled Koupparis, who was short, to
crowd tall Haythorne in the ring and hound him to a draw, despite
his lack of height and reach which brought him a broken nose from
Haythorne's long left. It enabled them collectively to shrug off
dislocation of expectation, finding they had to go on when they were
expecting to go in, or go back or do it all over again when they
thought they had finished. It was what kept them coming back for
more and making light of it. It forged a common bond of respect
and affection that enabled them to stand shoulder to shoulder
against all-comers, an attribute upon which they would draw
heavily in the times ahead. The 'thing' was in their minds, an ovary
fertilised by training, whose purpose was sometimes far from
apparent, especially to those going through it. But it worked, the
embryo grew and it produced the goods.

In the words of the Team Leader, "What this thing is all about is
standards, and their attainment." In the words of their officer,
"What the Royal Marines is all about is the Marine." And in the
words of Smith... "Well fuggin' whoopee! Can I have some sleep,
please?"

The pace quickened as the squad, with the bit between their
teeth, sensed the end was in sight.

★   ★   ★

A captain, the Personnel Selection Officer, addressed them, a
biro and the squad nominal lying on the table before him. His job,
the disposal of fully-fledged Marines about the Corps.

"The very first thing I have to say to this squad is that I need half
of you to go to 40 Commando in Northern Ireland. They need a few
more bods.

"Now, are there any volunteers?" asked the Captain without
much hope.

There was a conspicuous silence. Then slowly and very self-consciously, half the squad raised their hands. Whereupon the remainder burst into spontaneous applause. Like performers at the end of a show, the volunteers stood and took a bow, graciously acknowledging their squaddies' appreciation of such noble and virtuous selflessness.

"Thank you lads, now I can bronzy in the Med!"

"Give my love to Paisley ..."

"Ouzo ten mils a bottle in Malta, runs-ashore in Cyprus ..."

"Nail-bombs for breakfast, riots all night, you can stick Ulster up yer flippin' jacksie ..."

"Well," said the PSO with a smile, relieved that the unpleasant business of having to nominate people was dispensed with, "Just keep your hands up while I make a note of the names."

"It's not war. It's urban terrorism. And there is a considerable distinction despite what you would read. Unlike conventional warfare, where lives sometimes have to be sacrificed in order to attain a specific objective, in this business it's not necessary for you to die. But a lot o' people have. Far too many. And if you do too, it means that either *you* or your *oppo* hasn't done his fuckin' job properly."

The subject was Ulster. The speaker one of the Corporals on the training team, vividly reinforcing his points in the manner of every good instructor with illustrations drawn from his own experience. With their respective fates now confirmed, the squad hung avidly upon every word that could mean life or death to them, delivered—with stimulating irony—by an Irishman from the Republic.

"Too many soldiers have died over there already. And when you look into it, **no way** was every one of those deaths unavoidable. One thing led to another, one circumstance to another, something got forgotten or overlooked and somebody got zapped or blown up. Had the right thing been done at the right time by the right person—it wouldn't have happened. And the right person is **YOU**. So **SWITCH ON**, men. Or some *bastard* will switch you off for good. If you get yourself killed because of your own fuck-up then it's your own fault. That's not so bad. But if your oppo gets killed on your account, you're gonna look pretty fuckin' silly. So watch the rooftops, the windows, the alleyways. Watch your oppo's back when he's doing somethun'. Don't get caught out. Accepting a cup o' tea

which turns out to be poisoned. Opening a door which turns out to
be booby-trapped. Going to a house and gettin' yourself machine-
gunned to death. Because that's what it's all about over there, okay?
Your job is to keep the level of violence down. And if you needlessly
add yourself to the statistics, you're not doin' the job the taxpayer
pays you to do. Alright, fuck the taxpayer. But you're still dead.
D'you follow me?"

Sometimes 'The Mick' would point out that no fewer than 80,000
Irishmen from the Republic had soldiered for Britain during the
Second World War. And it was his considered opinion — when
discoursing over a pint of beer in the Junior NCOs' Club — that his
compatriots were still the backbone of the British Army, something
of which he was distinctly proud.

"Now I know these people. I lived twenty-two years among them
and I know their ways. I've got a brother in the IRA and if I saw
him tomorrow I'd shop him. Because for a long time over there, on
both sides of the border, killing has been going on for killing's sake.
To a lot of people, especially youngsters, who get drawn into it, it's
FUN. Look at all the sectarian murders. The cause is only a pretext,
an excuse to do it. And because these people are not subject to
a code of discipline such as a soldier is, once they've got involved
and got used to it, it's very, very hard to stop. And that's where you
come in.

"Your job is to get in amongst the civil population and winkle
these little bastards out. And the dividin' line between keepin' the
majority of people sweet while you're doin' it and drivin' others into
the hands of the extremist groups is a thin one at the best of times.
For a start you're at a disadvantage because soldiers amongst
civilians is not a popular thing. But given the situation it is
necessary. There again you have a natural advantage. You look well
turned out and fit and ready for any funny business and people
respect that. And there'll be plenty o' funny business. They don't
mess about over there. That's why we teach you all this unarmed
combat. So you can handle yourself. And when they start rippin' up
the railings and chuckin' them at you, you'll know all about it.
When you're stood in the middle of a riot protectin' Old Mother
Reilly's sweet shop and someone blows a whistle; and they all lie flat
and you're left standing there like a spare prick at a weddin'; and
there's a big bang and one o' you drops dead, you'll know you
should've reacted sooner. They'll pull every trick in the book and a
lot that's not in any book. That's just one o' them."

He picked up a gas mask and held it up. It was covered with
congealed blood and one of the eye-pieces was shattered.

"When the bullet went through that eye-piece, this respirator was on someone's head. We keep it to show you.

"Terrorism is a nasty business, men, and not just for you. One teenager with a Thompson sub-machine gun can terrorise an entire neighbourhood and I've seen it. More to the point I personally had the satisfaction of catching one o' the bastards once. People are afraid. If they see an incident they won't come forward and say so 'cos one o' these nasty little *thugs* will come around and **beat** them up. You'd be surprised at the amount of mail the company commanders get from people who live in the areas each company patrols. Thanking him for our protection. Some of it anonymous, a lot of it not. So don't be contemptuous of them. They live with that threat every day of their lives. The police especially.

"The majority of people just want to get on with their own life and they'll look to you to be able to do so. So be aware. If you see some-thun' that's suspicious, find out what's goin' on. Stop people. Get to know 'em. You're empowered to do so. Don't be abusive. Be polite but firm. When you get a load of abuse from someone *then* you can tell 'em to fuck off, *not* before. Because in the long run it's counter-productive to your own efforts. The hours you'll spend patrolling the streets, searching derelicts and so on. A friend of mine in the Army was fined seventy quid by his company commander for spitting at someone who was givin' him a load of abuse and who had spat at *him*. You'll get plenty of that, so don't worry about it. But there's a standard of behaviour which you're expected to maintain, even under those circumstances. And you're under pressure all the time. So like anything else in the Marines, what it boils down to is using your common sense. The old CDF. Common Dog Fuck. Think of it this way. For seventy quid, you can have a fuckin' good run ashore. So don't go spitting your money away.

"Now I would be less than truteful, if with a hondred and more soldiers dead, I were to say there was no chance of you catching it up. Like the booty who got shot at point blank range through a window—there will always be that chance. But what I will say is this. If you put into practice everything we've taught you in training, and you stay switched on—toroughly switched on   you *won't* catch it up. And that I will guarantee. So don't make the mistake of becoming fatalistic about any of this. Like a lot of the Yanks in Vietnam. When they considered themselves dead before they'd even fuckin' got there. You're in charge of your own destiny. It's up to you and your oppo."

Smith KEN staggered up the stairs with a 20lb box marked
'EXPLOSIVES' on his shoulder. He had just drawn it from the store.
During the final exercise he was to share the carrying of it with
Taverner. Their orders stated it would be required on the sixth
night. He kicked open the door and mopped his brow. Taverner was
adjusting the straps of his pack.

"Phew!" said Smith, the box still on his shoulder. "It ain't 'alf
'eavy. The Mick reckons this is what it says. I reckon it's sand."

Slowly, as though watching an experiment, he let the box fall.
Taverner dived behind his locker, knocking over a chair.

The box bounced off the bed and fell onto the floor with a heavy
thud. There was silence.

"FUCK'S SAKE!!" screeched Taverner, "If that'd gone off it'd have
blown us all up!!"

"It's sand," said Smith. "How far's the yomp in?"

"Twenty-eight mile."

"Okay, I'll take it for the first fourteen, you take if off me ..."

"Here," said Taverner pointing a pencil at the map.

"Right."

Smith bound the box onto his pack then stood up and heaved it
onto his shoulders.

"Cheerio," he said to his mattress, "Happy Thursday, Friday—see
ya Sat'dy."

They went outside and joined others heading for the transport,
each with the gloomy air a man has when he is about to hurt
himself.

It was Sunday.

Silently they shipped their paddles and slid over the sides into
waist-deep water, steadying the inflatables as they passed their packs
out of them. Then they formed up in groups and set off at a
cracking pace through sleeping villages ...

He went down on one knee, sweat dripping off his impudent ski-
slope nose in the moonlight. This hill was a holy bastard and getting
steeper.

"There ain't ... many ... fights ... I've ... backed out of,"
breathed Smith ... "But this ... might ... be oneuv'em."

"Never thought I'd hear *you* say that," said Taverner, passing
him.

"Take over wi'ya?"

"We change at the top, not half way up."

A glint of vengeance entered Smith's eye. The world was gonna pay for this.

"Pusser's bastard, Tavernah!" he muttered, sweating after him. "Plastic explosive, my arse! It's nothing but a lousy stinking shitty box of fucking pissing *sand* ..."

At the top they exchanged packs. Gingerly Taverner put his arms through Smith's pack with the box strapped onto it. Smith hauled him to his feet.

"It's PE," muttered Taverner.

"It's *sand*," said Smith.

"It's bloody heavy, whatever it is."

"You're not wrong," said Smith who had just carried it for fourteen miles.

Day Two

The weather clamped in; rain and mist. Visibility—200 metres. An OP party struggled to the top of a tor. Taverner dumped the pack.

"Careful!" said Smith.

"Whaja mean 'careful'?" panted Taverner. "It's *sand*."

"I dunno," said Smith.

Day Four

Driving rain. High wind. Visibility—2,500 metres.

"It's gettin' heavier," said Smith, pulling on the pack.

"Then it's definitely sand," said Taverner. "PE wouldn't absorb the wet."

Day Six

Solid rain. Visibility—500 metres.

Under a camouflage net stretched between rocks, Taverner struggled with the decoding of a radio message, trying to shield the pad from the wet with his body. Smith crouched 'outside', lighting hexamine blocks to make a brew. He tipped water into a mess-tin.

"Trouble with this '58 pattern webbing," he said, "is it gets heavy and unmanageable when wet."

"So do I," said Taverner, morale at rock bottom. The paper on which he was writing began to dissolve.

"Same with that wooden box," said Smith. "It's soggy and splitting round the nails."

"Like my fingers," said Taverner irritably.

"If there was PE in it, it'd be metal," said Smith.

"I know," said Taverner.

"We bin carting a poxy box o' sand around for the last four days."

"I KNOW!" said Taverner.

Smith shivered.

"Can I come back into our little home now, be it ever so humble?" he asked.

"Ah look, GIVE US A BREAK, SMITH WI'YA? I'M TRYING TO DO THIS!"

There was silence save for the static hiss of the radio set.

"This damp is ruining my perm," said Smith, wringing out his cap-comforter. "I must have a new blowjob when I get back. Go with the new beret."

Taverner had it. First word 'MOVE'. Second word 'TO'. Third word, a grid reference.

"Pack up," he said, "We gotta move again."

"*Move?*" echoed Smith, "Are you sure??"

"Bin it, Smudge," grunted Taverner, "Whaja think it was, a pay rise?"

"If it's within the guidelines I'm not accepting," said Smith.

With superhuman deliberation he poured the lukewarm brew-water back into his water bottle, capped it and began to roll up the camouflage net. Finally temperament got the better of him. He smashed his heel down onto the hexamine blocks, extinguishing the flames. Sheets of rain drifted across the hillside.

Night Six

Along the wood. Skirt the bog. Up the re-entrant. And ...
"There it is. Down." The demolition party went to ground.

On a signal from an instructor, Smith heaved off his pack, drew his bayonet and broke open the box. A torch revealed rows of explosive charges, all neatly wrapped in greaseproof paper. His mouth fell open.

In the Eastern bloc, inmates of forced labour camps rose to start their day. In Western beds, children and parents slept soundly in warmth and safety. On a UK training area, Democracy's young defenders melted silently into the night.

★　　★　　★

"Planning ... preparation ... and precision of performance ... equals PER-FECTION! (Ain't that right, Timber.) We've planned. We've prepared. And when you pass out on this parade tomorrow ... your performance is goin'ae be nothing less than PERFECT!!"

Like the rolling hills around the Firth of Tay, the First Drill's voice rolled with the resonancy of his Dundonian origins.

"YOUR BOOTS WILL SPARKLE LIKE *DIA-MONDS* ... AND YOUR BAY-ONET ... WILL HANG BY YOUR SIDE *LIKE A JEW-ELL!*"

The contrast between the men who a week earlier had clambered stiffly off the trucks and limped painfully back into the barrack-blocks and those who now ran a final duster over their brasswork, could not have been greater. Then they were more like zombies, having endured a week of unrelenting movement day and night in all weathers with barely time to smoke a cigarette or change a sock let alone seek shelter. Now, the morning after the First Drill's pep talk, they reached into the dark recesses of a locker and gingerly lifted out a pair of parade boots, each one a gem, a priceless work of art deserving of a place of honour in the Louvre. Unwillingly, they unwrapped gleaming toe-caps, reluctantly surrendering to the tarnish of ordinary atmosphere hour upon hour of loving spit, polish and elbow-grease. Patiently, they inspected their brasswork and bayonet yet again, minutely examining the chin-strap of the pith helmet for the slightest vestige of brasso upon the leather backing or tell-tale slivers of yellow duster fluff upon the chain-mail. Like daughters dressing for a coming-out ball, they climbed into their Blues tunics, its insignia and glittering buttons outdone by a simple piece of white cord entwined for this one occasion only around the left shoulder. The prized lanyard of the King's Squad, the senior recruit squad, which now they were. By braces that ran over gawdy, bawdy or insubordinate T-shirts, they adjusted the hang of their trousers so that in rigid uniformity each man's broke over the second lace-hole of his boots. In pairs they bound scrubbed white belts about each other, a two-man job, one hauling in the jacket from the rear, the other fastening the shining brass locket-union at the front. More primly than prima donnas, they brushed each other down, pouncing with fantastically developed eye upon every last tiny fleck of dust or fluff. Studded boots rang upon the landings as they began to foregather in the stairwell, primping themselves in front of full-length mirrors like actors and models, centering the belt, twitching a moustache to left and right, aligning the immaculate pith helmet, whitened with the delicate artistic brush-strokes of a squad of Picassos. Outside in the clean air, they removed the very last trace of barrack-room dust with the assistance of sticky-tape. Then they walked down the path and began to form up in the roadway, testing the rifle sling against slackness, adjusting the lie of the bayonet frog over the left hip, running a white gloved finger round the collar of the tunic where it was already beginning to cut into the neck. The day promised to be warm and they cursed the dust that was already forming a film over their glossy boots.

Critically Timber surveyed them.

"Stand properly at ease!"

They braced themselves. All talking stopped.

"The KING'S SQUAD ... **TUN-NER**! SHOWL-DER ... *HARMS-ER!* Cut hand away SHARPER! Look up! All of you! Neck-in-the-back-o-the-collar! Look your own height! (S'bettah.) **MOVE**—TO THE RIGHT—IN THREES ... RIGHT—*TAARN-ER!"*

On tiered seats either side of the saluting base, people began to congregate. Curious people, excited people, nostalgic people. Wives, parents, relatives, other servicemen, Joe Public. Women with bare arms, a pleasant fragrance and sun-specs shielding their eyes. Women who dripped jewellery, leaked perfume and whose sun-specs shielded the top of their heads. Men in blazers and regimental ties, men in shirt sleeves with gold expandable watchstraps. Kids in shorts, kids in bobby socks, kids with ice creams, kids with other kids. All sat surrounded by the fertile richness of Raleigh country, green lawns and trees with pink blossom, looking out over a parade ground marked with decorous corner flags. Awaiting a spectacle, an event, watching the sun play silvery upon the river and gild young fields of yellow corn beyond. Powderham Castle across the Exe. The heart of Mother Earth. Devon.

Out of sight, formed up in three ranks behind the Royal Marines band stood the King's Squad, nervously fingering a chin-strap, a collar, a belt, waiting with the impatience of thoroughbreds at a race meeting. No artist, no performer, no competitor had ever known a moment such as this.

Resplendent in Blues uniform and white pith helmet, with Sergeant's chevrons gold upon red and pacestick under his arm,

Timber addressed the squad, white even teeth flashing like a movie star's, eyes blazing with emphasis on certain words, chain-mail chin strap catching the sunlight, handsome symmetrical face occasionally relaxing into a malicious grin of supreme confidence. The Hollywood Director motivating his youthful protegés, immaculately trained, groomed and attired, dominating them, coaxing from them an Oscar-winning performance.

"This is your moment. Your passing-out parade. Solely, exclusively, utterly—*yours*. Never again will YOU be the King's Squad. Never again will you come together as you are now at the end of months and months of training. This is your *peak*. Your *pinnacle*. So do it justice. Do yourselves justice and everything you've worked for. I want you to go out there and bring off a performance that's nothing less than PERFECT. Relax. Concentrate. Forget about everything and everyone else. Listen to ME. To MY word of command. I want you to show ME! Everything that you've been through I want you to put together on this parade."

He stepped back and shook a white gloved fist at them.

"DO IT! FOR ME!"

The message went home and he noted with satisfaction how it lifted them, how they even paled a little like men about to go into action, about to brave death.

"Look *up*!"

Their hearts fluttered with the flightiness of debutantes.

"THE KING'S SQUAD .. TUN-NER! SHOUL-DER ... ARMS!"

With a timing that was flawless, forty hands cut from the stock to the side in a single white-gloved flash. Ramrod stiff they stood, clasping the pistol grip, pressing the butt into their side, pulling the silver ceremonial bayonet back into the shoulder.

For a second Timber watched them, savouring the moment before his word of command set them, the band, the whole parade into motion. Jaws jutted resolutely, eyes stared straight to the front. Such a moment presidents and prime minsters would look upon with envy, themselves wielding less power, having less earned authority.

"BY THE LEFT ... QUICK-*MARCH!*"

As one, forty left heels struck the tarmac, leaving little arcs in its softening surface. Twice the drums and cymbals of the band thundered out a three-pace roll before the musicians broke into the regimental march, 'A Life on the Ocean Wave.'

As he watched the King's Squad swing past him, gloves flashing, bayonets glinting, rounding the corner into full view of the spectators, proprietorial pride surged through his chest. His squad. HIS SQUAD.

"NOW SHOW OFF!" he screamed, "SWANK! SWAGGER!!"

There are no leaves upon the trees. The sky is squalid with rain. An icy wind howls across the parade ground bearing sleet, freezing them to the marrow. Uncomfortable in ill-fitting denims, unbroken boots and puttees, they shiver, are screamed at to stand still and placed on extra parades. For a dull toe-cap, a slackly knotted tie, a loose foresight they are punished. They do defaulters' drill, drill at the double. It is unpleasant. They are untrained. They do things wrong. They must be hammered into shape. Wearily they laugh. They volunteered. With frenzied patience the magnificent Timber says, "Alright. I'll show you again. Look this way. This is how the movement will be done. And if it's not right this time, you'll be out here one-o'clock in the morning if necessary." Puddles turn to ice. Snowflakes fall upon their heads. There are no flags. The benches are bare.

The March On. The Inspection at Open Order. The Commandant tours the ranks. In the background the band plays quietly. Harmonious brass blends with mellifluous woodwind. Music to grace an occasion. A Royal Marines band ... Wrong notes not issued.

The Display of Silent Drill. The Advance in Review Order. The presentation of the King's Badge for best all-round recruit.

"Well done. Keep it up. Are you going for a commission? Good show. You can wear this badge for the rest of your career, even if you get as high as me. It's a great honour.

"Thank you Sergeant, bring up the rest of the squad will you? I'd like to have a word with them ...

"Your report makes worthwhile reading. It's gratifying to read phrases such as 'A good overall reaction to discipline,' 'Ability to work as a team,' 'A determined approach to the commando course,' and so on. From now on you are Royal Marines. And as such a very valuable national asset. We know not what the future holds but we must be prepared and able to meet whatever situation arises. You are part of that preparedness. A significant and important part."

Mounted on horseback, the Adjutant led the squad down one side of the parade, sword unsheathed for the March Past. Against the thunder of the band behind them, Timber opened his lungs.

"THE KING'S SQUAD ... WILL ADVAAANCE ..."

Marching to the right and rear of them, he waited for the precise moment, watching the right boots of the rear rank lift and pound like synchronised metronomes.

"... LEFT ... **TAARN - ER!!**"

WHACK!

Forty right parade boots smacked the tarmac together, instantaneously turning the squad from three ranks back to review order, marching in three ruler-straight lines abreast, a movement fearful in its expression of power, precision, unity, perfection.

"EYES - AH ... RIGHT!!"

As they marched past the saluting base, head-and-eyes canted over to the right, they looked directly at the Commandant who took the salute. All except Haythorne, who ignored him. As right marker, he stared straight ahead, fixing his gaze on a tree at the far end of the parade ground, keeping the squad on course, his left glove flashing in and out of his vision, his right pulling the rifle into his shoulder until it hurt.

And as they marched, they talked, like ventriloquists, through lips as immobile as the opening of a letter box, the sound masked by the band ...

"Watchyadressin' — WATCHYADRESSIN'!"

"Mindyabay'net! DOUG! Pullyabay'netback!"

"Dress back Dave, DRESSBACKYACUNT!"

On the far side of the parade, the King's Squad turned once more into threes. The Adjutant led them back past the dais and through a gap in the tiered rows of spectators. As the band changed the tune into 'Sarie Marais', so the rhythm lengthened slightly into a pace that enabled the squad to literally swagger off their own passing-out parade. The spectators cheered and applauded and photographed them. Underneath the pith helmets, short-cropped hair stood on end at the enormity of the feeling.

Outside the barrack-block the Adjutant looked down on the latest batch of fully-fledged Royal Marines Commandos, surveying their upturned and expectant faces from the saddle of his charger, each one burning with the question "How were we?", eager for any complimentary morsel that might come their way after *all that*.

Timber stood behind them. In about a week he would pick up a new squad, fresh off the train at Deal.

"Thank you, Sergeant," nodded the Adjutant, sheathing his sword unsmilingly. "Not too bad," he condescended, riding off in the direction of a stiff gin.

"The Adjutant's a difficult man to please," the Team Leader explained the world in a single sentence; "But you made me a happy man, and that means ...?"

"WE MADE YOUR WIFE A HAPPY WOMAN!" responded the squad for the very last time.

Around the corner, turning cartwheels and doing handsprings, bounded Ricardo.

"Now, you bastards," he cajoled, shaking a finger at them, "You gonna buy me dat fuckin' beer!"

"Off pith helmets, on Green Berets, into the Naafi five minutes from now—SCRAM!" said Timber.

TORQUAY

She hung round his neck, pushing her pelvis into him. He leant back against the sea wall and explored her mouth voraciously. There was sand under their feet and the water's edge not far away. Other late-night couples strolled overhead, under the fairy-lights along the front. Occasionally they stopped and lingered, looking out to sea, unaware of the mounting passions below them. Slowly he unzipped her jeans and pushed them down. Pale legs in the shadows. Further round the bay, a seafront clock struck twelve midnight.

Three of them had come to the resort, others had gone elsewhere. Many had gone home for the week-end, travelling by train all over the country. Koupparis to London, Mazzi to Worcester, Hill, Douglas and co. to Manchester. Even now Dave Smith was still sitting on a train making the interminable journey to his home at Newcastle-upon-Tyne. Gilbrook, as he alighted from a taxi in front of his home in Northampton, took from his pocket a small round piece of cloth in order to show it to his mother as he walked in the door. She had been too ill to attend the ceremony. Umpteen times in successive buffet cars on the way up, in front of mounting piles of beer cans, he had stared at it, mumbling over and over again, "I got it. I bloody got it. I thought Haythorne would get it. But he didn't. I got it." Earlier in the day the Commandant had pinned the little cloth badge to his left shoulder. It bore a royal cypher in gold on blue. 'GR.' Georgius Rex. The King's Badge. Given by a grateful monarch, George V, in recognition of services rendered by the Corps ashore, afloat and in the air during the war to end all wars, 1914-1918.

Somewhere in the shadows further along the sea wall were the other two, similarly occupied. Teens, twenties, northern accents, out to sample the resort's fleshpots. They had met them in the Yacht, taken them up Casa's, plied them with drinks, made out they were a cross between millionaires and war heroes. ("Cor, listen to 'em, don't they half go on? What are they? Marines? S'pose they must be with haircuts like that," whisper-whisper, giggle-giggle ...) "Come on girls, what's with all the whisp'rin'? You ain't much cop at this subterfuge lark!"

He felt the warm soft skin of her supple stomach and ran his hands up underneath her bra. Mmmm ... nice, deliciously firm and nibblesome. The good things in life. What a man needed after all that running about. A decent late-night knee-trembler was one of life's rewards really. Relax, easy, plenty of time dear, I'll have it out in a minute. Alright, careful with the zip, there's two and quarter pounds of rampant spam-spanner in there. Mmmm ... okay, there we are, it's out and sniffing the night air, warm and throbbing in her tiny hands. ('The world's not ready for this, you spent so much time talking about it but when you had one in your hand, actually had it *there* ...')

He reached around her hips, pulling her towards him. Better than the Endurance Course. Was it.

She hit him across the face. Hard. He winced.

"Blimey!" blinked Smith, "is this a noo game or jussa variation on the old one?"

"If it's sex you want I'm not that sort of girl," she said, pulling up her jeans.

"What madeja think that?" asked Smith, genuinely astounded.

"Well, I'm not."

"Nah, look Doris ..."

"See, you don't even remember my name!"

"Deirdre, I mean. Look, y'know we had a few sherbets 'n' I was kinda gettin' the message, y'know ..."

"I know what kind of message you were getting."

"Well lissen darlin', blesh and flood, I mean flesh and blood can only stand so much."

"I'm going."

"Nah, Deirdre, look you don't unnerstand ..."

"I understand," she said, disappearing down the beach, "All your lot are the same!"

"No we're not!" he called after her, "There's two uv'em dahn vair gettin' their rocks off!"

She vanished. Smith swore with all the malice of a robber robbed.

He hitched up his trousers and walked slowly along the beach, stopping near the steps up which she had just rushed, heels clacking away into the distance. Venomously he struck a match, lit a cigarette, drew on it and flicked the match away. The smoke seemed to calm him. He put the packet back into his jerkin pocket, turned and sat on the steps.

'Smithy, ole boy,' he thought ruefully, 'You just become one of Her Majesty's men and God don't work two miracles in one day.' He shook his head and gave his luck two fingers. 'Come Monday morning, you ain't gonna get so much as a whiff of a woman for four whole months. So best you save your luck for that. All the same ... so near, yet so far. It's a travesty of justice and no mistake. And after all a man has gone through ...'

At length he finished his cigarette and walked over to a deck chair. He picked it up and carried it up the steps, across the road and along the other side to where was parked the car he, Haythorne and Taverner had on hire. He put the deck chair inside. Then he walked back a little way, crossed the road once more and leaned against the railings, lighting another fag and looking out to sea.

From left and right of him, on the sand twenty feet below, the urgent sounds of heavy petting assailed his ears in stereo. He blew out, soured with jealousy.

When finally, the other two appeared, girls in tow, they all walked back to the car. Smith jumped into the driver's seat.

Parked in a side road at the top of the town was a police car. The two constables in it were actually talking about cars when a Mini went past. There was nothing spectacularly unusual about Minis, even in Torquay at this time of night. No, what was interesting about this one was that it had a deck chair sticking out of the window ...

"AND ..." stormed Smith after they had been stopped, lecturing the policemen with all venom of a Cockney who considers himself on the end of raw deal,"... IF YOU WANNA BOOK US, YOU'LL 'AVE TO SWING IT WITH HIS OLD MAN ..."—pointing at Taverner—"'COS HE'S A JUDGE! AND HE'S PRICEY AND ALL, I'LL TELL YA! TWENNY PERCENT O' YOUR WAGES FOR THE REST O' YOUR TIME ON THE FORCE, THE PAIR O' YA!!"

CHAPTER 2

Gauntlet

BELFAST

Haythorne was nearly killed on his first foot patrol. It was at night and the corporal in charge was nearly killed with him. In the centre on one side of a six-man patrol, he closed up to the front man, the corporal, covering him as they prepared to turn a corner in the criss-cross streets of the New Lodge. The NCO paused before he went and in that moment they presented a double target. From a street leading the opposite way from the one into which they were about to turn came a burst of Thompson sub-machine gun fire directed at them.

Both men threw themselves flat, Haythorne catching a glimpse of the flashes out of the corner of his eye, astounded at the amount of noise in the confined space. As he went down, he felt he must surely have been hit. But barely had he time to register the spattering of rounds into the brickwork behind him when he was amazed by something else. The furious reaction of other members of the patrol who unleashed a fusillade of shots at the flashes before running *at* the firer so close did he seem to be. By Provisional IRA decree, how-ever, the doors of the New Lodge were kept open at night. Part of the job of the youth organisation, the Fianna, was to report any that were not with a view to sanctions being taken against the house-holder. Ten year-olds tried front and back doors of Coronation Street-type houses at dusk. For anyone foolish enough to bar his door against the entry of a fleeing Provo after dark, it meant a savage beating. So the gunman escaped and all the hot and sweating Marines had for ten minutes of chasing shadows through back alleys was twenty spent cases of ·45 calibre ammunition found in a passage between houses whence the flashes had come.

From the cases, the weapon and the circumstances, Special Branch and Intelligence pieced together the picture of an 'outside' job. Not the Czech or the German. Nor the man with dark glasses, a Latin-American accent and a Terror International tie. But someone

from the Ardoyne. A Volunteer trying to step up his competence by
going for the jackpot against a fresh unit in their first twenty-four
hours on the ground. Seeking the high financial reward known to be
on offer for the killing or capture of a soldier. A member of an active
service unit of one area ordered to do a job in another by PIRA
superiors increasingly aware of their factious and informer-ridden
organisation and unable to count on the unswerving loyalty of the
Catholic community among whom they moved. A man who had
graduated from the University of Everyday Brutality, passing
courses in simple beatings and the tarring-and-featherings of soldier
and Proddy-lovers. Someone who had majored in the use of the
handgun, studying its practical applications in the knee-capping of
touts or informers before gaining honours magna cum laude for the
murder of an off-duty UDR man. And now going for his master's
degree against the Royal Marines in an attempt to find an eternal
place of honour in the IRA's hall of fame. He failed.

It was not hard to speculate why. Nervous at finding himself in a
strange area, lacking confidence in his colleagues, probably without
proper night vision and conceivably inexperienced in the handling
of a Thompson, all together undoubtedly saved the lives of
Haythorne and his patrol commander. But not by much. He fired a
full magazine at a range of less than forty metres. They paced it out
the next day and examined the chipped brickwork on the wall where
they had been standing. The marks were high and slightly to the
right, characteristics of both an indifferent marksman when firing
at night and of the weapon itself when held slackly.

Twenty-four hours earlier accompanied by kitbag-small and suit-
case-green, the Unit had made the crossing from Liverpool to
Belfast by fleet auxiliary and by ferry. Most had been to Ulster
before at some point in their careers but whether or not they had,
those aboard the British and Irish Lines' 'Ulster Prince' used the bar
sparingly that night. They sat over halves in the saloon, talking
quietly amongst themselves, becoming acquainted or re-acquainted
with the plaintive accents of the province for which they were bound
and observing tribal demarcation which was already making itself
felt. One one side sat the Irish. On the other side sat the other Irish.
Both pulled faces and mouthed obscenities at each other. In the
centre stood the British soldier unable to resist joining in with any
old song regardless of its sympathy. Whereupon both sides seemed
to want to talk to the soldier-boys, summoning them with shouts of

'Hey Tommy!' and 'See yew, big fella!' Soon the bootnecks mingled freely, crossing or re-crossing the divide to join in a new conversation when bored of an old argument without ever losing their monopoly of the bar. Occasionally they would be exhorted 'not to talk to those people over there, Tarmy, they're not nice people.' With the sort of outlook that can only be obtained at an optician's each side blamed the other exclusively for the troubles, some even apologising for the involvement of the British soldier, urgently tugging his sleeve in order to impress upon him the fact that either 'the Irish are the friendliest people in the world' or 'the Northern Irish are the friendliest people in the world' depending upon which side of the saloon he happened to be.

The words of Orange songs they knew less well and as these expressed the hopes and fears of a beleaguered community with flag-waving and patriotic fervour, sentiments that are not always shared by British soldiers whether Field Marshals or foot sloggers, they became polite interludes for topping-up. Green songs, made famous by republican exiles the world over, they joined in with heartily. Even a Somerset schoolboy like Haythorne was acquainted with Dominic Behan and it was with lusty irony — in view of what was about to happen to him — that he sang ...

> 'We're off to Dubble-in in the green, in the green,
> Where the helmets glisten in the sun.
> Where the bayonets flash and the rifles crash
> To the echo of a Thompson gun.'

It was not Dublin but Belfast where they disembarked the next morning, to be met by a convoy of empty trucks manned by the grinning Marines of their brother Unit, the outgoing 42 Commando. As the convoy passed throught the city on its short journey to the area of responsibility which the Unit was to take over, it stopped at a traffic light. Silent and watchful men looked out of the backs of the trucks. A foot patrol of men in green berets was working its way up the street towards them, warily watching the rooftops, themselves outlined against the smoke-blackened walls of bombed and gutted buildings. On the wagons, the stomachs of old hands and newcomers alike tightened. They gazed at the patrolling Marines, at the broken buildings, the littered streets, at the dogs sniffing amongst the rubble and most of all at the people who moved around them. People without apparent pride or self-respect. People who seemed to have abdicated responsibility for their own future to others or to fate. People who allowed intimidators, murderers, maimers, assassins and proxy bombers to move freely amongst themselves and to feed off them. There in the pale morning sun lay a city pervaded by enmity and degradation with its shabby streets and hopeless populace, unwilling or unable to help themselves, a populace who blamed every turn of events upon something or some-one else. From where they sat, the newcomers caught their first real whiff of the atmosphere of Belfast, whilst the memories of the old hands awakened. Memories one, two, three even four years old now. Memories of a city festering like an abscess, perniciously infected by the feculence of its own population, the moral responsibility for whom now lay in the hands of those in the back of the trucks. Few would envy them their job. They got paid for it. But that was about all.

In England a few months earlier, the IRA had started a new campaign beginning with the Old Bailey bombings. The attitude of the troops to this event was 'At *last* somebody might wake up a bit now.' In the Province itself, the IRA's loosely controlled campaign wavered between sporadic shooting at random targets and bomb attacks upon the main centres of habitation. Within days of the unit's arrival, there occurred the sort of nasty incident that happens when large sections of the population are in possession of a multitude of firearms which they discharge hapazardly at soldiers, neighbours, passers-by, men returning from work, even no-one in particular. On this occasion it was at no-one in particular and again it was at night.

Down a dark alley lurked a foot patrol keeping an eye on a more lighted thoroughfare which ran across the end of it. The men wore flak jackets, useful for protection against blast, flying nails and the cold but not much else. Many were sceptical of their use. One Marine was crouching against the side of the alley which was the wall of a house, when a window opened behind him and a pistol, poked out at right angles, was discharged six times before being withdrawn and the window shut. The rounds went everywhere, most striking the wall on the far side of the throughfare. One, however, struck the ground behind the crouching Marine which made it start to tipple end over end in flight. Ricochetting upwards it would have passed harmlessly within an inch or two of his ribcage but for the protruding flak jacket whose inner face it caught. Turned inwards, it entered his body below the right ribcage and gouged a trail round his stomach until it struck his left ribcage from the inside whereupon it turned again and began to travel upwards in the direction of his heart. In agony, the bootneck got up and ran forward round the corner where he was tripped up by another member of the patrol who thought he was running away in panic.

"I've been hit! I've been hit!" he gasped as he lay writhing on the pavement.

The casualty evacuation procedure swung into action. A woman came out and compassionately gave him some water. Whilst waiting for the ambulance to arrive she equally compassionately pinched his beret.

It took all the surgical skills of the staff at the Royal Victoria Hospital to save the young man's life. When the round was finally located in his body it was found to have come to rest within a quarter of an inch of his heart. With internal injuries so grievous, the operations were delicate and complex and his convalescence long. One of the first to visit him in hospital was his oppo who had tripped him up. Eventually he was downgraded to permanent non-combatant status. Whereupon he determined at least to recoup financially from a self-absorbed taxpayer on whose behalf he had bled and suffered without complaint.

★ ★ ★

"They normally have a go somewhere round here," said the man in front, indicating Unity Flats, "So if you get the chance, blat 'em back."

A mobile patrol passed between the two sides of the foot patrol, rounding the corner into North Queen Street. Smith eyed the flats, standing rearguard as the rest walked forward. He counted. Then turned and walked forward himself, knowing from the rhythm of the patrol that his opposite number had stopped and would now be facing the rear. He was. Smith rounded the corner in time to see the second Landrover draw level with the front pair of his patrol.

There was a series of cracks like someone snapping twigs, and a ripping sound in the air. At the same time the tarmac in the road just ahead of him began to make odd alarming noises like a sewing machine. He realised rounds were striking it and he leapt down at the pavement, wriggling like a dog on heat for the cover of a tree in front of him. The cracks and bangs from up front were unnerving alright but the tarmac ripping up nearby terrified him. He cocked his weapon and as he did so he heard the bark of a self-loading rifle.

The next few seconds were grotesquely confusing. All he could think of was 'KER-IST! There's people up there trying to take MY LIFE AWAY for THEIR ENDS! SHIT!!' He wriggled as close to the plane tree as he could get. He distinctly remembered it was a plane tree from its scaly bark. As he peered round it he saw the man in front look back at him. He was taking cover in the same manner and his face was white. Completely white.

A dilemma presented itself. The flats about which he had just been warned were behind them. But they had been fired on from the front and Smith's job was to guard the rear. Either way he faced he had the tremendously uncomfortable feeling that at any moment he might be shot in the back. Nevertheless he turned round to face the rear. The feeling that followed having placed his back towards the direction from which they were actually being fired upon was nothing less than excruciating.

"Just watch the rear, watch the rear!" he kept muttering nervously to himself, gripping his rifle, searching every window with his muzzle up. Why were they static? This wasn't the aggressive reaction to enemy fire he had been taught. But he kept covering the buildings behind them, swinging the muzzle wherever he looked, a deterrent, a simple procedure to put off gunmen, planted and nurtured and honed into instinct on close quarter battle ranges, now emerging in time of crisis as a support. Soldiers exposed on the streets, gunmen hidden in safe houses. But they *disliked* having muzzles pointed at them. It made them shy.

"MOVE UP! MOVE UP!"

He leapt to his feet and ran forwards in little adrenalin-charged bursts, starting and stopping ...

"DOWN!"

Into a fire position again, swivelling on his feet as he went down to watch the rear once more. Trust those in front to watch your back, they're trusting you to watch theirs. From up front came more SLR shots, then they were up and running again and as he ran he became stabbed by a new fear, he became terrified that they would be shot at from yet another direction, that they were running into a trap, a box formed by the high-rise flats ahead. The men in front slithered down. Smith followed suit, a piece of grimy stone wall to his left spattering off near his head, leaving a clean white mark ...

'So this is what it's like,' he thought, heart pounding, head throbbing, blood coursing, muscle fibres twitching in anticipation of further demands about to be made upon them, weak at the knees, stomach churning, guts heaving, hot and cold, eyes everywhere, thoughts in a turmoil, wringing wet, flinching inside his flak jacket at every fresh outburst of firing ...

'IT'S NOTHING LESS THAN BOWEL-BOILING TROUSER-SOILING PANT-CRAPPING FEAR! IT'S LIKE NOTHING ELSE ON EARTH!"

Shock and fear had released into his system enormous amounts of adrenalin generating a vast amount of energy which required translating into instant action. All this stopping and starting made him like a cat on hot bricks, utterly unable to stay still.

'I'll clean the heads forever, Corporal, if you just get us out of this! I'll use me own tooth-brush, anything ...'

"GALLAGHER'S ROOF! THEY'RE ON GALLAGHER'S ROOF!"

The roof of the tobacco factory. Grimly Smith sighted his weapon back and forth across the windows and rooftops of the opposite direction, safety catch off, first pressure taken, deterring anybody from doing anything except breathe ... lightly.

'You or me, baby,' he mutely challenged his unknown assailant, 'And the man with the greater instinct for survival will survive. Lesson number one. Learn it here and now, and live. LIVE!'

Every few seconds he shifted, making a hard target of himself, hating having to stay put whilst a gun battle raged behind him. He looked at a doorway which seemed to offer more cover than the open pavement with its solitary line of trees but he checked himself because he saw they were derelict and you never knew what was behind derelict doors. So he looked behind him and found that the rest had slunk forwards, seeming to share his impatience at being pinned down. He got up and ran forwards a few paces, sliding down in front of another tree, hoping it would somehow protect his back.

To his left, slewed round in the road, was one of the Landrovers, the one that had been the original target for the gunmen. Crouching behind it was the driver whose job in a contact was to stay with the vehicle. Smith glanced at him and saw him peep over the gearbox at what was going on up front. Men were shifting fire positions, shouting instructions from one to another, coping, getting a grip on things. The driver sneaked down behind the bonnet again. Their eyes met. Then in a gesture Smith would never forget as long as he lived, the driver grinned at him, jerked his head casually towards the firefight and waved a hand over his mouth as though to stifle a yawn.

'You blasé bastard!'

Smith grinned back weakly, trying to look like a veteran himself, and in that moment it suddenly became funny, funny-ridiculous because other people were trying to take his life away and he saw himself as he really was, hot, afraid, grovelling and singularly unheroic. The driver had seen it all before, of course. Perhaps to an old Borneo hand, a grav-turned-driver, urban firefights really were boring. Smith felt ashamed. Ashamed that he had been so scared and panic-stricken and confused and he desperately hoped he hadn't done anything wrong and that his fear hadn't showed. He hated the street, he hated it lying out there without cover. He wanted to be anywhere else but where there were bullets cracking about but it had to be done, he was one of six, there were five others and he had to do his job, it was the only way, but God Almighty, was it frightening.

He glanced behind him again and saw other green-bereted
bastards handling the situation, knowing what they were doing and
exhibiting a seemingly unshakeable belief in themselves, a belief
that had almost completely deserted Smith in his first moments
under fire. But not quite. He still loathed the street, he still wanted
to be anywhere but there, he felt hugely envious of the driver who
could produce such an imperturbable reaction at such a moment
and he knew he always would be. Nevertheless because of him, a
little confidence and determination began to ebb back slowly, right
there by the plane trees and the Landrover. A confidence in their
collective ability to meet and deal with the situation. And the next
moment he was up again and running ...

★   ★   ★

Around them in the dark came the muffled sounds of those about
to go out on patrol trying not to disturb those who were not. Pulling
on a beret, fastening a flak jacket, slipping a rifle sling over a gloved
hand, flicking a torch on and off before stowing it in a pocket.
Whispering diminished, rubber soles retreated, the hut door closed
a final time. Silence. Men breathed in slumber.

It had been his tenth patrol, the ding-dong in North Queen
Street. Was that all? Smith had worked it out that on his present
routine of alternate days of patrols and guards he would have done
about 180 by the end of the tour. Ah well, only 170 to go. Apart
from the first one he could barely recall the rest, even now. Like
your first woman, you never really forgot your first foot patrol, far
less your first contact. Yet within hours his memory of that first one
was jumbled, hazy, sketchy. He remembered the fleet-footedness of
his opposite number in the centre, a young boyish-looking 2nd
Lieutenant who had joined them for his own initiation, a sixth
former with ink on his fingers, logarithm tables in his back pocket.
Impressions remained of them lurking in shadow, nipping across
pools of light, creeping forward on the outside edge of the foot, the
collective pace slowed practically to a halt, eyes, ears, every sense
extended like radar. Listening halts, the surreptitious examining of
things, the constant awareness, the neck-pricking, armpit-leaking
sense of danger; the sudden heart-stopping alarms, a black window
hole that could conceal a sniper, a smell like marzipan that made
you freeze, a metallic click that made you die. The fast pace in
response to a call on the pocket-phone, the significance of a solitary
snap of the fingers and the ability of six men to move with the stealth
of a cat. More than anything he remembered at the outset the flash
of a torch upon a little painted notice which hung just inside the

location gate. In the light of the beam that cut a swathe through the darkness were the words 'STAYING ALERT EQUALS STAYING ALIVE.'

In the quiet of the hut he lay on his pit thinking about it, musing over the events of the afternoon, eyeing the bulge of the mattress above him where lay the recumbent form of the corporal who had steered them through the gun battle. To him it had been just another contact, a lot of rounds, a nip of the flea and dissatisfyingly inconclusive. In Aden, the corporal said, patrols downtown were only of ninety minutes duration, that being considered then the optimum time a man could stay alert and effective. Here they were three hours. No unit had the amount of men needed to cover the ground twenty-four hours a day in ninety minute packets. So three hours it was. Sometimes it was longer. Fifteen or twenty when things were really buzzing wasn't unknown. But Smith was content to live for the present and the present was until twenty minutes to two in the morning. Till then the last lot out had the pleasure of coping with beered-up-and-raring-to-go-Provies trying to shoot the heads off British soldiers with their 'little Armalites.' Till then Smith had his pit all to himself, just him, the little bit of Belfast he owned, sheets two, blankets two, pillow one, pillowcase one. Two hours and forty minutes of unadulterated bliss till he had to wash his face and pull his boots on again. Heaving a sigh he pulled the grey issued blankets round his shoulders.

The advantage was always with the terrorist and the odds stacked against the soldier he knew, simply because the former had the element of surprise, the choosing of time and place, the initiative. But notwithstanding that, it was how you reacted to them that counted. Because of that the soldier had to endure hour after hour, day after day of nerve-snapping tension, pacing himself over the tour, tautly wound up to produce a reaction without ever knowing when it would be required. The only relief came with a meal, a film or sleep. Smith smiled sardonically at the memory of himself in his first contact. Hours were spent re-living the experience afterwards. Everyone needed to talk it out of their system. Well, he Kenneth Eric Norman Smith had now paid his dues under fire. Could he go now? Was he excused the rest? He dismissed the thought. Because subconsciously he already felt set apart by the experience he had just undergone. Vaguely, without being able to put a finger on it or even pausing to consider it for long, he felt something more had happened to him than just being shot at. He was right. He had just gained admission to a fraternity whose membership transcended all known parameters. No longer did he have to doff his cap to the foolish exhibitors of wealth and status, to the possessors of great

social, academic or political qualification. Somehow he sensed his
loyalty would always now be with those who had shared experiences
similar to his own on behalf of those others. For more than the
physical knocks and shocks it was the emotional bruises and heart-
ache suffered by ordinary mortals under fire that bound them
together and conferred upon them an inner dignity the like of which
mere immortality seekers would never know.

In another location men sat in a darkened television room, a hut
furnished with old sofas upon which they rested their feet. Plastic
cups of coffee to hand, served from a dimly lighted hatch by a
Pakistani—the goffer-wallah—they idly watched a film concerning
cowboys and Indians. One of those present appeared to be watching
with the help of a deaf-aid. But the wire from his ear-piece went not
to a set of batteries inside his shirt but to a pocket-phone radio he
held in his lap.

"Two One Bravo contact Upper Meadow Street!" he suddenly
announced, turning and taking out the ear-piece. Someone leapt to
turn the television set down.

The pocket-phone crackled an acknowledgement, its words
spoken by a signaller in the communications centre, another hut not
far from the tv room.

"Who's Two One Bravo?" whispered someone.

"Carver ..."

"Sssshh!" The man who held the radio turned up the volume.

Tense and frowning they held their breath and listened whilst the
screen continued to play to its lost audience. Indians circled a wagon
train, cowboys shot back through spokes. A half-mile away one of
their patrols was getting it. Even now a Marine might be sprawled
lifeless, his spilt guts held in place only by his flak jacket, his life
blood pouring out onto the street through a hole in his body.

They all knew him, some well, others to nod to. A cheerful bloke,
a corporal who always gave the chefs a hard time when he came in
for a meal. Now they pictured him, groping for cover, trying to stay
alive, taking charge, staying in control, carrying out his contact
drills, keeping his men alive, his headquarters informed, trying to
collar the gunman before he collared him and all with the aid of an
ordinary human brain, a cataclysm of pressure and stress that would
fuse a mere computer. The eyes of those in the goffer-wallah's hut
flicked about in the dark, resting nowhere, waiting tensely for the
gasping voice on the radio, strained and breathless and several
octaves higher than normal from its brush with death, that would

tell them the only thing they really cared about — whether there had been a casualty.

The radio went quiet, the prelude to a transmission...

Outside another hut stood a figure, about average height, iron muscled and grey haired. He was thirty-four and the lines on his face reflected the action he had seen as a lad in Cyprus during the 'fifties and in Indonesia during the 'sixties where he had established a reputation as one of the best jungle trackers around. The accent was South Walian but his heart lay in the swamps, rivers and mountains of the Far East, in places as remote and beautiful as Kedah and Sabah. The mention of leeches, lalang, rain forest, uncharted territory, all brought a knowledgeable gleam to his eye. All anyone knew of his private life was that he was a happily married family man. Once he had been a sergeant but a spell as a civilian had not been to his taste and now as a corporal, he was waiting to regain his former rank after re-enlisting. He stood checking his watch, ready to go, listening to the sounds of shooting coming from the Falls, Distillery, Unity, the Turf, neighbouring Ardoyne and the heart of the New Lodge. Two electrifying blue and white flashes lit up the sky one after the other, two thunderous explosions obliterated the night. The bombs were nearby.

"Looks like they're having a go;" a worried NCO hurried past, his brow furrowed by sudden foreboding.

The Borneo Man said nothing. He cocked an eye at a single tracer round which careered harmlessly into the air, his lips pursed, his hands clasped thoughtfully round the barrel of his rifle which rested on its butt between his feet. Other figures appeared wraith-like beside him. He counted them. There were five.

"All here?" he said, meaning 'Is everyone here who should be?'

No-one spoke, silence somehow implying assent.

"Right, Kiwi... front. Geordie 'n' Tug, rear. You two can have the middle ton..."

A series of angry cracks interrupted him. Some of the men started at their closeness. They stood, awaiting his word to move down to the main gate.

"Okay," said the Borneo Man when it had gone quiet again, "There's a lot of shooting going on tonight..."

They waited for the rest of it. 'Watch out. Watch your oppo's back. Move like cats. If a man gets hit, the nearest to him grab his weapon and stay with him, the rest do the follow up. Stay on the

ball. Don't bunch. Watch out for light. Be faster off the mark than
a sprinter. Don't get caught out..."

But all he said was...

"You all been paid recently? You all got paid okay last time, did
you?" They nodded.

"Okay," he breathed, "You draw your money—you take your
chances." He looked at them.

"Let's go."

In a sangar near the gate, a sentry watched the six souls flit past
him and out onto the streets, six prowling, creeping, lurking souls,
flitting through shadows, alleys, bombed out sites, time suspended,
bastard creatures possessing no future and no past, no wives or loved
ones, homeless, kithless, disowned, orphans of the Belfast night.

It was daytime. The sort of day when nothing much was
happening. The sort of day when business was slack and reflexes
slackened, the sort of day when a good unit consciously fought the
temptation to relax and other units simply thought, 'there's nothing
much happening.' The sort of day when the beginning was long
forgotten and the end not yet even considered, when the well-oiled
machinery ticked over without any prompting, when officers
scanned the editorials, sergeants the property columns and Marines
the sports pages. The sort of day when Westminster MPs and
ministers made plans for their summer recess and the rest of the
nation bound rubber boats onto their roof-racks and headed for
Blackpool, Brighton or Biarritz. The sort of day in Belfast when
guards were mounted and patrols and OPs undertaken with
mechanical punctiliousness. The sort of day when a Marine lay on
his pit and prayed for something to happen to relieve the monotony.
And usually it did. Though never in quite the way he hoped for or
envisaged.

In a hut with the figure '6' on the door, men rose for breakfast.
Others didn't, having just got their heads down. Back again, the
breakfasters cleaned out their living quarters, quietly sweeping
round their sleeping comrades. Men formed working parties and
went about obscure tasks collectively or individually. Then they lay
on their pits for a few moments before going out on patrol. Marines
came in, discarded flak jackets and took a late breakfast. Others
donned them and went out. The morning wore on. Work, eat,

patrol, the unvarying routine. Early lunches for Marines going out, late lunches for those coming in. Working round the clock, chefs kept a constant supply of hot food available, roughly suited to the time of day. Afternoon working parties were formed and fatigues undertaken. Galley fatigues, painting, area-cleaning, sandbagging, making the location safer, more habitable. Men donned tracksuits and ran, worked out or played games of volleyball or football, shielded from snipers by tall, corrugated-iron screens. Early suppers, more patrolling, another guard, another OP. Marines ate, donned flak jackets and went out. Marines came in, downed flak jackets and took a late supper. Throughout the night Marines watched, guarded, patrolled, each duty, every time, carrying the same simple reward. A hot meal, an egg banjo, some sleep. In other huts, in other locations, in other towns across the province the same routine went on day in day out, week after week, month after month, with unceasing vigilance and unstinting effort, doing the job, seeing it through.

★   ★   ★

With a rattle and a bang Six Troop's door was flung open. In the doorway, blocking out the light, stood an ominously tall figure. The Company Sergeant-Major.

"Where's the Borneo Man?" he demanded in a voice that spelled doom for anyone unfortunate enough not to know.

"Down there, Sir," said a Marine quickly, happening to be nearest and therefore the most imperilled. He indicated the far end of the hut where the corporals slept.

"Better be ..." grunted Gentleman Jack. He loped off down the length of the hut, implied threat underlying every movement.

A countryman by birth, taller than everyone else and with the sort of hands and feet of which people took care to keep clear, he possessed the mannerisms of a backwoodsman, the manners of a gentleman and the manner of a gamekeeper, which once he had been. Autocratic, authoritarian, utterly loyal to those with the same interests at heart, he was the core of the Corps, truculent, compassionate, big hearted, a professional infanteer to the bone, the personification of the axiom that power ultimately rests upon fear, yet paradoxically no tyrant. He had no need to be for he took the line — and in this no-one had ever cared to challenge him — that he could out-yob the yobs, out-slob the slobs, out-soldier the soldiers and out-old soldier the old soldiers. He ruled with the unassailable combination of size, ridicule, wit, low-comedy and threatening gestures. A leer from Gentleman Jack could freeze water whilst the jab of a finger left all sensible bootnecks treading very lightly indeed.

Five minutes later he passed by again. On his way out he stopped and looked at Taverner who in the meantime had grabbed a broom and was looking busy.

"I wanna see you, don' Oi?" said Gentleman Jack, eyeing him.

"Don't know Sir," said Taverner quickly, hoping like hell he didn't.

"I DO, DON' OI?" he asserted, glowering menacingly at the Marine.

"Very good Sir," said Taverner, picking his words with care. Marine Commandos began sliding into lockers and disappearing into holes barely big enough to accommodate woodworm.

'Yes I do," decided Gentleman Jack. "I'll have a word with you out here."

They stepped outside.

The Sergeant-Major assumed the manner of a long-suffering landlord dealing with a peasant noted for his obtuseness.

"Taverner, old boy," he began matily, "Ja know a Marine Haythorne, by any chance?"

"Yessir."

"And a Marine Smith? KEN? Wha'bout him?"

"Yessir."

"Oh you do. 'Ow ja know 'em like?" asked Jack as if he didn't know.

"We were in the same squad in training, Sir."

"Oh...!" said Jack, feigning enormous enlightenment, "Were you now? So you, Haythorne and Smith KEN were in training together were you?"

"Yessir."

"Mmmm. And did you happen to be in Torquay together, the night you passed out of training, by any chance?"

"Yessir," said Taverner, the blood beginning to drain out of his already pale cheeks. He looked distinctly uncomfortable.

"Nice down there was it? Have a good run didja?" said Jack, piling on the agony. "What sort uv place is it, like? I mean, Oi've always wanted to *go* there."

"It was alright, Sir," said Taverner quickly, waiting for the sarcasm. But Gentleman Jack switched tactics.

"You go to the beach a lot, ole son, do ya? Y'know, the one at the seaside, that's the one I'm on about..."

"Yessir."

"And s'posing you wanted to sit down on the beach like, what'd ya sit on? Y'know, 'part from the sand itself?"

"I'd sit on my towel, Sir," answered Taverner, playing for time.
"Oh ...?" said Jack, interested. "The ole pusser's green towel, eh?"
"Suh."

"And what else ja think you could sit on, y'know I'm thinking of summink the council might provide for the likes of ole Bert 'n' Florry, y'know, when they've finished their paddlin' with the ole rolled up trousers and knotted 'andkerchief on the 'ead sorta routine, whereja think they'd sit?"

"On a deckchair, Sir?" conceded Taverner at length.

"Ah!" exclaimed Gentleman Jack, "Ah! A deckchair! Now we're getting somewhere, aren't we? And s'posing they couldn't find one, s'posing there wasn't enough to go round, why ja think that'd be?"

"Maybe the council hadn't supplied enough," said Taverner, fighting a stiff rearguard action.

"OR ...?" said Jack, crowding him.

"Or ... um ..." said Taverner, cornered.

"OR MAYBE SOME LIGHT-FINGERED BASTARD HAD NICKED ONE. DID JA EVER THINK OF THAT? EH?" thundered Jack bearing down aggressively upon the Marine.

"Suh."

"I'll bet you did! I'll bet that's exactly what you thought the night you, Haythorne and Smith lifted that deckchair. The adjutant's up to *here* with you three ..." The CSM made a gesture lifting the back of one hand up to the level of his face; "... he's got a file *this* thick on your fookin' deckchair. All of it letters from the police concerning you three twats. We've got better things to do out here than worry about your last run ashore! The Adjutant has! And OI have, certainly!"

"Suh."

"Somebody said you're old man's a judge, Taverner, is that right?"

"Magistrate, Sir."

"Well, s'posing the police decided to press charges and you wound up in front of your ole man. You'd look a biff, wouldn't you?"

"Yessir."

"And when you got wheeled in front of the CO for consequential punishment you'd look an even bigger biff, wouldn't you?"

"Yessir."

"Well, you're a biff anyway," said Jack putting it in the sort of everyday English people could understand.

"Pick up all the gash round the galley and the gash bins and underneath the vehicles in the MT park. Everybit of it! Sweet paper, chip paper, fag paper, wrappers, dog ends, everythink. I shall be walking across here in half-an-hour and it shall be spotless."

"Suh. Sir?"

"What?"

"I'm on foot patrol in twenty minutes."

"Well you'd better move your fingers then" chided Gentleman
Jack. He considered.

"Alright. I shall be walking across here breakfast time tomorrow,
and it shall be spotless then. Right? The whole o' this area..."

"Very good Sir."

"Right. Hop it. Taverner!" The CSM called him back.

"Yessir?"

"'Ow shall it be?"

"Spotless, Sir."

"Right. And Taverner! If ya come across any deckchairs on ya
travels tonight, leave the poxy things alone."

"Suh."

★   ★   ★

Next morning the area round the galley, the gash bins and in the
MT park was as spotless as the good Sergeant-Major could have
wished. But it nearly wasn't. Because at the end of an otherwise
uneventful foot patrol, one hundred metres and two minutes from
home, Taverner nearly got wiped out. Again tragedy struck at
Belfast. Only this time it missed and hit pure farce.

On this occasion, shortly before eleven at night, six members of
Gentleman Jack's company were making their way out of the network of back-to-back housing and high-rise flats that was the New
Lodge, prior to crossing the Antrim Road and heading for home.
Once across it, they would take a dark narrow street between houses
of a more grandiose design — tall three storey houses that had seen
better days — which led them back to a Territorial Army centre in
the grounds of which their huts were located. This manoeuvre was
complicated by a number of things.

For a start, because the TA Centre only had two entrances, the
manoeuvre formed the beginning and end of almost every patrol
venturing into and out of the New Lodge which was the company's
main responsibility, and therefore it created in the mind of an
observer a pattern of time and place which troops worked
assiduously to avoid, even to the point of the individual varying in
which doorways he paused for cover or upon what paving stones he
trod. Second was the fact that each patrol took its toll physically,
mentally and emotionally of the men who carried them out and in
the middle of a tour it wasn't only teenagers who found it difficult to
maintain the necessary high state of nervous awareness to the end of

the allotted amount of time. Third was the fact that at that time of night, the Antrim Road bore a fairly heavy stream of traffic because despite the troubles, the city of Belfast had not yet become the entertainment desert it would later. And if there was one thing a man on foot patrol disliked, it was getting caught in someone's headlights. To him, the sudden glare of light spelt ambush.

Parked at the side of the Antrim Road near where they would cross it, was a car. Even as the patrol worked their way out of the New Lodge, a Marine in a nearby observation post overlooking the area, suspicious of its presence, was relaying details of the car to his Company HQ for checking out. The patrol moved on and up towards the Antrim Road, pausing before crossing it between cars one at a time, each man making for the dark narrow street on the far side in a diagonal run that unwittingly took him away from danger. For what no-one knew at this stage was that the parked car—a stolen Cortina—contained a bomb. A pattern of time and place had been established. The terrorist was about to strike.

Finally there remained Taverner who had been watching the rear whilst the others crossed. With the sort of instinctive timing possessed by a member of a section who have worked together for months, he rose and slipped round the corner just as the fifth man reached cover on the far side. Momentarily he sank into the recess between two bay-windows before making his run.

The windows were shuttered and of a jutting, squarish design, offering a recess deep in shadow. For this reason they were the best cover available for five or six metres either way, but like anyone, Taverner took care not to use them too often in order not to develop an observable habit. A charge placed inside a building directed at someone outside was one of the terrorist's not-so-pleasant party pieces. As a result, he had never noticed just how deep the recess was, turning whenever he went in there to face immediately outwards, all his attention being focused at that point upon the road and the movements of the other members of the patrol.

He leaned forwards, holding his muzzle down, looking to left and right, assessing his run. The others were in position, covering him, waiting for him to complete the collective bound before moving off again. There were no car lights. He paused, counted two and stepped out.

At that precise moment the Cortina blew up. A hot blast hit Taverner, enshrouding him in a glow like a tropical sunset. At the same time something plucked hard at his elbow which was the forward-most part of his body, as though someone running past had grabbed him, trying to get him to come along too. Twenty-five

metres away, metal and glass disintegrated with a roar like the day
of judgement whilst the blast blew out windows, dislodged tiles and
ripped down the street, hurling, clutching, tearing...

"'FUCK-SHITT!!'"

Instinctively he rammed himself backwards into the recess,
wondering in shock and bewilderment what bloody fool had shouted
so close to him, feeling hotly angry with whoever it was for having
startled him; then realising with a kind of acute irrational
embarrassment that it had been himself, that the words had been
involuntarily torn from him as though, by ludicrously trying to
match the noise of the explosion, he were somehow persuading
himself he was still alive. Shaken to the core but miraculously
unharmed, he sank to the very back of the recess whilst Marines
crouching or lying across the street bowed their heads and hugged
the ground against the possibility of a second bomb.

Expecting his shoulders to touch the wall of the house, Taverner
leapt in renewed alarm when the back of his flak jacket touched
something soft that moved. His deductive processes weren't working
too well but realising someone was standing behind him, he whirled
round in agitation, thinking he had erroneously supposed the
Marine in front of him to have crossed when he hadn't. Seeking
reassurance and unable to see in the pitch black, he called his name.
There was no answer.

It was at this point that events turned into sheer farce. With
bounding heart and fluttering hand Taverner groped for his torch
and flicked it on. What he saw in its lurid beam stupefied him.

There was not one person but two. Over her shoulder, the pale
pinched face of a Belfast girl stared at him with curiosity. Behind
her, leaning against the wall, was her boyfriend, staring at him
incuriously. He assumed he was her boyfriend because they were
engaged—coitally. The torch picked out the details. The youth's
jeans and underpants lay round his feet. Nearby were those of the
girl. Her white shiny bottom was gripped by him, her legs were
entwined round the bare flesh of his midriff and her narrow bony
knees bore slight scrape marks where they had been coming into
contact with the wall.

Taverner stood struggling to cope with the myriad of conflicting
emotions passing through him like an electrified express; shock,
anger, embarrassment, renewed terror ... Now, with envious and
lecherous eyes, he felt like a guest at a party who, about to leave,
wanders upstairs and finds two people having it off in the room
where he left his coat. Forced out of hearth and home by the
presence of a parent, to two teenagers desperate to do it, a pair of

bay-windows in the Antrim Road must have seemed like an ideal place, a quiet nook for nooky. Trousers were dropped in the dark and furtive hands run over trembling white flesh. Connection was made. Slowly at first then faster, as rising lust began to gallop them towards the edge, the girl's knees thumped the brickwork. Then suddenly the youth had frozen, signalling silence — 'Sssh!' — in her ear. There, not a yard away, was a bootneck with rifle and beret in the entrance to their hidey-hole! Seconds later he disappeared. Seconds later there was another one. Then he left and another one appeared. ('Jesus Christ, how many more ...?') Heavy breathing and aching loins were agonisingly held in check. Finally, at the very moment the last one quit, a monstrous explosion heralding the end of the world occurred, flinging a Marine backwards upon them and causing coitus interruptus for streets. Deaf and disgruntled, but not quite disengaged, they stared at the intruder.

Taverner's ears rang like the bells of St. Peter's. From a million miles away came a voice. Like people at the seaside who are forced to take shelter from a rainstorm in the same place, the youth felt obliged to venture polite conversation about the circumstances which had brought them together.

"W-was that a bomb?" he stammered.

Having come within a whisker of being blown to bits by it, the Marine struggled desperately to find a suitably scathing reply. Or indeed, any reply at all. It was hopeless. His benumbed brain was utterly unequal to the task.

The girl took his silence to be contemptuous. Shifting her coital position, she rounded on him in defiance.

"*Ay* thought ut wawse..." she said.

It was too much for Taverner. He left.

★   ★   ★

A bomb had been thrown into a pub packed with Sunday dinner-time drinkers. Haythorne was a member of the patrol first on the scene.

A car shot out of the street where the pub was, revving wildly and clearly bent on escape. Some cocked their weapons. But they hadn't *seen* the bomb being thrown from it ...

They were there within seconds.

"TOO LATE! TOO LATE!" screamed agitated onlookers. "YOU'RE ALWAYS TOO LATE, YOU FOCKIN' BRITISH SOLDIERS ...!"

The unit ambulance team worked to evacuate the wounded and dead, hindered by a crowd whose mood and intentions were verging on hysteria. Haythorne stood in the cordon keeping them back. But they pressed forward and milled around, taunting the rescuers and getting in the way, the situation approaching flashpoint.

Within minutes of the explosion a huge crowd gathered, some running the entire length of the New Lodge Road to catch a ghoul-like glimpse of the carnage, others, seeking stimulation from sight and smell, arriving plainly determined to work themselves into a frenzy in order to attain some macabre sort of sexual and psychological release in provoking a greater bloodbath. And when the first camera-toting newsman arrived and the crowd began to play to the gallery, the fate of a good many people present was sealed.

An old man, a lifetime of drink and futility behind him, stood flinging his arms about, sobbing and guffawing with anger and hatred, uttering noises like an animal. Spying Haythorne, he wobbled over to him and stood, his face inches from the Marine's, ranting and raving, spittle flying ...

"WE HATE YOU, YOU BRITISH SOLDIERS!" he screamed, his voice cracking with emotion, "WE FOCKIN' HATE YOU! DON'T YOU ONDERSTAND THAT? WE FOCKIN' HATE YOU, YOU FOCKIN' BRITISH SOLDIERS ...!"

He spat at Haythorne. The teenager stood his ground, eyeing those who would do him harm, outwardly calm, inwardly his heart crashing like timpani, his face bearing a vaguely puzzled expression, like that of a schoolboy struggling with a quadratic equation he cannot solve; 'Please Miss, I can't do this...' Tears fell from the old man's eyes as he hopped and jumped about on the edge of apoplexy, inviting, begging the 'British hero' to hit him, to shoot him, to make a martyr of him, to put some meaning into a life that had never known any but the bottle. Whilst inside Haythorne's head, the voice of another Irishman, demure and serious behind the humour, said, 'Think of it this way, men. For seventy quid, you can have a good run ashore. So don't go spittin' your money away.'

The riot spread like wildfire, the first stone coming from a group of Protestants standing jeering at the end of the street. Instantly, an enormous man in Green Beret and Dennison smock, with cauliflower ear and face like thunder, shouted orders. Marines ran with their Commanding Officer down the street with the crowd, sprinting to get ahead of them in order to create a No Man's Land between the two factions, where they stood, alternately facing, viciously stoned and bottled from both sides, six bootnecks and one Lieutenant-Colonel.

The air was thick with missiles. Brick-ends, bottles, stones, concrete...

"PETROL BOMB...!" shouted the CO in furious warning.

A flaming bottle came over. The line moved and the bomb shattered harmlessly in the road, its evil sticky yellow liquid igniting in a lethal pool of flame that sent up a weird glare. Newsmen jostled to film their reporters with it in the background.

("Well, I'm standing here among the bottles, bombs and bullets of Belfast ... Silly Woofter, news at Big Ben ... ") The schmucks.

Elsewhere, Sunday newspapers rustled as people put their feet up to watch the afternoon weepy. Across the water, sophisticated intelligentsia discussed life and art over coffee sipped from ornate Coalport, whilst armchair-hugging moralists handed round expensive cigarettes in silver cigarette boxes that reposed upon Chippendale and debated the state of their consciences, damning the government for physically repressing and terrorising the population of Ulster.

And in Earl Street, Haythorne thought, "Remember the drill. Stand still. Don't move. Keep your eye on the ball. Watch your oppo's back and we'll get out of here alive ..."

★   ★   ★

Bored between spells on watch in an observation post, Smith finished reading a letter. Mail from the outside world — from anyone anywhere — was a highly prized affair. This one particularly. It was from his mate, Taverner.

Delighted at hearing from his old mucker, he went straightway in search of pen and paper. Though based only a mile apart, they hadn't met in months.

'Mama Grumble's Slightly Polished
Coconut Dancers.

'Dear Soul brother,' he wrote;

'Well Kiddo, I have had it. This whole N.I. bit is giving me the shits and there is every chance I shall go screaming into the nearest potato field and do meself in.

'Anyway bruv, it's great to hear from you from half way round the world, well just down the road anyway. Oh yeah, is a dwarf on the French underground a metronome? Send your answer on a postcard size tricolour.

'Life in this neck o' the woods has been somewhat interesting of late. We were shot at AGAIN the other night, not your average cowboy shooting but from VERY close to. Jeeze, I didn't just shit a brick, I nearly laid a house. Why me? Am beginning to think someone up there doesn't like me. However, we ignored the initial reaction to change our underpants and just made like Boy Rugsy for a bit. Y'know the game—leaping over fences and generally acting the cunt. Unfortunately didn't catch the bastard but maybe that

was more judgement than luck. Apart from that I come from a long line of Terror Strickens.

'Anyway son, stay bright, keep yer 'ead down and stick it out. (Mind you, Custer did and look what happened to him.) Don't delay, write today - or tommorrer. Smudge.

'PS. Notice the Cockney accent. I refuse to be bludgeoned by numerous Scots, Brummies, Yorkies, etc. into speaking like the lower forms of life that exist north of the Watford Gap. No surrender. Yeurghhh!

'PPS. Do you 'spose if I opened a stall in Brixton I'd be a black marketeer? No? Oh well...'

The sun was out. A group of girls wearing Doc Martin boots and half-mast jeans walked down a street chanting a current pop song, its words adapted to carry a meaning clearly special to themselves.

"'Get yourself a Luger or a Mauser gun,
  Nice to kill a British pig;
  Shoot him in the face and watch the blood all run,
  Nice to kill a British pig...'"

But apart from them, it was a lovely day. The leaves on the trees in North Queen Street were turning a beautiful golden-brown and there were autumnal mists at night. And that meant one thing. Time was wearing on. The end was in sight.

★   ★   ★

A group of fifty women rushed about from one man to another, engaging each one in strident 'conversation', snapping brittle, emotion-filled questions at him. The atmosphere grew tense and as other housewives and mothers joined in, attracted by the mocking shrieks of their neighbours and swelling their numbers to a couple of hundred, Marines began to look uneasily at one another.

Suddenly, they all turned on the NCO in charge, surrounding him and pressing in upon him from all sides, hurling questions and statements about grievances real and imagined in high-pitched neurotic frenzy. The atmosphere turned electric. In the bat of an eyelid an ordinary street in the middle of the working day was transformed into one about to witness an 'incident'.

The patrol was a standing patrol, keeping an eye on the employees of the tobacco factory, mainly girls, who had the habit of airing their sectarian differences during their lunch break. Buying pasties from shops on different sides of the street, they formed groups and harangued each other before curiously going back to work in the same place when the hooter sounded. Frequently, it wasn't only abuse or pasties that were shied across the street. Unless quickly checked, full-scale riots developed, riots which had the potential to spread district and province-wide, topple governments and start world wars.

It began simply enough, with two girls having a kicking, screaming, hair-tugging match. Whereupon the NCO in charge, who was the Borneo Man, intervened, telling them politely to knock it off. But a big hefty woman, taking the side of one, weighed in with, "What right have yew got to tell horr to do somethun'? Eh?" The NCO walked away and it seemed the incident was over. But the woman, wanting to make something out of nothing, kept up a torrent of abuse and because the patrol were obliged to stay where they were until the all clear, it simmered on. Now they were surrounded by scores of women all howling with derision and seeking an incident. The situation was poised on a knife-edge. The slightest gesture, the minutest motion and a woman would fall to the ground, 'beaten senseless', sparking off a riot as the rest went completely berserk. Crouching bootnecks eyed the inauspicious size of some of them. At the hands of two hundred maddened, hysterical women they were mincemeat and they knew it.

In the centre of it all stood the Borneo Man, looking for all the world as though he were unconcernedly chatting to fellow passengers at a bus stop. For long critical minutes he fielded their wildest allegations, keeping his cool, exercising judgement and self-control in the face of vicious squalls of verbal assault. Little by little, he managed to undercut the collective desire for violence, taming the incident-seekers with poker-faced patience and deadpan humour, giving away not a clue, not a twitch, not even the slightest twinkle.

"YEW!" yelled one, pointing her finger at him, "I REMEMBER YEW! ARE YEW HERE TO TORTURE OS AGAIN? ARE YEW HERE TO MURDER OUR PEOPLE ...?"

"No," he calmly rebutted the accusation, "As a matter of fact, we're not ..."

"THEN WHADDA YEW HERE FOR, IN GOD'S NAME?" she shrieked apoplectically.

"'Cos we like it here," he said, "We find it very agreeable. We like to see all your charming, smiling faces. In fact we like it here so much, we're here on leave at the moment ..."

Disappointment and vexation showed as it began to dawn on them they weren't going to succeed in winding him up. For a brief moment they were at a loss, uncertain what other tactic to try, and in that moment the Borneo Man did a singularly intelligent thing. Slowly and calmly, so they could see he was not doing something hostile, he reached into the breast pocket of his flak jacket and withdrew a pipe which he put into his mouth. Then he took out a lighter and with slow, calculated flicks of the thumb, ignited it and applied it to the bowl of the pipe which contained tobacco.

It was the turning point. It was more. In the circumstances, it was an act of such intrinsically courageous quality that the press would have done well to record it. Robert Capa Award-seeking photographers might have got the shot of a career: exclusive — 'The Crowd-Tamer.' But they were all in the bar of the Europa Hotel with their newsmen, tapping out Belfast stories of a different kind over their third double Scotch of the day. Seeking sensationalism — like making comparisons between Ulster and Vietnam which no-one really believed — for the sake of newspaper sales and job security. A bomb was news, its defusing not; a riot an event, its defusing a non-event. So here was no 'scoop' for the press. The very lack of sensationalism precluded it. The lighter was applied not to Viet-Cong huts or to Belfast buildings but to the Borneo Man's bent and battered Falcon pipe. And the smoke that drifted into the crowd was not that of burning flesh or timber, but a secret mixture of quite unbelievable pipe tobaccos known only to the Borneo Man himself and called by him 'Old Socks'. Perhaps for that reason alone, people began moving away. It was hard enough to argue with a benign pipe-smoker at the best of times, let alone one smoking that stuff.

Grabbing eating irons and cup, they nipped across to the galley for a late lunch, picking up stainless steel meal trays and standing in the queue.

"Ah well," boasted a bootneck triumphantly, "We just about averted World War Three again s'morning, down the bottom o' the Lodge ..."

Gentleman Jack glanced at his contemporary, the Borneo Man, in sympathy; then at the members of the patrol, a look of withering sarcasm on his face.

"I wish I could pay you fooking blokes more ..." he said.

The INTELLIGENCE SUMMARY stated, "... These and other sources confirm that the Provisional IRA are now definitely planning to hit us in our final week. They haven't had much luck with us so far and are therefore desperate. *Don't give them the*

chance. Stay alert and alive for a well-earned leave." The signature
was that of the Company Intelligence Senior NCO.

With rumours of impending mortar attacks also flying around,
Smith sat down and addressed himself to Taverner, from whom he
hadn't heard for a while.

> *'The Incredible Shrinking Man's*
> *Tombola & Euphonium Players'*
> *Reedy Voice Snail Choir.*
> *B F Pissed Off.*

'Hello soul bruvver,

*'Fuck me, I gonna crack. "Damn it Sidney, it'll be over by
Christmas." Like I was saying, as I haven't received communications
from you since before Corunna, my simple mind deems it necessary
to enquire "WHERE THE JERKIN HELL IS MY BODY BUILDING
LITERATURE?" As you may have gathered, the threads are beginning
to snap. At present am suffering from triple creeping leprosy of the
left side. I've got so much poison in my system after four months in
this circus, I'm going to need "milking". And what with the budgie
going down with malaria and the dog 4 streets away committing
Hari-Kiri in the shower, it's been a bloody awful week.*

'We returned from guard at the Crumlin Road Zoo yesterday for
the last time but one thank gawd. It is only now after numerous
sedative measures, several Newcastle Brahns to be exact, that I can
talk intelligently about our forays into that particular unknown.
Glubling! There is a faint sniff of incongruity about watching over a
crew of twisted killers and bombers playing a harmless game of
football. Their primitive mind patterns!! Dunno what I kept
expecting them to do—strangle the ball or something.*

*''Phoned the Old Queen yesterday, tell her when we'd be home.
Just about stopped her catching the next ferry out. I keep on looking
out for you, incidentally, in case you're hanging onto some localised
sort of mortar rocket. But being as that mode of travel is still in the
experimental stage, I shall expect to see you on the ship.*

*'Anyway me old china, roll on 'ome. And you're paying for the
nosh by the way. Nothing too ostentatious. Prawn Cocktail, Filet
Mignon, a couple of quick flashes of Escargot finishing up with a
turreen or so of Pusser's custard and rice. But it'll probably be a
double dollop of egg & chips!*

*'And now my son, the Commando man with his brief case full of
jelly babies will head for the big divide just outside of Wapping.
Thee you tweetie! Smudge.'*

*The Crumlin Road Jail.

Pinned on the notice board were a number of letters addressed to the company commander, the handwriting and spelling of which often betrayed the unfamiliarity of the writer with putting pen to paper. All, however, expressed gratitude. The heartfelt gratitude of those who lived in the shadow of violence and who derived from the company's presence comfort and reassurance for themselves and their families. Their sentiments were conveyed in religious and sometimes stumbling phrases. One, from a woman, read simply,

> *'Dear Sir,*
> *Thank you and your brave men for being here. I pray daily for you all. I hope you will soon be with your loved ones again. May the Good Lord watch over you wherever you have to go. God Bless you all.'*

The paper was small and ruled in straight lines and the address was in the heart of a hardcore area. Others were written on cards. One depicted Lourdes, another the Virgin Mary.

The final week was a microcosm of all that went before. Reacting to a massive explosion in his area of observation, a Marine manning an OP radioed laconically, "Hello Two, that were the York Road railway station just went oop ...!" Minutes later came savage comedy as the dazed and grazed driver of a light vehicle reported hesitantly, "... the blast has blown my landrover over, over."

Dusk was falling as a woman approached a Marine on foot patrol.

"God bless you, son," she whispered.

"Eh?"

A door opened.

"I said 'YOU FOCKIN' BRITISH SOLDIER!'"

"S'more like it ..." observed the bootneck.

Curtains moved. A hand appeared, waving, beckoning. With elaborate caution a patrol approached, wary of a 'come-on'. Inside the house was a distraught and frightened woman.

It needed meticulous planning, preparation and execution. A fullscale covert operation was mounted. Armed with special equipment of wire, plunger and rods, the patrol returned under cover of darkness, gaining entry and going to work with shielded torches. Their mission: to unblock her drains without the neighbours knowing. The stairs ran with sewage. For days she had been unable to bring herself to ask for help, petrified of reprisal.

Then it happened.

A Marine was killed. Not at the the hands of the Provisional IRA, but speeding across the city in response to a 999 call. As the mobile patrol crossed a road junction, the rear Landrover was hit by a car.

Marines spilled from it, one of them cracking his head against a bollard. He never regained consciousness. This time the surgeons could do nothing. But his mates, typically, did something.

Gentleman Jack presided over the sale of kit, auctioning off the dead man's military property in a ceremony that reflected the attitude of those present to life and death. Hardly sombre, more a pantomime, an irreverent gathering of the company to which people came in order to pay their last respects to one of their own who had died sharing the same risks, to bid astronomical prices for a piece of his webbing, a water bottle or medal ribbon and thereby to provide something for his family, themselves a part of the larger family, the Corps.

A pannier-dragging storeman, rumoured to be in league with Jack, artificially bumped up the bidding, crossing and re-crossing the compound with shouts of "FIVE! FIVE! Awright—TEN, then!" before disappearing; then reappearing at a crucial stage to give a wave in what always cunningly contrived to be the penultimate bid as Jack harried and cajoled and browbeat the bidders into parting with their money.

"... Forty, forty, forty, do I hear forty-five? Thank you, fifty, fifty, fifty—c'mon you tight bastards, cough up! YOU, you 'avent't bought nuffin' yet, 'ave you? Well, how about it? Right, sold to that man there—the web belt. Whaja mean the buckle's broken? Whaj'expect for fifty quid??

"Right next lot—a pair of long, olive green shreddies—look good in bed with the wife with these on, eh? There's elastic round the top and a slit down the front so's you can lob it out in case you want a bit. Now who'll gimme five? Thank you. Do I hear ten, ten, ten—ten for a pair o' passion-killers ..."

And when the last lot was gone and the kit-bag itself had been sold, there stood a four figure sum for a nineteen year-old widow.

There was vengeance too. A highly satisfying, personal vengeance. The capture of a man wanted for the crippling of a Marine of another unit.

★   ★   ★

On the corner of two streets is a house and at the corner of the house, a door. The door is at forty-five degrees to both streets and it is watched from opposite by a man who has placed an explosive charge at ground level behind the door.

Concealed in another house, he waits, keeping apart two wires that will complete the circuit and blow the charge. A patrolling

Marine pauses in the doorway. The wires touch, the door erupts and the Marine falls to the ground, his feet and ankles severed from his body. Quietly the man leaves as the smell of detonated explosive mingles with the blood and groans of a young bootneck in the throes of death.

In silent fury, the others bind first field dressings onto the shattered stumps of his legs. A sergeant kneels beside him, cradling his head, calming him, reassuring him, urging him to hold on, to fight the waves of pain and shock that threaten to send him under. Life flickers in him as feebly as a lightbulb with a faulty connection. Before the ambulance arrives to rush him to hospital, one booted foot is found in the gutter nearby, the other lying a distance up the street.

For days it is touch and go. But deep down amongst the trauma that wracks his body and psyche is a tiny nugget of willpower, the will to live, the desire not to be beaten but to embrace life again on any terms. Bit by bit, his mental attitude pulls him through. After a month filled with alarms and set-backs and lapses, he is photographed again, smiling.

But for someone who knows the perpetrator of the deed, the awfulness of that night will never recede. For months they will it to —to no avail. Finally, their conscience can stand it no more. With trembling hand, a receiver is lifted, a voice speaks in a whisper ...

"Listen, y'know the Shandon Street bomber? Aye, the one who did fer one of your boys? Well listen carefully, you'll find him at ..."

The procedure was good. Slickly the machinery went into action. Men took up positions knowing exactly what was required of them. Gentleman Jack reserved the main role for himself.

The Shandon Street bomber was watching television. When he saw the Sergeant-Major, he leapt up. For a second they eyed one another.

"There's two ways of doing this," Jack told him, "And neither of them looks good from where you are."

The man hesitated—then chose the first way. He leapt over the furniture in a bid for the back door. Jack got there first. He swung a fist like a cylinder.

Into the dark serried mass of backed up waves, the 'Sir Galahad' and the 'Sir Percival', two vessels of the Royal Fleet Auxiliary, snubbed their stubby bows. Flat-bottomed landing ships, they rose and pitched and corkscrewed in the teeth of an easterly, riding in the manner of their design, not through but over everything the sea put before them to the intense discomfiture of all on board. It hardly mattered. Liberated after months under a restrictive routine and the daily threat of death, the atmosphere on board was euphoric.

Everyone was talking at once. Queues for six-packs and Naafi goods wound round the galley flat. Cans of beer pished and frothed and cigarettes were hoarded as old oppos, long separated, sought each other out. There were only two topics of conversation; the tour behind them and the leave ahead of them. Conversation piled upon conversation, laughter obliterated laughter. In a corner, a television set flickered, its screen crackling with interference in the middle of the Celtic Sea. Football fanatics watched as England failed to qualify for the '74 World Cup, beaten by Poland. It mattered not. Each man's presence on board was his own personal victory.

In a passageway jammed with noisy burbling bootnecks sat Smith and Taverner, clicking cans, hoovering ale, planning their leave.

"A week's leave is forever," said Smith.

"Too right," assented Taverner, leaning back playing with a can of beer, "What'll we do?"

"I'll come to your place," said Smith.

"Then I'll come to yours ..."

"Right. Then we'll go to Phil's."

Smith belched. A gassy nauseous mixture of air and alcohol shot from his gullet.

"Where is he, by the way?" he asked suspiciously.

Haythorne appeared.

"Where you bin?"

"Spewing," replied Haythorne weakly.

"Seasick?" echoed Taverner, "But you're a Marine!"

"Whaddya wanna drink the sea for?" enquired Smith, "We're on beer ..."

Haythorne sat down.

"I feel ill," he said, "Canned beer in this sea's murdering my guts ..."

"Here!" remonstrated Smith, "If you're gonna give it Burt 'n' Harry again, go somewhere else."

"Burt 'n' Harry?"

"Buuuurrrpppll—'Eaaaarrreeeghll!" explained Smith trying to make him feel better.

"Why didn't I join the Pay Corps?" moaned Haythorne.

"'Cos fate wouldn't allow it," pronounced Smith sternly, "You

had to be a hero. What's the crumpet like down your way, Tav?"

"Wonderful. Truly wonderful. There's this bird I know called Gina ..."

"Tasty?" asked Smith, "Bit o' class?"

"She is — gorgeous. She's a barmaid ..."

"Ah," grunted Smith knowledgeably.

"... and she's about nineteen but you can't get near her for the queue."

"See. Beer 'n' women," said Smith taking a swig. "That's all the other ranks think about. I read it in a report. Beer and women ..."

"There's no such thing as 'other ranks' in the Marines ..."

"No? What are they then?"

"Bootnecks. Marines. Howling commandos. Men of action. People who can hack it after the rest have jacked it in ..." said Taverner in a 'Nigel-Green-in-Tobruk' voice.

"The chaps," said Haythorne in an officer's voice.

"That's it — the chaps," said Smith, hoovering more ale, "Here's to 'em. The Chaps. Good 'ealth."

They clinked cans and drank.

> "'Aye aye-aye-aye! Me and my soggy sombrero!
> Sombrero sombrero sombrero sombrero—
> Sombrero sombrero sombrero ...'"

"Ahh ..." breathed Smith, wiping his mouth, "This canned's alright but I couldn't half go a pint o' the old wallop down Shoreditch or Essex way. Ho, I can picture it now — a sleever set up on the bar of the William the Conqueror, froth jus' running over the edges ..." A look of longing entered his eyes.

He blinked.

"This Gina," he said, "Bit of alright, is she? Why don'tcha give her a ring?"

"Goo' idea, mate," nodded Taverner, "Tell ya what, she's got the loveliest pair of ..."

"Eyes, did you say? Tell ya *what* — there's more ex-bootnecks down the Bill than almost anywhere I know. You won't have to put your hand in your pocket hardly when we go down there ..."

> "'It's a shame these slugs ain't real
> I love to hear those convicts squeal
> At the local hop, at the local county jail
>   Whatcha gonna do about it, whatcha gonna do?
>   Whatcha gonna do about it, whatcha gonna do?'"

"Hah, a whole week's leave ..."

"It'll be like living."

"Will it ever ..."

"Whaddarewe gonna do?"

"Right, let's go through it again. Take notes. You come to my place ..."

"No, I don't, you come to my place first, then we both go to Phil's."

"No we don't. You come to my place and Phil comes to my place, then we all go to your place, then we all go to Phil's place."

"Look, start again. I come to your place, right? Then what happens?"

"I dunno. I don't care. It's gonna be great—it's gonna be great anyway. There's gonna be some o' this and plenty o' that and some o' the other ... Wall-op!"

> " *'Sergeant Baker faced the crowd with a ball-point in his hand*
> *He was cool, he was calm, he was always in command;*
> *he said "Blood will flow—*
> *here padre; padre, you talk to your boys—*
> *God will surely find a way ..." '"*

> "'*Load up, load up, load up with ru-bber bullets*
> *Load up, load up, load up with ru-bber bullets ...*'"

On Wednesday, 18th October, 1973 the Commando concluded a tour of internal security duty in Belfast, two below approved complement. One wounded, one dead.

★ ★ ★

Haythorne's girl-friend looked at him on his first night home.

"You've changed, Phil," she accused, "You're all sort of hard and not like you were at all. What are you looking at me like that for?"

Haythorne was taken aback. He hadn't realised he was looking at her like that. By the end of the evening he had realised it was time for a new girl-friend, though. Off with the old and on with the new.

Smith vowed he was going to have a woman every night of his leave. But he needed a car for the purpose, so with two hundred notes in his pocket, saved from the tour, he went off in search of one. At a garage in East London where a number of his old mates worked, he ran into aggro in the form of Harry, a local wide boy. Harry seemed to object to Smith. There was a stand off. Smith eyed Harry—then dropped him. But Harry raided a tool box and came up with a starting handle and for a moment it looked as though there might be serious trouble until Smith's civvy mates obligingly intervened, not wishing to miss out on the fun.

"Leave the soldier-boy alone, 'Arree ... (dink, dink) ... leave the soldier-boy alone, I *sed*!"

Harry left ignominiously, swearing vengeance. Everyone felt
better for the little rumble bar him, but that didn't matter—he was
from Hoxton and thus off limits. Smith bought the car, a Vauxhall
—"Lovely job, Ken, nice little runner. Come in handy for a bank
job ..."—then celebrated with a midday sesh in the pub. The same
afternoon, the western world was rocked by the doubling of oil
prices—"Oh, charming, that. Alright, which one of you's the spy?
Who's bin on the 'phone to Sheik Yamani telling him I've just
bought a motor ...?"

All three bootnecks exhibited marked reluctance to walk
anywhere without fixed purpose now. When his mother suggested
he go out for a breath of fresh air one afternoon, Haythorne
explained he was on leave. Also, women apart, things which had
interested them previously now bored them. None of them watched
television any more, having had a surfeit of media and politicians
over the other side. On the other hand, they found that the petty
tensions of everyday life now tended to pass clean over their heads.
In particular, Haythorne and Taverner liked to lounge around on
the carpet in their homes. It was luxurious to them and they
couldn't seem to get comfortable on the furniture. Much to their
mothers' consternation, they even took to sleeping in front of the
fire. Constantly stepping over him, Haythorne's mother found
herself wondering if this great big long-legged creature was really
her son. He'd grown so much since he first left home. A year ago he
had been such a pleasant boy—the captain of the school football
team. Now the word 'boy' didn't seem to apply to him any more.

There weren't any carpets in Smith's home. There was a lot of
love instead.

All three swore they were going to sleep for a week when they got
back but none of them found they wanted to. They got up early
every day. Smith hammered on the door of his local if it didn't open
bang on time; he then spent the rest of the day in there playing
euchre before coming home for a bath at five and setting off on his
rounds of pubs and clubs at seven-thirty, finally winding up at a
Chinese or Indian restaurant after midnight. Taverner went fishing
in the mornings, then over to Chatham during the afternoons where
he was doing his bit for inter-service relations by keeping a naval
two-and-a-half's wife warm whilst her husband was at sea. She
excused him clothes all afternoon. Haythorne sat in a Glastonbury
café the first couple of mornings, flirting with schoolgirls and
wasting no time in dating one. It was freezing when he first kissed
her goodnight outside her home, but slipping a hand inside her
coat, he soon discovered a place of infinitely more charm, all warm,

wet and inviting. Whereupon they consummated the evening in the woodshed. The next day she was sixteen.

When they visited Shoreditch and were surrounded by the saw-toothed accents of London's East End, Haythorne and Taverner found to their surprise that Smith's accent had in fact yielded to the assorted Jocks, Brummies and Yorkies with whom he had been consorting over the past year. The Old Queen fussed about, making them tea, whilst Smith's dad 'Scrapper,' an ex-pug now down to one lung, occupied his favourite threadbare armchair—from where he shadow boxed, compulsively unable to keep his hands still as he talked with his son's mates.

"See, loneliness is endemmick to the 'uman race (pow-pow, jab-jab). But not me ... (straight right) I can't get away from people enuff! (Feint, duck, weave) I goes to the park, don' I? (couple of lefts). It's empty, beautiful (floating like a butterfly) ... really quiet, peaceful, tranquil (stinging like a bee), I'm enjoying every minute of it, ain't I? (hands and shoulders going). Then along come anuvver geezer (covering up defensively) the whole bleedin' park an' he has to sit next ter me (combination punches) ... Starts talkin'—'Fink it's gonna rain?' ... (left to chin, right hook, KO)"

"Cuh ...!" he confided in Haythorne, "When it come to them teligraph poles I 'ad me dahts about him, I fought no way is 'e gonna make it, 'e'll be back 'ome soon ...

"'Ere! You didn't like luggin' them teligraph poles abaht in training, didja?"

"Whaja think I was gonna do," retorted Smith, pulling a face, "Jack it in and become electricity linesman?"

"Haaaagh!"

Henry Cooper, Jimmy Greaves and Bobby Moore were all 'good boys,' Reggie 'n' Ronny were part of local folklore and Nipper Read who put 'em away, he was not a bad lad either. Respect for the Ole Bill certainly, but in the East End of London 'fings do have a habit of fallin' offa back o' lorries, I 'spect it's the same dahn your way ...' Scrapper Smith was also a living encyclopaedia of local boxing lore; So-'n'-So out-pointed Whatsname, Young Kid drew wiv Basham at Stepney but Geezer went dahn Wappin' and was laid out flat on the canvas inside o' free! Mind you, he had him back, he got him wiv eighteen inches o' lead pipe down a dark alley one night—haaaagh!

Taverner's folks had prepared a formal dinner-party for him on his first night home, inviting people in for the occasion. He hardly minded; he was too happy just to be home safe and sound and in

pleasant surroundings once again. But he found himself sitting next
to a woman in educational administration, a highly politically
charged person with ambitions to stand for election somewhere.
Election to what was not exactly clear, but with hair cropped short
on top, straggly below, a table cloth for a dress and her every
reaction wired into social guilt, it was soon apparent that nothing
escaped her condemnation. Everything was either bourgeois or
fascist or repressive or something. As for the Armed Forces, the
whole subject was like a red rag to a bull. There were only two
reasons why anyone would join up; either they were too stupid to
earn their own living or they were possessed by a raving blood lust.

'Such a balanced person,' thought Taverner, 'She'd make a good
cabinet.'

Upon learning that he had just returned from duty in Northern
Ireland, she rounded on him.

"I suppose you've killed people over there."

Taverner looked at her.

"Hundreds, actually," he replied matter-of-factly. "Why do you
ask?"

The woman recoiled visibly—then tried again.

"Couldn't you have joined a more thinking profession than the
Army?"

"You mean—such as your own?"

She glared at him.

"I'm not in the Army, anyway," he volunteered, "I'm in the
Marines."

Her knife and fork were set down with a click.

"They're worse," she snorted, incensed, "They're nothing but
animals."

Taverner repressed a grin.

"I'll pass your views on to the Commandant-General," he
rejoined, "I'm sure he'd be interested."

"We're going to disband your regiment when we come to power."

He groaned inwardly. He was about to reply 'And sleep the
sounder for having done so, presumably' when he stopped. There
was no point in pursuing conversation with her. She was a moron;
dense, impassioned, bigoted, power-hungry, pompous, petty and
pathetic and as such, ideally suited to political life. 'Who didn't eat
their greens up for lunch, Mr. Speaker, anyway—eh? Nair-nair-nair
...' When, as now, reasoned argument failed, the party cassette
simply took over.

He half-listened to her well-worn clichés as she launched into a
political tirade. Her drivel failed entirely to impair his appreciation

of his mother's food and father's wine, however.

"... my party is determined to end all exploitation of the masses and repression by the forces of the state ... the Army the last bastion of privilege ... the masses are on the move ... the embodiment of fascistic state capitalism which we are determined to dismantle ... new freedom ... democratic and socialist era ... determined to end oppression and self-interest and social inequality and injustice and social iniquity ..."

'Fine words,' thought Taverner, 'Great words — but apart from being her election ticket, what does any of it mean?'

"I mean, you take the miners ..."

Yeah, take 'em. All the way to Butlins.

Hurrah. Hallelujah. In the words of the prophet — Sock it to 'em, baby. The speaker raises her hands. The audience leaps to its feet. Applause pounds the platform. The masses burst into the Internationale and march outside to victory and annihilation. Godhead. Deity. I'll promise you anything if only you'll elect me so I can be up there when the party leaders hug. Up there amongst all the power and the glory. Gloria in excelsis. For ever and ever. Amen. Now get stuffed.

Taverner tuned into the young lady on his right. A rich man's daughter up at university reading the rich-man's-daughter's subject of sociology. No chance of a leg-over here, Mummie hasn't shown her what it's for yet.

Chauvinist pig.

Precisely.

"Are you an officer?"

"No, I'm one of the trogs."

End of conversation.

He listened to her holding forth on the sociologist's favourite theme — class warfare. Nowadays, it seemed, the nation was no longer divided into the three old traditionally implacable classes of upper, middle and working. Today, thanks to sociology, it was divided into six new 'classless' classes, social class one, social class two and so on. This was an enormous advance! At the top now were people with degrees who had got there by a new thing called 'merit.' It was triumph for social engineering. No longer did the unskilled labourer have to doff his cap to the gaffer, etc. etc.

Taverner couldn't help observing that the most unskilled labourers he knew were people who possessed degrees.

"Have you actually met the working classes yet?" he enquired, "Or are you still on the theory?"

If looks could kill, the budding sociologist would have succeeded where the IRA's Antrim Road car bomb had failed.

"Well now," intervened the JP diplomatically, casting a benevolent eye over his son, "What are you going to do for the rest of your leave, Neil?"

"Fish," answered Taverner, "Or I might trap. Phil and Ken are coming up anyway."

★   ★   ★

Inside the 'Pilotage,' an old coastal inn near the north Kent village of Saltsea, a huge log fire cast dancing patterns over the carpet and around the walls. Outside, fog rolled inland off the Oaze Deep. Behind the bar an attractive and vivacious girl served.

Taverner ordered three more pints and watched Gina refurbish their glasses. As he reached back to place two of them in his mates' outstretched hands, he wondered how the hell Smith did it. Within minutes of entering he had made himself the centre of attention whilst all other competitors for the barmaid's eye stood around him looking on like bit-part players, required only when Smith required them. As talkers they were simply not in his league. Smith had sometimes laid claim to possessing more rabbit than Sainsbury's and tonight his two muckers were beginning to think him right.

By the time 'Last Orders' came—"Shoot me!" shouted Scrapper's eldest, and there were those who wished they could—it was crystal clear who Gina had eyes for. Her telephone number, scribbled down and torn off the bar pad, proved it. That prized piece of paper was in Smith's pocket. He was in love. "She's essence—I'm smitten," were his precise words.

★   ★   ★

In dusty Nicosia, the sons of EOKA murderers renewed an old oath.

"Makarios preby na pethane."

"Makarios must die."

"How soon, Nicos?"

"Soon, my friend, soon. Then all Kypros will be ours."

At an army staff college near Ankara, a Turkish General tapped a file marked **Top Secret**.

"We have made many staff studies of the invasion over the years, but the political opportunity is now with us. Once we have launched *ATTATURK*, neither the Soviets nor NATO will intervene. Both will be aghast at the prospect of another European conflict."

CHAPTER 3

Armed Predicament

CYPRUS 1974

Over the shimmering Mediterranean island the midday sun climbed to its zenith. Beneath its scorching rays which bore down upon bended back and reddened skin, men dug in stifling heat. Picks thudded into parched earth, shovels clinked against stone, flies droned. In growing slit-trenches and gunpits, sandbags were held open, filled with spoil, and passed up to be used with rocks and natural features to throw up defences. Rivers of sweat streaked olive green-clad bodies. Covered head to foot in a film of light brown dust, troops built road blocks and observation posts overlooking key routes and approaches. A man paused, straightening up to mop his brow on his shirt. Round about him, the countryside lay ominously quiet.

Work

Dig

Sweat

It was two small enclaves of land on the south coast of the island that the pickers and shovellers were preparing to defend. Two territories at Dhekelia and at Akrotiri, separate from the island's republic, sovereign base areas retained by the British, each with its own autonomous police force. Around these enclaves lay a countryside dotted with dark green orange groves, tall trees and shining flat-roofed villages distinguished by parapets, pointed bell-towers and basking domes. North of Dhekelia stretched the Mesaoria Plain; inland, watching over Akrotiri, brooded the Troodos massif. Across that plain, behind those mountains, an event was taking place which lent urgency to men's actions. Armour was rolling ashore in the region of Kyrenia on the north coast.

75

Further inland, paratroops had landed, seizing routes for the island's capital, Nicosia. Turkish forces were invading.

Work

Dig

Sweat

A day or two earlier, Archbishop Makarios, the island's president, had fled to Britain, toppled from power by a former EOKA gunman, Nicos Samson, backed by the junta in Greece. Whereupon the Turks mounted an amphibious landing on Cyprus on the pretext of being alarmed for the safety of the Turkish Cypriot minority. In the face of the invasion, the everyday deep-seated fear, suspicion and hostility which existed between the island's two communities now burst into open conflict. Greek Cypriots held Turkish communities hostage; Turkish Cypriots fled to the British-administered Sovereign Base Areas for protection; Greek Cypriots fleeing the invasion did the same. Intimidation, arson and looting were widespread; property was destroyed; Nicosia was bombed at the hands of the Turks; Famagusta burned at the hands of the Greeks. British and American retirees and vacationers sheltered in the basements of their shattered homes and hotels.

With mutual hatred and palpable anti-UN feeling reigning on both sides, once again the bootnecks found themselves in a three-cornered contest. Local politics were obscure, even capricious. The EOKA B, successors to the anti-British EOKA of Grivas in the 1950s and still bent upon union with Greece, were known to have infiltrated the island's Greek National Guard. London newspaper reports of atrocities committed by that organisation therefore incensed the Greek community. Additionally, the influx of thousands of Turkish refugees into the Sovereign Base Areas where they were fed and accommodated by the British, lent weight to the universal Greek belief that the British troops — who were preparing to defend the island against its Turkish invaders — somehow harboured pro-Turkish sympathies. Used to such paranoia in another part of the world, the troops themselves simply shrugged at it.

Within nineteen hours of the invasion, the Commando, which was the United Kingdom spearhead unit, was landed by air at Akrotiri. Straightaway it set about defending the western base whilst Marines of a brother unit, choppered in from the carrier 'Hermes,' did the same at Dhekelia in the east. Both units began to control the torrents of panic-stricken refugees, mounted sorties to evacuate the wounded and homeless UK and US citizens to HMS 'Hermes' and USS 'Trenton,' and prepared to defend strategic points across the island. But the Turks, having established a salient which reached down as far as Nicosia, paused to consolidate. At the same time, Britain, a signatory to the tripartite agreement of 1960 guaranteeing the island's independence, despatched tanks with supporting infantry to the two Commando units. Behind the scenes, politicians talked. On the ground, the troops watched, waited and continued to reinforce their positions in preparation for the expected Turkish break-out. AIR ARTY MOR TKS INF—the hardware keeps pouring in.

Work
Dig
Sweat

Deliberate defence ... concealment, depth, support, 'range to that road junction there'; priority and extent of work, sandbags against 155 millimetre guns ... "Don't waffle about it, just fill the fuckers up." Track, supply, tunnel, sewer and deception plans.

Ground ... approaches, obstacles, natural features, friendly positions; ground of our own choosing, ground affecting the plan, dominating ground, high ground, low ground, soft ground, hard ground, dead ground, killing ground, denial of ground.

Enemy forces, friendly forces, attachments, detachments, reserves, battle casualty replacements, us, them, the politicos.

Mission: 'to defend ...' repulse, repel, drive out, oust, bump, crack, slot, flatten, hammer, mallet, barrel, welly, zap, smash, cream, crunch, splunch, yomp, blat, neutralise, destroy, eliminate, obliterate, annihilate ... 'to defend'. Co-ordinate, deceive, dominate.

Communication, anticipation, target indication, target pre-registration; the battery, base-plates, anti-tanks, recce, AE's, sigs; grid, add, subtract, in clear, encode, decode, code-word, nick name, act upon—'Now!' The artful skills of the Marine Commandos.

Enfilade, defilade, fixed lines, interlocking, locked against rotation, swinging traverse; Schermuly, trip-flare, HEAT round, HESH round, beaten zone, accuracy, hard-hitting power, reference points, strong points, gun emplacement, 'able to withstand,' danger arc in rear, 1020 feet per second, available alternatives ....

Boot, butt, bayonet, belt, banjo, nut, knuckleduster, cheesewire, Jo-Jo, To-To, Killjoy, MANDI, QM's Delight, GRENADE A PERS, Perce ...*

'Fire ...' fields of fire, deliberate fire, rapid fire, sniper fire, harrassing fire, defensive fire, pre-arranged fire, sustained fire, high concentration of fire, final protective fire. All arms shoot to *kill*.

Tactical requirements, high degree of protection, efficient distribution, maximum exploitation. 'Exploit, *Exploit*, EXPLOIT!'

In the shade of two Landrovers the CO made his dispositions:

*Perce: Short for 'Percy Pongo,' a generic term for members of the British Army. Note also the Latin: *Pongo Britannicus*.

"Ian, I want you on the left flank; be particularly careful, they may try and turn you on the flat ground between here and the sea. Jumbo, you're to hold the middle ground here, you'll probably take the main weight of their thrust—don't worry about it, I'll have Duggie in reserve right behind you. Alan, I want your assault engineers to string out some surprises for them up on the high ground here to convince them that this is the way to come—if the armour pull their finger out and get here on time, I'll give you a couple of tanks to cover this defile with; meanwhile it's down to you alone. Mike, I'm going to stretch you to the absolute limit, all that stuff and nonsense you learned at Warminster about battalion frontage you can forget because you've got this bloody great feature here to contend with and I can't spare anybody else to help you. Happily, it's wooded ..."

"No, it's not, Sir, the map's wrong, we did a recce on it this morning and it's bare-arsed as hell."

"Is it? Well, fine, splendid—you never did like woods anyway, so that's absolutely ideal ..."

"Message from HQ Middle East, Sir ..."

"19 Brigade on land line, Sir. Brigadier wishes to speak to you personally, Sir ..."

"Signal from 'Hermes', Sir ..."

"Signal from 'Trenton', Sir ..."

"Message from Four-One, Sir ..."

"Brigadier now at twenty thousand feet, Sir ..."

Break out.

Deliberate defence.

"When the push comes ..."

Field glasses sweep the terrain.

"Don't much like that there";

"Not good for our friends the armour, if and when they get here ..."

"Abysmal field of view."

"Whoever drew this border up ought to be bloody well shot."

Work

Dig

Sweat

Crouched in the shade and cover of some bushes not far from a group of Marines was a man. He watched them as they worked on their position. He had the sunburned features of the Middle East with long, shaggy black hair and he wore an unkempt and piecemeal uniform. There were others with him, a couple of dozen, and their uniforms were similarly hung about with badges and knives and bandoliers of small-arms ammunition like bandidos in a spaghetti western. They watched the Brits at work. The leader scratched his beard and counted them. There were eight. He grunted in satisfaction and turned to the man next to him.

His men were armed with an assortment of firearms, mainly rifles and sub-machine guns inherited from previous campaigns and they outnumbered the OP party three to one. Further, the leader had the soundest military tactic on his side. For in the absence of a border — which existed only as a boundary line on a map — he had been able to close to within a short distance, thus ensuring he would take them with maximum surprise. Even a Cyp, theo thelontos, couldn't miss from forty metres. He touched the arm of his marksman and with the same hand pointed at the nearest Brit.

"Pyrovolise afton..." ('Shoot that one...')

His intention was to shoot one outright before capturing the rest and making off with them to another part of the island where he would hold them hostage. After drawing world attention to his cause, 'Enosis', the union of Cyprus with Greece, by placing demands with the British government, he would casually demonstrate the bona-fides of Ethniki Organosis Kypriou Agoniston (EOKA) by publicly executing the hostages one a time, shooting them in the back of the head before tossing their bound and blindfolded bodies off the roofs of buildings in such a way that all the world could see EOKA's methods matched its fanaticism. Few, if any, would have much sympathy for hostages who were soldiers, particularly British ones, the 'lame dogs and lackeys of neo-western imperialist capitalism.' And with the island already being invaded by Turkey, their eight lives, individually spent with the maximum publicity, would gain Enosis huge moral support. The marksman put his weapon to his shoulder and fired, twice.

Everything happened at once. A Brit folded to the ground like an empty sack, the rest dived for cover and the EOKA fighters stepped from the bushes.

Marines rolled in the dirt, going for their weapons. They looked up. Twenty-four muzzles stared at them. To make the slightest move was death.

"Paradotheite ...!" ('Surrender ...!')

Slowly, they stole a look at the section commander, caught like a waxwork with one hand round the pistol grip of his rifle, the other raised bidding his men hold their fire, seeking a way other than mutual annihilation at point blank range. For century-long seconds, the crushing weight of having to make a decision that would set the whole hash of international politics reverberating bore down upon the young corporal's shoulders. In a blink, he had to resolve a matter with which not the highest nor most exalted councils at Westminster would care to be faced.

Like a frozen tabloid, the two groups faced each other. Narrowed eyes. Sweat trickling down the back. Decisions, decisions ...

Men's lives, other lives, orders — 'You are to observe and report ...' The groans of a dying mate crumpled on the ground before him. Twenty-four muzzles, twenty-four itchy trigger fingers, three to one outnumbered and outgunned at point blank range; soldiers, guerrillas, civilians, Turks, Greeks, who the hell were they? What part of his orders covered this? Political incident, villain, hero, dead hero, not much difference. Court-martial, God, answerable for the rest of your life; loyalties, the CO, the men, orders, the situation, size it up and figure it out. To act, to take action, must act, regain the initiative. How? What action? Open fire like hell, at the same time throw yourself at 'em, they're edging closer. If you're going to die, die going forward, out of the front-door, in a blaze of glory — there's a chance Lloyd's and Ladbroke's would laugh at that someone might get away with it. In the words of the prophet, you've always got a chance left as long as you've got a throw left.

"Paradotheite ... e pyrovoloume!" ('Surrender ... or we shoot!')

What chance here? No dice left, no throw left, no nothing. Death in an orange grove, that's all. A body like a colander for the first man to move. Look at their faces, search their eyes, find the weak link, pray for a distraction ...

"Dostou pende defterolepta ..." ('Give him five seconds ...')

The EOKA leader's words, spoken almost as an aside to his own men, provided only the merest distraction — but it was enough. For significantly, he had already miscalculated. Evidently the EOKA leader had never been a student of British military tactics or organisation. Had he been, he might have known that a rifle section, infantry or commandos, comprised not eight men but nine. Which simple shortcoming on his part was about to have a telling effect upon his plan.

Lying off to one side unnoticed in the shade was the section GPMG gunner, watching over his companions. It was he who now with commendable initiative brought the impasse to a swift and sudden end. Slowly, as from the first appearance of their adversaries, he slunk round, swivelling the muzzle of the gun in their direction without drawing attention to himself. Between him and the EOKA contingent were the rest of the section. It was a difficult shot.

Carefully, he angled the gun. As he did so, he heard the leader's sotto voce words and sensed his meaning. Whereupon, with deadly accuracy, he rifled a single shot between the legs of an oppo at the foremost hostage-taker.

The result was as unexpected as it was instantaneous. A guerrilla fell mortally wounded whilst the rest, imagining this to be a foretaste of greater things to come, fled into the bushes.

Marines scrambled into all-round-defence. Then, when the EOKA showed no sign of coming back for more, two of them rose, icy with adrenalin, to examine the wounded.

A large shadow alighted upon the guerrilla as a bootneck stooped over him to tend his wound. First the bootneck picked up the unconscious man and removed him to some shade.

"Shouldn't play with guns, butty," he gently rebuked him as he worked, his voice as Welsh as Cwm Rhondda, "'Sdange'rus .. din' you mam never tell you that?"

They did what they could for him but a stomach wound was bad and despite being evacuated to hospital within minutes, after two days he died. The wounded bootneck, however, hit in the shoulder and thigh, recovered and before long the incident was dubbed the 'Three Round Shoot-Out.' Some considered it barely worth an entry on the books but the feeling of having come a bit close to their ticket was something the nine Royals wouldn't forget. Laugh at it they might — and certainly did — but like a lot of things, it looked better in retrospect.

"What the fuck took you so long, Taff?" the corporal chided the machine-gunner, "I thought you'd got your bleeding head down!"

"You ace shot!" expostulated the bootneck between whose legs the gunner had aimed, "When did you last do a range course? The flash git nearly shot my fucking goolies off ...!"

★   ★   ★

"Looks like Aden ...," said Gentleman Jack, sweeping his field glasses across the arid countryside in the direction of the mountains. The Turks were still ensconced behind their salient, the Gunes Lines.

"Well, if they're going to come," said the company commander looking in the same direction, "That's where they'll be coming from ..."

Clerides had replaced the gun-toting Samson as president and there was a feeling, it was said, that behind-the-scenes talking might be enough to stop the Turks from breaking out. At the moment, nothing else would if they chose to.

"But," said the Company Commander, "If the politicos do their stuff, all might be well."

"And if they don't" added the Sergeant-Major, "It'll be down to us again."

★　★　★

Commando HQ was in a grape factory. A shed in which obsolete presses and wine-making machinery had been pushed aside was the domain of the Intelligence Section. A member of that organisation stood outside in clean denims and shirt watching a line of dusty gravel-bellies marching towards him. They carried packs and rifles after a spell in the forward positions and the one at the front possessed a brassard bearing the single chevron of a Lance-Corporal.

"Smitten!" shouted Taverner catching sight of him. He veered the line towards the Int. man. "How's the 'big picture'?" he asked, coming closer.

"Your mission, Corpse," intoned Smith sonorously, "should you choose to accept it, is — in the event of a major push by Johnny Turk ..."

"Major Push? He's my old company commander," quipped Taverner;

"... to skirmish back in *pairs*," continued Smith ignoring him, "shouting 'BANG' five times for every live round fired to assist the general economic situation, and to make a last stand at the Naafi under cover of drunken singing provided by Perce. Any questions?"

The men walked by, grinning. Lance-Corporal Taverner stopped of his own volition as befitted one now in the big time of the promotion stakes.

The Commando had been recalled from week-end leave to fly to Cyprus and when the last man had deplaned, as the CO was happy to be told, not a single member of it was missing. Its swift dispersal to action upon arrival, however, meant that for weeks afterwards everyone was still catching up on how everyone else had been reclaimed from bars, cars, pubs, clubs, nurses' quarters and nunneries the country over when the balloon went up.

"Where were you?" enquired Taverner, "When the trumpet sounded ..."

"You mean when the shit hit the fan?" said Smith, "10 Downing Street, Wapping. Nah, Gina's actually. Matter o' fact, we were just on our way down the boozer when a copper come to the door with the magic words. 'Course, it had to be this happy bunch o' morons, didn't it?"

"How did Gina take it?"

"Well", Smith looked askance, "from what I could gather, in between all the sobbing and the hullabaloo, she didn't seem too impressed."

★　★　★

After three weeks, with a political settlement nowhere but the Foreign Office playing it all down and authorising the brass to return the troops, the unit was released and ordered to emplane for England. Speeding past the salt flats that bordered Akrotiri airfield, Smith dispassionately eyed them from the back of a four-tonner. All the indications were that he would never see them again in his life but — he couldn't say he was unduly worried by the prospect. It was evening and they'd soon be on their way. That was Cyprus that was. Bit of a garbled spree.

At which point the Turks chose to break out of their salient in an armoured drive west towards Morphou and south-east to Famagusta. There was nothing to stop them now. British units were in the act of leaving.

Most of the emplanement was halted in time, one 'plane actually having its clearance for take-off countermanded whilst carrying out pre-takeoff checks on the end of the runway. But a number had already left, the first one, on which Smith found himself, by as much as a day.

At Plymouth he oiled up his weapon, housed it in the armoury, locked up his locker, wrote an address and telephone number on his recall card and caught the London train, his mind now firmly fixed on the favourite occupation of single off-duty servicemen. Cyprus '74 was behind him.

Gina greeted him at her front door with the words 'Banana Boat'. Smith did a double-take.

"You're jokin' .." he said, "When did that come through?"

"An hour ago. It's from your unit, isn't it?"

"Yeah."

"What does it mean?"

"It means — the Turks are still messing about in Cyprus. But I'm over here and so is half the bleedin' unit. The CO must be doing his nut! This is not one of the Foreign Office's better days."

"Britain needs you," she mocked.

"Not for half-an-hour it don't," retorted Smith and shut the door.

A bead of sweat trickled round his neck. He watched it fall onto Gina's. It was incredible how much loving you could pack into half-an-hour when there was a chance you might never see each other again.

"Listen," he said, holding her and breathing hard, "I don't wanna rush things but ... there might be a scrap, so ... will you marry me?"

Her lifelong vision of being proposed to by someone on bended knee whilst taking a romantic moonlight stroll through swaying cornfields vanished instantly.

"Yes," she said simply.

"Good," said Smith and kissed her, 'That's that jacked up then. I was gonna write to you about it but I wasn't sure how to spell 'diamond ring.'"

"Liar. What about a ring for my finger, anyway?" asked Gina.

"I'll buy it from the Naafi," promised Smith generously.

The following day after commuting back to Cyprus aboard a VC10, he eyed the dried-up salt lake once again, thinking savage, unspeakable thoughts. Next to him on the back of the truck an NCO destined to spend his honeymoon in a slit-trench did the same.

Fighting flies and boredom back in the forward positions, Taverner whiled away the unforgiving minute by noting:

'With the Turks now on the move across the island, the situation has suddenly hardened and we may be called upon at any moment to go and stop them. That certainly is the message I get from the battery of artillery, naval gunfire support team and forward air controllers who have just been added to the unit. Just when and where, politics will do much to decide and of course the blokes who actually fight the battles are always the last to know about it beforehand. But as, additionally, the place is seething with pressmen and they're not here just to gaze at the view, maybe we are indeed in for the big one. The mere thought of this has ensured that we now spend every spare moment of the day cleaning, oiling and canoodling the weapons, magazines and ammunition we hope will keep us alive when the crunch comes. Tony lavishes care and attention on the GPMG as though it were a musical instrument of rare quality and after being fucked about as much as we have of late, the desire for blood throughout the unit in general is of an extremely high order. Whichever bunch of indolent shiny-arses was responsible would do worse than stay at home well out of our reach.

'I don't think the PM is going to allow the Turks to flatten the island or its Greek Cypriot population, whatever the difficulties of the past with that particular community (as 'A' Company found out the other day.) At any rate, we were given a briefing on the way events might unfold by one of our own (RM) generals yesterday. He ended with such a forceful pep-talk it was practically a bollocking!

This was highly effective stuff, actually, and all the more so because he looked like a man of action himself. He had a distinctly villainous turn of phrase and a group of blokes who've been flown out straight from training to join us for 'phase two' stood there quaking, wondering what on earth they'd let themselves in for. Marine George Seward, however, like the old sweat he is, remained totally unmoved and not quite inaudibly hummed 'Land of Hope and Glory' throughout. 'Bung' Haines turned round and gave him a look such as only RSMs can.

'The long and short of it is — there may well be action. It is worth recording that this piece of information was imparted without the slightest hint of rhetoric and that it was received with a good deal of clear-eyed satisfaction all round. One day I may look back and find that quite extraordinary, perhaps even unbelievable, but at the moment I don't. It is perfectly in keeping with the spirit of this well-seasoned and remarkable unit. There are a lot of old hands from Borneo days kicking around, three-badgers just longing to see a bit of action again before they all become janitors, and I don't think they're particularly fussy who the enemy is. The Turks probably feel the same.

'HQ Company meanwhile, with the aid of boxes, benches and fresh white linen for table cloths (beautifully starched and bearing RAF laundry marks), have rigged up a bar in one corner of the grape factory yard which, needless to say, is proving to be a most acceptable place. (The word grape 'factory', which is what everyone calls the location, is in fact misleading; they are the outbuildings of a grape producing farm.) Anyway, vine-covered trellis-work and walls make the whole effect very Mediterranean and relaxing and it was here one night, doing just that as a guest of Smudge, sipping beer and ouzo by the light of a Tilley lamp, that we heard George Seward's philosophy of life and death. Coming from an old campaigner like him this was really something, a rare privilege not accorded to many and we hung on his every word. It was exquisitely brief and to the point and it fascinated everyone present.

'It seems there are three old hags (women) and they have a spinning wheel. The first old hag spins the web of your life. And when she's done, she passes your life to the second old hag — who measures the span of it which she enters in a ledger against your name. And when she's done, she passes your life to the third old hag — who blows it away, "Pooff!" He blew on his palm as though blowing away a spider's web.

'Now that's what I call a philosophy!

'As the unit ammunition storeman, George works very closely with the RSM. Despite coming from opposite ends of the country, however, George from Durham and 'Bung' Haines from London, the two of them come from exactly the same mould—only when the Good Lord saw what He'd created, He promptly broke that mould and chucked it away. I suppose there is about eight or ten years age difference in George's favour, but you wouldn't know it—they're both built like a pair of proverbial brick shit-houses, and the only difference of any substance between them is that George never bothered with the pedantry of promotion. There is a story which goes—arguing tactics in the field on George's umpteenth course for promotion to corporal, his instructor pleaded with him with tears in his eyes (so the story goes) to "Just *pretend* you agree with me, Corporal Seward (he was acting, unpaid at the time)—and I'll pass you!" There is, of course, no way of proving a tactical argument without doing it for real, so most people in George's position would have gone along with the Directing Staff's solution and collected their stripes and extra money into the bargain. That, however, was too much for one of his integrity. So with scintillating wit and presence of mind, he replied, "Bollocks ..." and has remained a gash-hand Marine to this day.

'Bung' Haines was having a beer with him that night and we then heard another gem of soldierly philosophy, this time concerning the hierachy's attitude to awards and decorations as told by the RSM himself. There was a helicopter crash in Borneo during the Indonesian confrontation. There were a number of people on board and it went on fire. (The mind boggles—flailing blades, holed avgas tanks, etc.) 'Bung', then a sergeant, happened to be nearby at the time and taking charge of some ground crew, piled into the rescue. "It was a bit nasty," he said. Some of those inside were dead from the impact, but others whom he got out lived to tell the tale, despite horrific burns. Whereupon the RAF recommended all the rescuers for an award of some kind which their own people eventually got. 'Bung' forgot all about his until one day when he was summoned to see his CO.

'"About this award," said the CO, "Well done, Sergeant Haines, jolly good, keep it up—but I'm not forwarding it because that's the standard of behaviour I expect from a senior NCO in this Corps ..."

'"So I dipped out, didn't I," growled 'Bung' dismissively, still apparently thinking it enormously funny and inclined to tell us about it at all only because he viewed it in the light of a good after-dinner joke.

'*21st August;* the Imprest Officer, on his way round paying out local currency, took one look at our shady parachute awning, log

fire, oranges, grapes and so on, and remarked, "By God, it's tough
at the front." Nice one.

'A week has gone by since the start of 'phase two' and in that time
absolutely knack-all has happened. We are now so docile as a result
of this existence that the first Turkish tank to appear would
probably finish us all off before we'd stopped gawping at it.

'We met some US Marines the other day, back at the Company
location. Just like John Wayne, they were. Part of the problem of
being a Yank soldier, one imagines, is that they're stuck with this
John Wayne image — stern, handsome, steely-eyed, gung-ho, gum-
chewing, chin-strap-dangling and white T-shirt wearing. The other
part of the problem must be that they like it. Anyway, whilst we
were talking to them, who should come by but our number one
Royal, our mascot, the man himself, George Seward; stripped to the
waist, shorts, beret, face like a mortar impact area, muscles like
Charles Fatlas, tattoos of every run-ashore from Plymouth to Hong-
Kong and back adorning his torso, carrying three full double
ammunition liners stacked up on each shoulder and singing, "Ging-
gang-gooly-gong."

'Kiwi Cargill suddenly snapped to attention, shouted "Ranks
standing about — tenshon!" and saluted George — "Morning, Sir," —
most efficiently with that bright breezy smile of his. One of the
Yanks said "Hi," in a slightly uncertain manner — whereupon
George stopped singing, nodded a greeting and proceeded to inspect
them, looking them over from head to foot. At the end of which,
without deigning to pass comment, he walked on, resuming his
singing, "Ging-gang-gooly-gooly-gooly-gooly-gong ..." etc. etc.
With the ammunition boxes on his shoulders, he looked like a
walking concrete bunker.

'Naturally they all wanted to know who he was. When Kiwi
explained that that was the company commander, they were all well
amazed. But one asked, "Like, what's with the ammo boxes, man?"
"Fitness," we explained, adding — "And when he takes them off, it
makes all the other problems bearing down upon his shoulders seem
that much lighter." This certainly appealed to the intellectuals
amongst them, and when Kiwi told them that George's family
owned Durham Castle (in point of fact, they own *the* 'Durham
Castle', a pub) our visitors went away convinced they'd met a truly
eccentric English officer and gentleman. It helped pass five minutes
of the day I suppose.

'Whilst there is an immediate kindred feeling for anyone in or out
of uniform who knows — or has known — anything of the hazards and
privations of service life, to say nothing of its undoubted bonuses

(such as compo), our American cousins never seem to have been much rated by us for their skill-at-arms. Trigger-happiness, indiscrimate bombing and massive civilian casualties are always the first things to be associated with them, and the tragically unskilful and bloody saga that was Vietnam with its staggering undertones of incompetence and ignorance at all levels has probably ensured that this will remain the case for a very long time to come. As a result, soldierly opinion about them ranges from informed professional criticism along the 'Errores Belli Americanorum' lines (our schoolie's polite Latin euphemism for what anyone else would call their 'fuck-ups') to quite open prejudice of the sort exhibited by Smudge that day, who eyeing them, said, "Great at moonshots and golf, the Yanks, but they ain't much cop at this game, are they ..." To which he added, "If only they didn't get so bleeding excited they might do better."

★   ★   ★

'The NCO I relieved today told me that last night he mounted a clearing patrol after hearing what sounded like a weapon being cocked forward of this position. Good work, I thought, mentally applauding him for going after them in the dark *before* he had a dead body on his hands instead of waiting till afterwards like he would have to in Northern Ireland. However, after an excursion into the republic, they found nothing. Whoever it was obviously got the wind up and buggered off. We jointly suspect it was more of those EOKA schmucks who vittled up 'A' Company.

'We have been given a ten-man tent to sleep in (luxury) and a union flag to fly above the position (highly tactical). The explanation for the latter is that it should help to avoid further incidents with the Greek Cypriot population; on the basis of 'Don't-shoot-we're-British', one assumes. Apparently, after the Three-Round Shoot-Out they apologised to the CO, claiming they had mistaken our lads for the invading Turks. (Oh yeah! Me, Smudge and George Seward are dining with Ari Onassis tomorrow night, too ...)

'Anyway, as the tent is the obvious target for anyone wishing to shoot us by night, I told the blokes to sleep away from it. It is a measure of how switched off we have become since falling into this deadening routine of waiting for an event which refuses to happen, that the reaction to this order was 'What the fuck for?' So when, having explained the reason for it again, they still showed dissent, I went bolshy too and said, 'Well you're fucking doing it anyway.' At times the weighty authority of one solitary stripe can be a bit on the thin side, especially when bending the collective will of five distinctly soured and disgruntled bootnecks into doing something they are disinclined to do. Still, even 'Bung' was like this once — acting, unpaid, inconsequential, etc — and a bit of chuntering in the ranks is no great hardship to live with.

August 27th. 'There was one of those funny/serious incidents this morning symptomatic of our general touchiness when I literally hoofed Jock Cochran out of bed. He was sleeping on a camp bed underneath an orange tree and I had shaken him as per normal, ten minutes before he was due to relieve me on watch at dawn. Fifteen minutes later I found him still there fast asleep. He's been a bit prone to doing that recently and when it's the end of your watch you don't take too kindly to it. So I booted the bed as hard as I could where it was bulging with his backside. The result was extremely funny (to me; he very nearly lost his cool), for the kick completely inverted the relative positions of sleeper and bed. He flew into the air, did a 180 degree roll to the right and landed on his front with his face in the dirt and the bed on top of him. There was a split second's silence whilst he registered his rude awakening, then he scrambled to his feet, shouting a torrent of what I took to be Gaelic, words which, if I heard correctly, all began with the letters 'F', 'B' or 'C'. I thought he was going to come up swinging but I just sort of stood there, giving him a stony stare and this must have had the desired effect because after picking up his rifle and kit, he loped off on watch. In that I'd never done this to anyone before the result was most enlightening and the general effect upon the rest of the section good from my point of view. We were all quite civilised to each other over shaving and breakfast. Since when I notice our timekeeping at the change-over of watches has improved enormously. Marvellous what a well-placed kick in the pants can do.

'In the past week even less has happened than the week before and a sense of frustration hangs in the air. The buzz is that the Turks are moving freely about the north part of the island and yet we *still* have not been called upon to do anything about it. Perhaps this is what's getting to Jock. He says he owes the Turks for a great uncle lost at Gallipoli. Apparently he was an Argyll and Sutherland Highlander aged nineteen. Meanwhile our routine, of which everyone is becoming heartily sick, goes on the same. The men want action — or something. Anything ...

'Three am really is the most deadly hour of the night. Jules was on with me last night, a little guy who has had some interesting experiences. Being shot in the knee in Belfast the year before last is but one of them. I shall never forget the complete and utter stillness that surrounds you at that hour though. It was as though the world

had died and we were the only two guys left. The moon cast deep
shadow everywhere and a noctural haze hung over the grove to our
right. Between the shadows of the tall cypress trees that line the road
we're straddling, its dusty surface shone like a river snaking down to
the border a hundred metres away. An old bus is parked down there
on the bend. It brings the grape farm workers in each day. Up front
it has little crucifixes and a religious shrine; down the back transfers
of lewd and leggy women showing their boobs. When it enters the
SBA we climb aboard for a perfunctory check. Some of the men
have wonderfully expressive faces, like wrinkled bits of leather and
many of them have surprisingly blue eyes, whilst some of the women
have red hair, which against bronzed skin is considered by Jules to
be 'essence'. He's not wrong. It's as attractive as it is unusual to our
eyes. There is no possible means of communication as none of us
have a word of Greek and none of them a word of English, so we
forego language and simply look at their sunburned faces and get
our meaning across with the use of nods and gestures and the
expressions on our own faces. Phrases such as "Thanks darlin'" and
"Cheers, drives, see ya tomorrer .." in fact are probably understood
from the tone of voice for simple good manners and respect for
human dignity is a matter of conduct not words. Anyway, with a
wink and a wave of the British Army thumb — or a blown kiss and a
pout — we send the old bus shuddering on its way and they always
wave back, the youngsters with great excitement. The bus is a very
ancient Thorneycroft and as the driver crunchingly engages first
gear, Keith, whose mechanical sensibilities have been refined by
three years on the motor cycle display team, always grimaces and
shouts, "Easy on the crash box, John, or you'll never make it in
tomorrer!"

'Some of the kids who are too young to work yet come and sit
around the position and pass the time of day with us. The extraordinary thing is they come not as might be expected, to barter or to
see what they can pilfer, but simply to be with us. The limit of our
conversation is to ask their names; "You ..." "Nicos." "And you?"
"Andoni ..." "And you?" "Mihale." They seem very pleased to be
asked their name and especially then to be addressed by it. We offer
them a tea or coffee when making it but they're not overkeen to take
anything from us except sweets perhaps, and they even bring us
offerings of cheese and kebab from time to time which makes a
pleasant change from compo. They attach themselves to different
members of the section and will sit by you loyally for hour after hour
when you're on watch, without saying a word. In fact, you're quite
sad to see them go in at night and always glad to see them back in

the morning. What a strange and simple thing, the yen of humans for company. Strange and simple but beautiful, very real and utterly natural. Politics and people are different things.

'Of course, should anyone at some future date ever read these scribblings which I very much doubt, time and distance will have altered the picture irrevocably and no-one will be able to believe that these kids came to seek us out not for gain or even for entertainment but in the cause of companionship. And found ours congenial. Or that we 'unthinking, unfeeling, brutal, callous commandos' felt the same way about them. Back in a world screaming with materialism it doesn't happen.

August 30th: 'Back at the company location. Saw Smudge on our way through. The trouble with these intelligence boys with their big picture is that half the time they know nothing but won't admit it and the other half they do but won't tell you. Everything, he says, depends on the Turks, i.e., the invasion force. Fine. At the moment they are consolidating their grip on the north part of the island. Marvellous. His own evaluation of this is that they may be preparing for a second push. Wonderful. Will they then attempt a sweep through to the south coast of the island? The answer to this, says Smudge, is definitely. Definitely maybe. Maybe they will and maybe they won't. Maybe they will just stay where they are, for the time being. And for the time being, we are to stay where we are just in case they don't stay where they are. It all depends on the Turks. Fan-bloody-tastic. I wish they'd make up their mind whether they want a battle or not. I feel like a member of a cup final team ready to kick off while the opposition won't come out of the changing rooms.

'He also said there was a CSE concert at Kourion amphitheatre last night with a couple of big names, a comedian and an actress whisked out from the UK to keep the troops happy. This was just the stuff for the men alright, comparable to the discovery of a goldmine in our present circumstances. Boy, could we have done with some of that ...! But it's always the base rats who get to see these things, never the combat troopers. Naturally Smudge wangled both a ticket and his duties, getting the adjutant or somebody to stand in for him while he attended. I'm glad I didn't know about it at the time. Leaning against a sandbag staring into the dark for four hours whilst that was on would have pissed me off no end.

'Kiwi Cargill, the New Zealand lance-jack i/c Three Section, has just returned from a six hour foot-patrol. He said they weren't exactly shot at from every bush but it was good to get on the move again. This I can believe. I remember a history master at school telling us that the British Army had retreated more than any other in the world. Which in the light of our present experience I can only consider a tribute to its discipline. Going forward with an immediate sense of purpose may have its problems but morale is not one of them. Nothing, on the other hand, hacks the blokes off more than to be stopped, bored, without immediate sense of purpose, not knowing what's going on, kept in the dark like a mushroom and fed on shit. That really does hack 'em off. As for going backwards ...

'The weather of course, is an independent factor. To hear a complaint about the Middle East sun from troops used to being as cold and piss-wet through as we are, would be surprising and there has yet to be one. When (forcing myself) I remember the unanaesthetised exposure to the elements on some of those cold weather exercises we did last winter, especially the defence ones when there was nothing to do but suffer day after day of mud and rain and cracked hands and nothing to look forward to but the next perishing dawn, weather-wise this is a positive dawdle. Sometimes you were so cold then it was like someone slicing your balls off with a razor blade. Jock Cochran, who's ex-Four Five, reckons he prefers both the jungle and the Arctic to the cold wet of UK. He's done both and neither are exactly what you'd call a picnic. He says he'd do anything to get out of another exercise on some rain-sodden, wind-blasted lump of shite like Dartmoor, the Beacons, Scotland or all those other boody awful places we train in. I know what he means. I once saw an entire line of SMG firers flattened by a single gust on some godforsaken range in Wales. They were in the kneeling position too. At the same time the targets were torn from their stakes and the patching-out material scattered to the four winds. I reckon if you can pass a range course in those conditions it's a fair bet you can shoot accurately anywhere.

September 1st. 'Good one from Kiwi Cargill last night, piss-taking colonial bastard that he is. "Never mind, we might be rubbish but at least we're *British* rubbish .." Said to Gentleman Jack, apropos of what I don't know. Jack, who was paying Three Section a visit, sitting at a table outside their tent, thought this highly amusing. It's good to know someone can make Jack laugh. He obviously derives enormous amusement from us on occasions but mostly it's at our expense and that's not quite the same thing.

September 2nd. 'It looks as though the war is off. Or at least indefinitely postponed. Ran down to the coast today for a swim and whilst there got talking to an army staff officer who was having a dip. He told us that the Turks have stabilised a line running right across the island from Pomos Point in the west, through Nicosia to Famagusta in the east. This is being referred to as the Attila Line and everything north of it, including the famous panhandle, now looks like staying occupied. Thus the Turks, by force of arms, have been able to establish a de facto partition of the island, in the course of which, the officer said, they have inflicted much wanton destruction, desecrated many monuments and much archaeological heritage in which the island abounds, and displaced some 200,000 Greek Cypriots. Why the Turks were not prevented from breaking out of the old Gunes Lines is a very good question and perhaps one that only the Prime Minister with his big picture—or possibly Smudge with his—can answer. When singly or jointly, they have released their memoirs, and these have been made compulsory reading for university entrance in a hundred years time, we may learn more. Until then, however, I am losing no sleep over it and neither, I dare say, are they. The staff officer also said it will be the end of the month before we go back.

September 10th. 'It's just been announced that we're pulling out in three days time.

'So there it is. Everything has changed and nothing has changed. The Greek and Turkish Cypriot communities still loathe and fear each other; the one wants enosis, the other partition and that, it now looks, is what they've got. Upon which note of bitter division, we shall stow our grenades, empty our sandbags, fill in the holes and prepare to take our leave of this sad and beautiful island.

'So now a question mark hangs over the whole place and its future looks far from certain. But we were here and we were ready and though we didn't have the scrap we expected—upon which matter as professional soldiers we voice no opinion—we did a lot of other things. We evacuated a lot of civilian personnel, holiday-makers and so on, from the wrecks of their places across the island, we patched up the wounded and we have looked after, fed, housed and de-loused refugees of both sides who have fled to us in their thousands. Most of all, the south of the island where we happened to be remains untouched and emphatically free of the depredations of the Turkish invaders. Our presence *just might* have had something to do with that. Jamal, the local policeman, certainly thinks so. Tonight he has invited the entire troop to his house for beer and kebab in the garden. He says (knowing us) that the whole village is likely to turn out to watch. I can imagine. This promises to be some ban-yan. A whip-round for booze, firewood collection and other preparations are already under way.

'But when in the future, perhaps over a beer somewhere, someone recalls this operation, all the hours of boredom and eye-strain and ear-singing silence will have shrivelled to nothing and then I will remember only one thing. When I recall this episode I will always think of an enormous Greek-Cypriot, a refugee, who drove into the sovereign base area one day in a dilapidated Morris Minor on top of which was lashed every single thing he owned. Chairs, table, a settee, crockery, pictures, a lampshade, bedding, the lot. Inside and in the boot it was the same story. Stuffed to the brim. In the left-hand seat sat his mother or grandmother, a frail wizened woman. Alongside her, the driver's seat didn't exist. He was so big, this Greek Cypriot, six foot six and with a massive girth, that he had simply removed the seat in order to be able to drive the car. He was like a vast podgy boy and he sat on a small box with his back against the paraphernalia cluttering the rear seat. This was only apparent after he had got out. Each tyre was as bald as a coot and as one of us strode across to examine his papers, with little more than a hiss it was so flat, the front right-hand one finally subsided. The pantomime that followed was straight out of Charlie Chaplin.

'Off-duty members of the section got the wheel off with the aid of a solitary spanner and no jack. The jack problem was solved by the Cypriot himself who lifted the car, mother, furniture and all whilst somebody shoved a rock under the axle. He didn't speak, he didn't smile, he just lifted. Then off went one of the blokes, rolling the wheel in front of him down the road like a ten-year-old. Eventually he gave it to a Landrover coming out of a side turning. Half-an-hour later the Landrover was back with the tyre mended. This time the blokes gave the Cyp a hand to lift the car. The wheel was put on, there was a solemn shaking of hands all round, again with no trace of a smile or words from this simple colossus, and with much smoke and swaying of household furniture, he lurched off in the direction of the reception centre. His final wave had us in stitches. A huge great hand came out of the driver's window — the steering wheel appeared to be buried in his shirt — and he gave us a wave like a child's. "Bye-bye ..."

September 12th. 'Everything is packed, our old positions have been demolished, we've unloaded and de-ammunitioned for the last time (I think). The RAF no longer trust us with bayonets as they did on the way out. We've had to hand 'em in. More nausea at the other end reclaiming them. Meanwhile we still carry jack-knives etc. Marvellous.

'We're spending our last night billeted in a school near the airfield. A Major in Army Movements who met us here was visibly shaken when we debussed to find we possessed no officers or sergeants. John B. (the senior corporal present) went forward to parley, but the Major, perhaps hoping for social equals with whom to

conduct negotiations, took fright and asked where they were. They
had in fact gone to their respective messes as guests of the RAF but
John, in light-hearted mood, replied that they'd escaped. What he
meant was that they'd escaped the clutches of Army Movements for
the night. The effect of this reply upon the unfortunate Major,
however, was nothing less than catastrophic. His mouth opened and
closed several times like an expiring fish whilst his imagination ran
riot and told him he was confronted with a mutinous band of
leaderless cut-throats and desperados just back from the trenches
having done in some of their officers on the way. It was too
delightful to be true. Wide-eyed with alarm, he stood waving his
brief-case at us to keep us at bay, ('But we're nice animals, Major,
throw us a peanut ...' was one comment), shooing John back to us
and ourselves into the shadows (perhaps we were too awful for him
to behold), whilst he remained in a pool of light (hoping someone
would see his predicament, no doubt), uttering tense little shrieks of
"Stay there!" and "Do as you're told!" — or presumably he'd stamp
his foot. He seemed terrified of someone getting behind him, having
heard and believed all those stories about us — which prospect
alarmed him the more I couldn't say. Altogether he behaved so
perfectly ludicrously it put us in top mood and quite set us up for the
remainder of the night.

'Tom has a bottle of Scotch, which, together with the noble
assistance of myself, Jules and Johnny Cochran, the four of us are
bent upon reducing to a blurred and hazy memory in honour of the
occasion. Having no glasses, we have requisitioned a large porcelain
pot for the purpose, into which we have poured the entire contents
neat. The milk of human kindness once again flows in our veins and
with my bottle of ouzo to follow — here's to Kypros. Bottoms up!'

On 13th September 1974, the Commando flew out of Cyprus after
an emergency tour of active duty. Complement complete — less one
wounded.

'What's next on this merry-go-round,' pondered Smith as they
took off; 'Back to Cyprus on Monday? Sort out some other triumph
for diplomacy on Tuesday? A honeymoon, a pools-win? Or Belfast
again, with the chance of a bullet in the guts for good measure ...'

CHAPTER 4

Broken Truce

BELFAST AGAIN 1975

A sign on the gate of the tin-city camp at Fort Monagh bore the unit's name. Outside a bombed-out and abandoned hotel in the Suffolk area and on the exterior of a wooden-hutted, corrugated-iron screened shanty-town complex in Andersonstown similar signs could be seen, such places being company locations, 'home' for the troops whose job it was to keep the peace.

Another tour of duty was drawing to a close. This time the unit's area of responsibility contained the Protestant-Catholic Suffolk interface, Ladybrook, the Lenadoon, Twinbrook, the Turf Lodge and other notorious West Belfast trouble spots, all staunchly Republican in sympathy and eager to claim the life of a soldier or three. It had been pretty much a standard affair—some bombing, some shooting, a little rioting. But generally the desire of the population to become hysterical at the drop of a hat had lost out to the infinite humour, patience and watchfulness of the troops which seemingly nothing could exhaust ...

Death misses the driver of the rations truck by four inches as he drives up Kennedy Way. He is photographed pointing to the hole in the windscreen. The smile on his face is a triumphant "Missed me, ya bastards ..."

At the wheel of a van, a drunk smashes into three parked cars at a time when people are returning from church. Hysteria mounts. The troops are blamed. A near riot ensues. As a mobile patrol approaches the scene, with people all around it, a youth takes an Armalite rifle and fires at it. Bootnecks dive into fire positions, people flee into gardens. Beyond all belief no-one is hit, but the youth escapes in the confusion.

Barely into their teens, four youths are apprehended trying to threaten farmers into parting with their shotguns.

In response to a 999 call, a mobile patrol races to a post office which is being held up at gun-point. The gang—members of an IRA youth organisation—are caught red-handed. Their get-away car won't start and they are pushing it. They have pistol-whipped the post-mistress. Blood pours from her face. One of the youths is wearing underpants on his head for disguise.

Beered-up and raring to shoot someone's head off, two men take a Garand rifle one night and fire at random into the tall screened camp from the Turf Lodge. A member of a foot patrol, lurking nearby, simply walks a dozen paces round a corner and wrests the weapon from the firer before apprehending them both. His act becomes the talk of the unit for a week but speculation ensues as to whether he could not with legitimacy have shot at least one of them within the rules of the Yellow Card. Mercifully, no-one in the camp is seriously injured. The tall corrugated-iron anti-sniper screen has done its job.

In response to an anonymous telephone call saying there is a bomb in a catholic infants' school, a mobile patrol is scrambled to the scene. Marines race through the building, searching, opening doors, checking, clearing classrooms, playrooms, staff rooms and lavatories of children and teachers alike. The NCO in charge questions the staff, the janitor, the boilerman on the likely location of the bomb, the lay-out of buildings, places to which someone might have had access and in which even as they speak, there may be charges within seconds of exploding. Outside, drivers draw up their Landrovers at the remotest corner of the playground to form a protective laager into which teachers hasten with their children. Men run with armfuls of tiny tots, who cannot, or not understanding what it is all about, will not, hurry. Others check the basement, store-rooms and boiler-room by torch, the very act of switching on a light containing within it the possibility of detonating the bomb. Still inside the school, the NCO questions the headmistress, calmly but urgently drawing from her all the relevant information he can whilst himself assessing the whereabouts of the terrorists' dirtiest trick, the pre-placing of a second bomb designed to catch those leaving the building en masse or congregating in the area to which even now he might be evacuating them. She is a greying, careworn woman, fraught with the daily responsibility for a hundred and twenty children in a city rife with terrorism and the

present cataclysm proves almost too much for her. Seeing her
obvious distress the NCO takes her arm reassuringly. Between
quietly voiced questions to her, he shouts orders to his men. She
presses her hands to her temples, swallowing with nervous stress,
eyes filled with the tears of fright. Her hair is pinned up, wispy and
unkempt and a lock of it has fallen to her shoulder. He notices a
hairpin about to drop from the back of her head and when it does,
he unconsciously stoops to pick it up and hands it back to her as they
hurry from the building.

The 'bomb' turns out to be a hoax.

After days, weeks, months of painstaking intelligence gathering, a
wanted man is lifted.

After days, weeks, months of diligent foot patrolling, vigilant
observation and scrupulous searching, arms, ammunition and
explosives are uncovered, not all of which are to be used against the
security forces, the public-at-large or specific innocents. The
Official and Provisional IRA, and IRSP and the emergent INLA all
have their differences. Political integrity frequently dissolves into a
welter of jealousies and recriminations, at the root of which is the
possession of the large amounts of money they receive from
America. Time and again, the Security Forces pick up the pieces,
the arguments solved by pistol-whippings, tar-and-featherings,
knee-cappings and merciless assassinations known as 'head jobs'.

And at Commando HQ, someone's job is to tot up the figures.

★   ★   ★

It was the early hours of the morning. In the Intelligence Section,
a naked neon strip-light burned. Filing cabinets and document
lockers stood open. Mugshots and statistical 'trends' adorned the
walls. It was quiet. Outside, the sky paled, very slightly.

Smith sat surrounded by paperwork. The Intelligence Officer had
to make his final report; Smith's job was to prepare the facts and
figures. Next door, in the operations room, an officer stared at the
wall, his thoughts uninterrupted by the static hiss of radio sets. The
unit's nerve centre. Even the IRA slept.

Taverner rose and slipped a file back into a document locker. He
breathed a sigh of relief. It had taken him all night to work his way
through the locker, certifying that every document was there that
should be in the final classified document check before handing over
to the incoming unit. Four months earlier he had signed for them,
each month he had mustered them and the unit second-in-
command had certified his muster. Now he could look him in the

face again. The carefully graded apportionments of responsibility. He closed and locked the locker, then stood and stretched, grasping his hands behind his head for long moments, filling his lungs to capacity like a waking dog. Finally, he resumed his seat.

Silence.

Smith yawned the sort of yawn that left his eyes watering. Elsewhere, men slowly walked the empty, litter-strewn streets. Cats, slogans, milk bottles, over-turned litter bins, gaunt curtained blocks of flats whose entrance and passages stank of urine. Those guarding the camp leaned and stared. At this hour Belfast was a morgue.

"What time is it?" asked Taverner.

"There's only one time in this Army," replied Smith, "And that's 'tup-free'! You ought to know that ..."

"Thank you," said Taverner patiently, "What **time** is it?"

"Oh-five-fifteen," answered Smith slowly, "In other words, a quarter past five. That is to say, in three-quarters of an hour's time, it will be the sausage-bacon-and-eggs time of six-o-clock. Any further questions for me, over?"

"You mean the big hand will be pointing at twelve?"

"Yes."

"And the little hand at six?"

"Yes."

"Then it will be six-o-clock?"

"In a word — yes."

"Ah! That's when Wyatt Earp comes out and points his six-shooter at Mickey Mouse on my watch."

"Likewise on mine," said Smith, "But those watches are only on issue to members of the Intelligence Section."

"Oh ..." said Taverner in an awed voice.

There was another long silence during which time Taverner rose and went out, returning minutes later with a bucket of steaming water and a mop, in the use of which he had been trained at the taxpayer's expense. With skilful professionalism he began to re-arrange the dirt on the floor, the silence broken only by the caress of the mop upon linoleum and water being squeezed from it back into the bucket. It was galling, unedifying work, particularly to someone with a year's accumulated seniority in the rank of Lance-Corporal and he knew that, without union representation he was unlikely to receive any thanks for it. He knew too that though Belfast was no place for heroes, it just had to be done. It was long, arduous, grinding work involving unsocial hours, little pay and nil recognition. It took him all of five whole minutes.

"Ta for doing the floor," said Smith.

"It was a holiday," replied Taverner on his way out, "Your turn to make the coffees."

When he came back there was one waiting for him.

"'Member when we first came here back in Feb?" began Smith. "We couldn't get out of the gates for snow ..."

"Yeah—but not only that, the Provisional IRA announced a ceasefire."

"Meaning they can shoot us but we can't shoot them? I remember ..."

"Precisely. Well, since then they've broken that ceasefire thirty-nine times in our area alone!"

"Discipline," muttered Taverner, sipping his coffee, "That's what it is. A well-disciplined rank and file. Imagine if they'd been using riff-raff ..."

"True," rejoined Smith, "But then one almost has to feel sorry for the poor old IRA these days, Neil baby, reduced to the three-day working week and crippled by appalling taxes as a result of the Common Market. I mean, fourpence on every Armalite round is a lot, y'know, 'specially the amount they use. Then there's donations from America drying up and the Garda nicking that boat-load of rifles on its way from Libya. That was a right kick in the bollocks for them! I mean, it's all very well for you just to sit there, smugly sippin' your coffee, but if you're an IRA man, totally dedicated to blowing people apart as your way of life—and you can't trust the Dublin government, well, who can you trust?"

Taverner nodded sagely.

"What the world needs more of today," he mused, "is people who can see both sides of the question. People who can see through all this narrow-minded clap-trap which simple morons like us can't. People of breadth of paunch and depth of dewlap. People who make profound statements over coffee at ten, barter human beings over lunch at twelve, take an afternoon nap full of caviar at two and chauffeur-driven car home at a quarter-to-four. Top people whose only concern is to brown-nose their way into the honours list. People of clarity of vision and clairvoyance ..."

"Claire Voyance?" asked Smith, "Who's she?"

"She is a naval nurse," announced Taverner, "Sometimes she has to work week-ends but she does get days off in lieu ..."

"Ah," retorted Smith, grinning, "But does she get any off in Liskeard?"

"Blimey, that's an old chestnut. Haven't heard that one since at least 1973. How about—'I was thinking of deserting last week ...'"

"'But I decided not to,'" answered Smith "'Cos I don't like

sand.'" He made a face. "The way some men amuse themselves when time hangs heavy on their hands. It's gotta be five-thirty in the perishing morning with stuff like that coming out!"

"Whaja mean?" exclaimed Taverner, "With gags of that calibre, we'll be topping the bill at the Sod's Opera next time we're embarked!"

"Topping up the bilges, more like," rejoined Smith. Taking his work out of the typewriter, he laid the facts and figures inside a folder, then pushing back his chair, picked up a printed pamphlet aimed at telling the bombed, bottled and bulleted British squaddy why it was all happening to him.

"Y'know," he said, flipping through its pages, "We were standing in the grand duchy of Duncairn Gardens one time last time out, and the sky was fairly teeming with bricks and bottles what the locals were heaving at us; dunno if you remember that place at all, do you?"

"On the edge of the New Lodge, wasn't it?"

"That's it. Anyway, what happens? For some reason the troop officer broke rank in the middle of it all, just when it was getting critical—and stepped directly in front of me. Wham! Gets a half-housebrick right in the mouth!"

There was a sharp intake of breath from Taverner.

"Well, naturally—*I* was grateful to him ..." said Smith.

"Painful!" commented Taverner, "Dentist?"

"Dentist??" echoed Smith, "I'll say! Smashed his jaw. I remember thinking 'Hallo, he's gone down like a bag o' spuds!' So anyway, later we went to see him in RVH. Gawd, what a mess ... jaw all wired up, stitching, stumps where his front teeth used to be, nose like a tennis ball, so much bruising he was like something out the Black 'n' White Minstrel Show. You wouldn't think a half-housebrick could do that much damage to a bloke's face. Or perhaps you would. Anyway, there by his bedside was one of these information pamphlets telling you about Ulster being founded in the ninth century, and the Danes and the Normans coming over, and de Courcy and de Lacy ..."

"And de Trouble-Makers?"

"Them too. Shuddup. So Jono picks it up and has a flip through while we're talking away; then he looks up and says 'This all you got to read, Sir? I'll get you the pamphlet on riot drill if you want!'"

"Pppphh ..." erupted Taverner. He got up and went over to the window from where he watched an early morning foot patrol make its way out of the camp and onto the streets.

"Y'know," he speculated with engaging optimism, "In five years' time, or thereabouts, there might be no further need for this place.

This camp might not exist. There might be a supermarket or something here instead ..."

Smith looked at Taverner indulgently. He went over to the
window and patted him patronisingly on the head.

"If there is, son," he said, "I'll be the first to use it. In fact, I'll
preside over the opening ceremony. Meanwhile, you stick to liftin'
heavy weights, eh? That's more your niche ..."

The glass communicating hatch between the 'Ops' and 'Int'
suddenly slid open to reveal the duty operations officer. The twin
black stars of a full lieutenant showed on the epaulettes of his olive
green shirt. The hair and eyes were unusually dark and the naturally
brown complexion was conspicuously weatherbeaten, almost like
someone returning from a good holiday.

"Sir?"

"McCracken. Desmond. What do we know about him?"

"How far back do you wanna go, Sir?" asked Smith.

"Well, is he actively involved for a start?"

"Involved? He's got shares in it!" said Smith, adding, "He got
himself a soggy leg the other night for his pains, an' all ..."

"That I know. What I want to know," said the officer, "is why?"

"Well, officially he was a Provisional but unofficially he was an
Official. If you follow that," said Smith. He opened the drawer of a
filing cabinet in search of the right card; "Which annoyed the 'law-
abiding' elements in both camps so it was only a matter of time
before he got his come-uppance from one or the other of 'em—
either the Provies or the Stickies. That's how he got his knee job.
Lucky it wasn't a head job."

Smith obscenely mimed the actions of someone drilling through a
person's knee-cap with an electric drill; "Ber-lack 'n' decker-
lack'n'decker-lack'n'decker—they oughta put that on the TV ads ..."

The lieutenant winced.

"Ah yes"; the bootneck turned up the card; "they figured he was a
tout running between the two organisations passing information. In
the end it was the Provos who got to him as you might expect. They
put a British Standard Whitworth three-eighths drill through his
left knee-cap twice, undoing the chuck and leaving it there the
second time."

He looked up.

"Such lovely people, Sir ..."

"Who found him ?"

"'S' Company foot patrol up the top of the Turf. He was trying to
do a runner at the time and getting nowhere fast. 'S' put paid to his
chances of the Olympics," he observed.

"Is there any chance of him claiming compensation, that's what I've got to find out," asked the officer.

"Pppfffhh! You're jokin', Sir! What, a feud between members of an illegal organisation? Mind you, you never can tell with our bureaucrats, can you? What with Elvis Paisley up for the Nobel peace prize ..."

"And Twogun Seamus in the birthday honours," agreed the officer, "Okay, thanks."

He shut the sliding window and immediately re-opened it.

"Go and present yourself to my troop sergeant sometime today, will you, Corporal Taverner; he wants to have a word with you."

"Okay, Sir. By the way, what's his name?"

"Sergeant Daffney," replied the officer, shutting the window again. Smith looked at Taverner.

'Who's he?" he asked, nodding at the hatch.

"Lieutenant Shutbridge."

"New?"

"Joined from the Arctic Special Group a couple of weeks ago."

"Blimey," Smith looked askance. "He speaks quite good English for an eskimo. Wuuh!" he shuddered, "I wouldn't like to meet him on a dark night, though. How come he's so bronzy?"

"Maybe they eat a lot of brown sauce ..." gurgled Taverner, shielding himself from the blows Smith rained upon him, "in the Arctic ... Aaagh! Assaulting a Lance-Jack! That's serious!"

He flung a back-hander at Smith, catching him on the jaw and giving him a livid bruise that to their concern would last over a week.

"Assaulting a Cockney! That's even more serious!"

Smith feigned injury, then pile-drove his Yorkshireman-dropping fist into Taverner's guts. Devoid of wind, Taverner went backwards, pulling Smith after him by the ears, tucking his feet up and throwing him into the air.

Smith somersaulted before landing lightly on his feet, closing the filing cabinet with his head as he righted himself.

"You thought I'd forgotten that one, didn't you?" groaned Taverner.

It was sausage-bacon-and-eggs time. The bridegroom went first, followed twenty minutes later by the best man. In two weeks time it was Smith's wedding to Gina.

★   ★   ★

The Reconnaissance Troop Sergeant Taverner found after breakfast in a group of wooden huts and Portakabins on the far side of the compound. It had just gone eight am when he strolled across and the day was sunny, the sky blue and cloudless and an air of peace and quiet pervaded West Belfast. High summer was just around the corner. Above, an aircraft droned lazily towards Aldergrove Airport and from across the Springfield Road there floated the sounds of a man tapping, mending a garden fence, the daily background noise of traffic not yet loud enough to obscure it. To foot patrols venturing up the mountainside overlooking the city it always seemed such a very small bowl of strife and today, more than most days, the sunshine brought with it hope. Normality was in the air again, for a very significant thing was happening. Slowly but surely, people were beginning to go about their everyday business — without fear.

The Sergeant was busy detailing off a number of Army ranks who had drawn the Marines for a brief initiation to the streets of Northern Ireland before joining their own units in the province, and from the expressions on their faces, some bordering upon awe of the man briefing them, Taverner concluded they seemed to adjudge themselves to be in good hands. And it was Daffney's hands, not his eyes, that were the first things he noticed about him. He was standing sideways on to Taverner as he walked in the door, tracing a big hand along a fablon-covered patrol deployment roster on the wall. On the middle finger of the left hand was a heavy gold ring whilst in the web between forefinger and thumb of the right was a small bird, the exquisite handiwork of a Chinese tattoo artist, its once colourful coat now beginning to fade. They were the sort of hands that hauled on ropes, whose skin was cracked and hardened, whose fingers one would think, might inadvertently snap a fountain pen in two whilst writing with it — if they ever picked one up to do so — and whose potentially sinister uses went better un-named. The face was boucanned, wind-blasted, weathered like moorland and its texture this morning was that of well-soaped saddle leather, durable and hard-wearing. Taverner saw how strikingly the wide load-carrying weight-lifting shoulders topped off the rangy trunk and legs, and he surmised that like water wearing down rock, the years of the Sergeant's service had smelted from him all that was luxuriant, indulgent or redundant, leaving in its place only what was remorselessly spartan, rigorously functional, ruthlessly expedient.

"Right, who's next? Corporal of Horse Franks of the Lancers — let's see if we can't fit you in with ..." the large hand traced a line across the roster again:

"It's just 'Corporal', Sergeant," ventured the Lancer.

"'Corporal Sargeant?'" echoed Daffney, looking at him poker faced, "I thought you said your name was 'Corporal of Horse Franks ...'"

"Just 'Corporal', Sergeant, not 'Corporal of Horse'";

"Oh," said Daffney, "You mean you haven't brought your horse?"

"No, Sergeant," replied the Lancer uncertainly, unfortunate enough to find himself the butt of Daffney's playful mood so early in the day. Army ranks, regalia and modes of address constantly fascinated Marines and the Sergeant was no exception.

"Oh," said Daffney again, feigning disappointment, "Well, have you brought your lance with you?"

"No, Sergeant," answered the Lancer lamely, still not sure whether Daffney was joking or not. This geezer might be one of those solid bone Marines he'd heard about.

"Oh," said Daffney a third time, turning away with a shrug, "Well, in that case you'd better go with our Corporal Phillips, there look, 12 Troop. You'll find him next hut over, down the corridor, last door on the right—hang on a *minute* ...!"

When he had allotted each one a section for the day, he addressed them collectively, telling them which were the easier areas and which were the more prone to trouble, advising them what to watch out for and informing them of the administrative arrangements in the camp, translating Royal Marine jargon such as 'galley', 'scran', and 'watch' into the appropriate Army vernacular of 'cookhouse', 'scoff', 'stagg' and so on. Finally, when they all seemed to have got the picture and there were no more questions for him, he wound it all up in the manner and accent of an American tour operator with the words,

"And so it only remains for me to wish you gennelmen a happy day on the streets of San Francisco ...

"Oh, Belfast, is it?" he shrugged indifferently, "Oh, alright then."

As the visitors dispersed, Taverner followed Daffney through an open door on which was painted a large letter 'S' with a Commando knife running through it and above which were the words 'The Big 'S'', the Support Company's self-styled nickname. Maps about the walls, large radio sets and grey blanketed tables made up the usual sparse furbishing of an operations room. At the far end, near the sets, an officer sat listening out, ready to answer any transmissions. Nearer the door, another officer, senior in rank to the first, sat at a table reading a newspaper. Stout of build, thirty-fivish and balding, his demeanour was that of someone who found complete and utter satisfaction with his allotted role in life. Feet on the desk, Captain Thomas Compton—"No relation to the famous cricketer I'm afraid,

sorry!"—was busy scrutinising an article written by a journalist who
had visited the unit during the course of its current tour of duty.

The company commander swivelled on his chair and quoted
aloud from the paper.

"Here, listen to this. 'The Marines are based in a number of
shanty-towns or tin-cities in the West Belfast area known as
Andersonstown. They call it Andy-Pandy town ...'

"I ask you! The facking nobber! 'Andy-Pandy town ...'" he
mimicked, throwing down the paper contemptuously. Occupants of
the ops. room grinned at the outburst, couched as it was in faultless
Oxford English.

Compton picked up the paper again and offered it to Daffney.

"Here you are, Sar'nt Daffney, have a laugh on me. I paid for the
bloody thing—should have known better!" His laugh was boisterous.

"Ah!" he exclaimed, spying Taverner, "This is the chap who
found the pistol used in that shooting a few weeks ago, he's a good
man! Special Branch have confirmed that now, y'know, so you'll be
involved as a witness. You'll probably be flown back from the far
side of the moon or somewhere, these cases never come up when
we're anywhere sensible, and when you finally get here and go to
court, they'll all change their minds and plead guilty, that's the way
it usually goes. Anyway, what's happening? Have you come to see
me about something?"

"No Sir; Sergeant Daffney," replied Taverner.

"Oh," complained Compton, crestfallen. "Nobody wants to see
me today for some reason. What a load of unsociable buggers you all
are ...! Sar'nt Daffney, this chap wants to see you. Can't think why,
you haven't had a big win on the tombola lately, have you?"

"Corporal Taverner, Sar'nt," said Taverner, choosing frugal
words with which to present himself to the Sergeant. Like anyone
meeting Daffney for the first time, he was immediately fixated by
the bright pink discolouration of the outermost part of the man's
right eye.

"You one o' the new blokes the boss is bringing into the troop?"
growled Daffney, scowling at him.

"Yes, Sar'nt."

"Right. The next time I wanna see you is first parade back at
Plumer Barracks. By which time the boss will have arranged for you
to be reverted to Marine Taverner again. We don't have Lance-
Jacks in this troop, he told you that, did he?"

"Sar'nt," nodded Taverner.

"By that time too, you'll have had a mother-and-father of a
haircut—none of this Fred Karno's caper, you long-haired yeti—

and third, you'll be fully fit or you'll go right back where you came from, *if* they'll have you. Then you'll have lost your stripe for nothing. Last, if we don't like you, we'll tell you. That's the deal. Get it? Any questions?"

"No, Sar'nt," answered Taverner.

"One more thing. Keep your links with the people you're working with at present, right?" The pink eye winked conspiratorially.

Taverner turned and walked out into the morning sunshine with the feeling he had just stumbled upon plutonium. On the way, he passed his new company commander.

"Are you joining us?" asked Compton, boots still firmly planted on the table.

"Yessir."

"Oh good show," nodded the Captain with approval, "Well done. Well welcome to the Big 'S' ...!

"CO sent for me the other day," he continued to the ops. room at large, "Wanted to know what was going on in our patch and why he hadn't heard anything. All I could show him was the radio log. All two pages of it for the past two weeks! If it goes on like this much longer, I said, I'll be inclined to believe the IRA have called in the receivers and gone into voluntary liquidation. 'I damn well wish they would,' he said ...! Ha-haaagh!"

The sun was hot and high when, exactly one week later, the first foot patrol belonging to the relieving unit ventured out through the gates of the camp. But it was past its zenith when the convoy of Royal Corps of Transport three and four-ton trucks returned to the ferry terminal laden with Marines. Alongside the quay lay the 'Ulster Prince', booked for use by the couple of hundred bootnecks unable to travel on the single landing ship available. Much to their taste, for the ferry had a commodity the landing ship did not; a proper bar where beer was served in glasses.

As the afternoon wore on and the boarding of personnel and loading of stores and unit vehicles continued, those aboard secured a bunk for themselves and headed for the bar which was open in accordance with the local licensing hours. Most sat around the saloon within easy reach of a refill but a number, attracted by the afternoon sun, wandered up to the top deck and there leaned against the wooden rail. On previous tours, sound common sense dictated against such a move, for sniping at departing troops aboard the ferry had been known. But on this day, at the end of a relatively quiet — and therefore successful — tour of duty, the possibility seemed remote enough, though each man gave it a passing thought as he stepped out onto the boat deck. Below their feet, the ship hummed and vibrated like a living being, resounding with muffled thuds and clangs as containers and lorries were stowed and secured in its holds and vehicle deck.

Pints in hand, a group of Senior NCOs emerged, Daffney among them. From the 'tween decks area emanated the buzz of conversation. Up top, Marines stood or sat, lounging around in groups, joking, chatting, making wry observations about the dockside activity. The sun was pleasant, the beer more so and some even dozed.

Some distance away from the wharf ran Corporation Street, sweeping past the front of the terminal building in a fast bend. On the other side of the road was situated a number of ramshackle warehouses and dockland derelicts, the nearest being only a couple of hundred metres from the ferry. From this area shots suddenly rang out. Being high up on the ship, the bootnecks found themselves able to look down into the pot-holed and dusty network of roads lacing that part of the dockland whence the shots came. Several, on hearing the outbreak of firing, which came to them as peppery little bangs, wisely moved to the other side of the funnel or judiciously opted to continue their conversations below. But a handful stayed, assessing the shooting. Then, having got the measure of it, deciding though they couldn't see the target that they were not it, this hardcore became interested and highly partisan spectators, shirt sleeves rolled up, beer glasses in hand. Clearly a sporadic fire-fight was taking place somewhere down there.

Attracted by the shooting, a mobile patrol of Paras swept round the bend in front of the terminal building, crouching in long wheel-base Landrovers, green and black painted, stripped down and open for easy abandonment. They circled the block and came back up to the bend more slowly a second time.

"Go on! Start poking down those side streets there!" directed Daffney, leaning against the rail, watching intently. Other Marines stood apart, their instincts even now being not to bunch. The Landrovers did another circuit amongst the traffic, coming more gently this time along the main road where it ran parallel to the dock. Then, on the bend, the front one pulled off and began to move gingerly down amongst the warehouses and derelicts, second one following.

"THAT'S IT!" shouted Daffney over the rail, knowing he couldn't be heard but living second by second with them, "THAT'S WHERE IT CAME FROM! IN THERE! GET IN AMONGST IT!"

Putting up a hand against the sun, the bootnecks watched in tense expectancy. Wary of being lured by a *come-on* setting them up for ambush, the Paras worked at snail's pace, Landrovers nosing along opposite sides of the road in bottom gear. Stock still, the Marines watched, knowing the feelings of their comrades-in-arms at this moment as they swivelled their eyes, adrenalin pumping, hair on the neck prickling, safety-catch off, first pressure taken, seeking the thousandth-of-a-second reaction that for them would split the difference between death and life. A Para in the rear Rover jumped out and began to walk along behind his vehicle, swivelling on his feet, watching doorways, windows, rooftops in case they were sniped at from behind.

"That's it!" chivvied Daffney, "Good instinct! Now let's have another of you this side, so you've got your rear cover set up!" Momentarily, the watching bootnecks broke their concentration to grin at the commentary.

The ship began to drift away from the quayside as another Para hopped out of the hindmost vehicle, leaving only the driver in it.

"Good!" exclaimed Daffney, "Well done the rear Rover! 2ic's switched on! How about all you in the front one doing the same, SECTION COMMANDAH ...!"

Even as he spoke, there came a burst of firing. Red-bereted figures leapt from the front vehicle, diving for fire positions whilst the two Landrovers swerved left and right across the street, drivers rolling out of them. The bootnecks watched helplessly ... then suddenly, as the screws of the ferry began to turn, they saw a Para kneel and take an aimed shot.

"GO ON! GO ON! YA BASTARDS!" they roared, "GIVE 'EM HELL! GO ON, THE PARAS! KNOCK TEN BELLS O' SHIT OUT THE FUCKERS, MEN! GO ON! TAKE 'EM OUT!"

They shielded their eyes and shook their fists and someone threw a beer glass in the general direction which landed in the harbour. Roaring, snarling and crowing, they cheered the Paras as though it were a gladiatorial contest, months of bottled-up frustration spontaneously given vent to by the incident taking place a few hundred metres away.

In the early evening sunlight, the 'Ulster Prince' slid into mid-river and went 'slow ahead both'. And there, plainly to be seen by astounded spectators on the dockside, was a group of cheering, jeering Marines crowding her port rail, supporting their comrades-in-arms in an incident ashore which those on the dockside could not see. Supporting them in the only way they could in the circumstances; with brutal vocal concern because they cared about

them being under fire in a way in which only those who themselves
have been under fire can do.

When they could see no more of it, they trooped below to seek a
refill.

"Who got who?" asked someone.

Another one shrugged.

"Be on the news," he said.

On 25th June, 1975, after a tour of internal security duty, the
Commando pulled out of Belfast. Complement complete.

Roman, Saxon, Viking and Norman had all at one point in
history or another, landed along the Kent coast and on the banks of
the Thames where it cut deep inland towards the old Roman town
of Londinium, founded by the Emperor Claudius in AD 43 and
without whose walls lay that part subsequently known as
'Schoredich' or Shoreditch, 'ditch running towards the shore of the
Thames'. And the warm summer day in AD 1975 when one of
Shoreditch's sons sat in the Norman church in the north Kent village
of Saltsea, awaiting the arrival of his bride at the altar, past, present
and future seem perfectly fused. Beside Ken Smith and likewise
resplendent in best Blues uniform and white carnation, sat his best
man, Neil Taverner. In front of them, on the prayer book shelf, lay
a small pad of velvet on which there reposed a commodity vital to
the proceedings—the wedding ring, gleaming and unforgotten.
Discreetly they gazed about them, at the colourful stained-glass
windows, at the organ pipes and commemorative plaques and at the
bright shafts of morning sunlight which played in the transept and
upon the choir stalls. Behind them, on both sides of the church, the
polished pews rustled with the filing in of relatives and friends,
relieved to have got at least themselves if no-one else to the church
on time.

Taverner opened the prayer book at the page entitled 'The
Solemnization Of Matrimony.'

'The man and woman to be married,' he read, 'having come to
the entry to the chancel of the church, together with their company,
the Priest declares the meaning and purpose of Marriage in these
words.'

'Company' was certainly the mot-juste this morning, he thought,
where the number of bootnecks sitting behind he and the bridegroom

were concerned. Already, against a background of quiet organ
music, there was an undisguised hum of conversation, as with hissed
greetings and cross-pew hand shakings, old mates, long time
separated, caught up briefly on the news of one another. In the end
it was the organist himself who quieted them by striking up
fortissimo with 'Here Comes The Bride,' the opening bars of which
refrain served also to remind them that though it was the occasion of
a grand re-union for them, the day in fact belonged to Gina, as
every wedding belonged always, exclusively to the bride.

As an usher at the back of the church, Phil Haythorne watched
Gina glide past him on the arm of her father. 'Ravishing,' he mused,
was a cliché the local newspaperman was bound to write about her,
simply because to such a man all brides were ravishing. Which was
why he was destined to remain a hack and his dreams would go
largely unfulfilled. Gina looked the way every bride wanted to on
her wedding day, and the word for that, thought Haythorne, was
'entrancing.' His eye followed her slim shapely form down the aisle,
two bridesmaids in attendance, one her little sister, the other her
cousin, to where Smith stood waiting. To one, like many of those
present, whose eye was accustomed to the squarish angular
uniformity of men, there was something particularly pleasing about
such a scene. 'Wholesome' was the word Phil Haythorne would use.
'Yes,' he thought, 'It's all distinctly wholesome.'

"Dearly Beloved," intoned the priest, "we are gathered here in the
sight of God and in the face of this congregation, to join this man
and this woman in Holy Matrimony which is an honourable estate,
instituted of God Himself, signifying unto us the mystical union that
is betwixt Christ and His Church; which Holy estate..."

"I Gina Hilary," repeated the bride, following the priest's
measured phrases, her right hand holding that of Smith, "Take thee
Kenneth Eric Norman to my wedded husband, to have and to hold
from this day forward, for better, for worse; for richer, for poorer;
in sickness and in health; to love and to cherish, till death us do
part, according to God's holy law; and thereto I give thee my troth."

Smith took the wedding ring from the priest and slipped it onto
the third finger of his bride's left hand. Then supporting her hand
in his he held the ring there, between his forefinger and thumb.

"With this ring I thee wed," he vowed, "With my body I thee
honour; and all my wordly goods with thee I share: In the Name of
the Father, and of the Son, and of the Holy Ghost. Amen."

"Those whom God hath joined," declared the priest, joining the
right hands of bride and groom, "Let no man put asunder."

The organ played quietly throughout their visit to the vestry—

then triumphantly it broke into Mendelssohn's Wedding March, heralding the newly married couple as they re-entered the nave and began to make their way down the aisle. Mothers struggled with perfumed handkerchiefs, fathers permitted themselves proud smiles. This time the bride and groom walked step by step in perfect harmony, mindful no doubt of the groom's words to his then bride-to-be at this point during their final dress rehearsal; "Now, forget about the talking, just concentrate on the walking here..."

Sunlight and confetti greeted them at the church door, and then there was the endless posing for group photographs whilst above, the church bells rang out. Peal after peal rolled out across the green and beyond, alerting offshore yachtsmen and fishermen alike to the fact that, for this couple today was no ordinary day. Today they would remember for the rest of their lives.

★　★　★

In the upstairs of 'The Pilotage Inn' a plush sit-down reception had been prepared, and it began, like any promising reception, with high decibel meetings and greetings, champagne and sherry thrust into everyone's hands and appetising frivolities being passed around on trays held by smiling waitresses. Hill, Douglas, Gilbrook, Mazzi and all the old squad were there, Dave Smith was already into the beer and little George Koupparis's grin stretched from one ear to the other. Each one of them had been tasked by Haythorne—quite superfluously—with keeping his own and everyone else's glass topped up, especially for the big moment, the moment of the toast to the bride and groom. Taverner manfully tackled a pile of telegrams that must have kept the post office up half the night— then towards the end of the meal, he stood up again, this time to make the best man's speech.

Best man, he began, was a misnomer—"miss who?" came the instant response from the back. A misnomer, he repeated—he was the second best man today. It was an old well-worn gag, now gently mellowing into senility, but owing to the large number of empty magnums stacked behind the bar, it fair set the place rocking. He was a good speaker and laughs were easily come by in the circumstances, but he knew that in the end he was going to have to concede the day to the groom. Speaking was only a matter of being versed in the art of what you were going to say. After that, it was entirely a matter of spontaneity. And in that department, of the two of them, the man whose turn it was to speak next had the major shareholding.

"And so," concluded Taverner propitiously, "It's my very great pleasure to be able to invite you to join me in a toast to the bride and groom. Ladies and gentlemen—'To Kenneth and Gina...'"

"Kenneth and Gina," came the universal response. Glasses were raised and the couple's future generously drunk. Mothers again swallowed lumps in throats and champagne bubbles went smartly up at least six noses present and equally smartly came down again.

The best man felt a tug on his jacket. Solicitously, he bent his head, anxious to know what could possibly be amiss with either the groom or his beautiful bride at such an exquisite moment.

"Pass the bottle over," murmured Smith in the manner of a conspirator, "We'll have a couple of slurps ourselves..."

They had about two weeks together. After that, the newly-weds would be separated for months. Some in Gina's position might have thought themselves hard done by. She was just grateful for their two weeks together.

★   ★   ★

The Officer Commanding No. 1 Parachute Training School gazed balefully at the lawns of RAF Brize Norton as his Administrative Officer closed a police report.

"Another pub punch-up involving parachutists," he sighed.

"But not **airmen**, Sir," smirked the AO, "The light blue escaped lightly again."

"That's not the point, Lofty. We're responsible for them all while they're here: foreigners, Paras, SAS, Marine Commandos, the lot. You'd better do something, or my OBE's a goner!" he added reflectively. The Squadron Leader fingered a pencil rubber—then impulsively flung it at the window.

"It's when it gets into *writing* that the mud sticks! You've got no friends at Group then, Lofty. Look at Hugo. Twenty-eight years loyal service, one untimely fart and they told him to stick his gong up his jacksie!!"

"Broke wind during the Loyal Toast, did he? The bandmaster has special music to cover that, y'know," observed the AO drily.

"Untimely 'indiscretion', if you like. Hugo tried to drive a golf ball over 15 Hangar; some sort of bet. He did it, but the ball went straight through the open window of the Air Vice-Marshal's car who happened to be passing on the other side."

"One of those things only fate can ordain," remarked the AO.

"Naturally, the meticulous Hugo had his name written on it ..."

"When your number's on it is one thing," smirked the AO again. "When *'To Whom This May Concern'* is as well—game and match to the AVM, I'd say!"

CHAPTER 5

The Silver-Blue Tail Fin

"UP EIGHT HUNDRED—THREE JUMPING!"
The Flight-Sergeant waited, looking back at the cable truck.

"Up eight hundred—three jumping ..." came the winch operator's distant response. The cable drum began to roll.

Surrounded by the redolent summertime smell of freshly mown grass, seventy parachutists sitting in neat lines, leaned back against their 'chutes and felt the leg-straps of their tightened harnesses bite into their thighs. Fifty yards away, awesome at ground level, a barrage balloon swayed slightly to begin its first silent, tremulous ascent of the day, permitted by its retaining cable. The eyes of all those destined to jump were riveted upon it as it rose. Suspended underneath was a box-like structure, a cage which contained the first three of their number. Accompanying them on their upwards journey was a sergeant of the Royal Air Force, a parachute jump instructor, there to despatch.

After drawing their 'chutes from the pantechnicon, fitting them up and being checked out by their instructors, the course—amongst them the as yet un-parachute-trained members of Lieutenant Shutbridge's Reconnaissance Troop—had lain back nervously awaiting the order of their fate to be pronounced. Finally, crew-cut and striking muscle-flexing pose, an instructor of the No. 1 Parachute Training School stood out front brandishing a manifest board. Those resting on the grass viewed him apprehensively, some clearly more in dread than anticipation.

"Right! Listen in! Number one stick: Francis, Stevenson, Gerson; number two stick: Burns, Taverner, Boult ..."

As he worked his way through the list, the bootnecks heaved a collective sigh of relief. First onto the chopping block at least meant less waiting around.

The PJIs they liked, for in training and despatching the military parachutists of all three services, their reservists and the occasional member of a foreign ally, the Sergeants of the RAF's Parachute Jump Instructor branch did their job with a flair and expertise borne of long experience at the game. They were full of sound practical and philosophic advice, such as 'Stand up, hook up and look up' and 'Fear dispels beer;' 'Feet and knees together, lads, protect the family jewels' was another of their favourites and sooner or later they always liked to ask the course a hypothetical question about the aircraft, a C130 Hercules.

"If this eighty-odd ton of iron-maiden came down in the sea, do you think it would float? Sapper Jones, a man with a technical background ..."

"Yes."

"Oh you do, do you? Well, there's hope for us all then."

Everyone watched as the first stick began to ascend for their first jump from the balloon. Those who knew them watched hyper-critically. Everyone felt fear. Fear was apparent in a hundred different ways—talkativeness, silence, fidgeting, introspection, sleepiness—and a face on which it showed was a source of endless encouragement and amusement to others, all trying to put a bold front on it, because it made them believe they were succeeding. Burns wondered what his face was like. He tried to assume an expression of interested indifference but the hand that was steadily twisting his guts made it difficult.

In the rising cage, Stevenson wore a very slight frown; which was obviously more than he wanted to, thought the watching 'Ginger' Boult, since fear, worry, anxiety, caution and associated sentiments were inconsistent with his desired public image. Gerson was trying desperately not to notice the receding ground but Francis, on the other hand, was leaning out of the cage, sucking on the corner of his moustache as was his habit, grinning and waving the standard British Army thumb at everyone below as though the whole thing were a fairground ride. Boult gave him two fingers.

The cable paid out, a flagman telling off to the winch operator as the markers came past. To the watchers on the ground it seemed as if the balloon were going to disappear. Eight hundred feet! There was no such height ...

"You'll all enjoy this jump," intoned the course officer, a flight-lieutenant, to those on the ground, keeping their minds occupied.

'What, jump from a swinging platform eight hundred feet up? You're joking ...' they thought.

"You WILL all enjoy this jump," smirked the officer with a slight alteration of emphasis, smiling at his own tremendous wit.

The flagman stopped the winch operator. On a sign from him, he indicated to the despatcher with his flags that the cage was now at the right height and the winch secured. A slight breeze leaned the cable off the vertical.

On the ground there was an air of tense expectancy. Resting their backs against their parachutes everyone looked up, shielding their eyes. No-one spoke, the box-like cage beneath the silvery-blue barrage balloon being the focus of all their attention. In the distance traffic hummed, barely perceptible against the murmuring of a warm summer's day ...

Something emerged and fell. A dot. A man! A sliver of material wound upwards in relation to him like a plume of smoke curling from a lighted cigarette. As it drew taut, so it mushroomed outwards, waffling then filling with air until there it was, a khaki canopy, beautiful and round, breathing its diminishing expansions and contractions until it settled into a perfect half-globe, bearing its human cargo to earth.

"There Y'ARE!" crowed the Flight-Sergeant, waving an arm as though demonstrating a miracle to non-believers, "The good old PX. No frills or spills or even thrills unless," he added, "... yer cock somethin' up 'cos yer warn't listenin' to me!"

The course officer took up a loud-hailer.

"All round observation ... open your legs and look down ... that's it. Now assess your drift ... feet together ..."

The PX buckled as Francis rolled on the ground. The canopy waffled, then folded down on top of him so still were the airs at ground level. Grinning all over his face, he walked back past the others carrying his 'chute.

"Alright?" enquired someone amongst the rows of watchers.

"Piece o' piss ..." answered Francis.

"Tea over here for those of you who survive," joked an instructor.

"Ta very much." The bootneck surrendered his 'chute and helped himself to a plastic cupful of tea, issue, milk and sugar already in. Then he came and sat down by the others.

"Whaja reckon?" asked Boult, keeping a tight rein on his feelings.

Francis looked into his tea, struggling to find any word or words which could possibly summarise the experience with the slightest semblance of adequacy. After a moment he gave up the struggle.

"I dunno," he breathed. "It don't feel that much different being a ... a 'parachut-er!'"

In the balloon the despatcher was telling another joke, worse than the one he had told at length on the way up. A smutty joke which would barely raise a laugh in any company let alone that of people about to make their first descent. Stevenson half listened, Gerson not at all. PJIs must learn them on their course, he thought ...

'Right, sit at ease, sit easy. The aim of this afternoon's lecture is to cover the jokes to be told to the novice parachutist on his way up for the balloon jump. Now, broadly speaking, these jokes fall into three categories. Vicars, tarts and wedding night jokes. Or to put it another way, smutty jokes, dirty jokes and downright filthy bastards. Take notes if you wish ...

'First we'll cover the vicar jokes then, okay? Right, there's this vicar and he's down the ole rectory one afternoon, lobbing it up this busty bint from the Lamb and Flag when alluva sudden the church bells begin to ring. Bells? he says, bells ...?'

Gerson stood with his head bowed, looking at the floor of the cage. He didn't mind the joke; he might even have found it funny in other circumstances. What he couldn't stand was being so high up. He loathed the humming of the wind in the suspension wires and the way the cage shifted about made him feel sick. If he looked up, he saw the horizon and that made him aware of how high they were and paralysed him with fear. Nervously he grasped the handrail, trying to blot out his view of the airfield, trying not to notice anything about this whole damn thing.

The balloon lurched.

'Oh gawd,' thought Gerson. 'Give over, will ya? JUST STAY STILL, WILL YOU? Oh christ all bleedin' mighty ...'

The despatcher finished his joke.

"Pathetic," snorted Stevenson, moving unbidden towards the door.

'Cocky bastard, eh?' thought the PJI. A lot of the booties he had had in the past liked to think they were hardmen, supermen, uncrackable, that type of thing. Here apparently was another. Throwing abuse and fishing for bites off the instructors all the first week, that was him. Needed taking down a peg or two. Well, there were two easy ways to do that from a balloon. One was to tell the man to go in his own time. That sorted the wheat from the chaff, that did. They just couldn't bring themselves to do it. Didn't have it inside 'em. But for the real hard nuts like this geezer, there was only one way. Which was to give them the 'Go' whilst holding onto the back of their 'chute, then pull them back in. It worked a treat. Every one a winner! They got all steamed up, went to jump, stepped off and found themselves back in the cage when they thought they ought to be falling. *It was a beaut!* It never failed. You should see their faces; panting, snarling, eyes like the proverbial racing dog's bollocks. It cracked the hardmen right open, that one did. Like throwing a firecracker into a greyhound's starting cage. A real peach. And Mister Stevenson looked like a suitable case for treatment. Calling his class instructor a 'crabfat!' Eh? We'll see about you, sonny.

"RED ON!" snapped the despatcher.

Stevenson slapped his left arm across his front-mounted reserve parachute.

"Now," cooed the PJI in a voice of honey, "Go in your own time, pal." His hand stole towards the top of Stevenson's main parachute.

"Just remember, son, don't look down, look ..."

Stevenson jumped. No point in hanging around. Silly twat might tell another joke.

Robbed of his little trick, the despatcher swore. Damn! His hand hadn't quite made it. Damn him! Ah well, he would get him back on the flight swings next week. Stevenson. Sarcastic bastard. He had only known him one week yet it seemed like forever. Now what a different sort of bloke Gerson was. Always happy, laughing, smiling, ready with a gag. Never down. Not this morning though. No. From the look on the guy's face this morning it was going to take all his powers of persuasion to coax an exit out of him, not a refusal. Small, pinched face; so white it was like a washing advert. He was looking humble, this character. About as humble as a man could be. Six helpings of humble pie up the Naff last night, that's what he must've had.

"In the door," commanded the RAF sergeant.

Like a man in a nightmare, Gerson moved in slow-motion toward the aperture in the side of the cage, grasping the handrail with the grip of a maniac. As he got to the edge, he peered out and quickly shut his eyes in horror. He jerked his head up. The tail fin loomed above him. He tried not to look at it or at anything. He felt weak. Weak in the guts, weak in the legs, weak in the head. Everywhere. He thought of his bed back in the grot. He thought of home, he thought of all the luscious girls down on Plymouth Hoe, he thought of all the pubs where he could be sinking kosher beer, he thought of all the jobs he could be doing the world over instead of THIS! But no, he had to go and be a hero ... And now he was going to die. He knew he was going to die and he knew he had to do it. But what a way to go! Impact from eight hundred feet. Death he could just about cope with. But not this. It was the uncertainty of it all, falling to his death, maybe it would open, maybe not. Oh shit! He had nothing left. Nothing at all. No physical strength whatever. He was completely drained of everything except a tiny amount of moral courage desperately fighting an almost overwhelming urge to say

NO! To scream out in refusal. It was all he had left. Just that.
Nothing else. Mere fumes after the petrol tank had run dry. His
heart beat to excess, his breath came in tiny shallow bursts. Beads of
perspiration stood out on his face and ran down his cheeks, soaking
into the leather chin-strap of his helmet.

"A good step out, now," urged the PJI; "Don't look down, look
out, head up ..."

He looked over the side at the flagman, checking he was clear to
despatch.

"RED ON!"

In a trance Gerson took his hand away from the stay-bar and put
it across his reserve. His eyes were round, huge, terrified. For a split
second he tottered in the doorway on shaky legs. Then feeling
himself to be in danger of falling out accidentally, he whipped his
other arm off the reserve and grasped the right-hand stay-bar to
steady himself.

A twinkle came into the despatcher's eye. In a kindly voice,
reminiscent of the headmaster of the South London school from
which Gerson had played truant as a youngster, he said,

"Alright, we'll try that again, shall we? Just relax, okay?
Remember what I said. Step well out, just like stepping off a
London bus."

Gerson tried to smile but his facial muscles were stuck. He closed
his eyes, took a deep breath and held it...

"RED ON!" screamed the despatcher in his ear. ..."GO!!"

Instinctively he stepped out, incapable of refusing. He tried to
scream as he felt himself falling, anticipating the shattering impact
as he plunged from bus to pavement 800 feet below but his scream
emerged as a breathy groan which only he himself heard. Then a
miracle happened. A huge hand slowed him down, more and more,
until he felt himself dangling, swinging in mid-air. He opened one
eye, then both, looking for the explanation. There was nothing
below him so he looked up, fearful in case the miracle should have
second thoughts. But there it was, sure enough, billowing above
him. A big brown canopy, gorgeous and buxom like the sun-tanned
WRAF corporal he'd been trying it on with down the bowling alley.
With exaggerated motions he went through his flight drills, anxious
to please. Anxious to please anybody and everybody after his
reprieve from death. When he reached the ground he made a
perfect parachute-landing-fall, then took a long time about
gathering up the 'chute until he had conquered the feeling of
wanting to cry with relief. Sheepishly he walked back.

"Good, no problem there, Royal," nodded the course officer,

easily seeing through Gerson's attempted air of indifference. "'Chute over there, tea over there ..."

Detachedly, Boult watched his right knee shake like a leaf beneath his denims as they ascended. He shifted his weight onto it to stop it; a moment later his left began to do the same. The cage gave a little jerk as the paying out stopped and there was a sudden uncanny silence broken only by the humming of the wind in the wires.

"And if you look over here," laughed the despatcher pointing towards Oxford, "You'll see a cemetery, ha ha ha ha ...! It really is a fine view, isn't it? We could stay up here all day, y'know, the old beer and sandwiches touch. Still, got to get on or we'll never get through the rest of the course. Number One in the doorway ..."

Burns, an ex-apprentice professional footballer whose career had come to grief after being hacked out of a trial with a first-division club, would have been quite happy to have stayed up there all day too. But as it meant parachuting down, the sooner they got on with that part of it, he felt, the better. He moved to the door.

Taverner watched him go, his face non-plussed by the new sensation of falling. A couple of seconds later there was a clink as Burns' break-ties parted, jerking the metal buckle of his static-line against the strong point in the cage. Then it was his turn.

He moved to the edge, determined not to look down, face pale, cheeks hollow.

"GO."

Taverner stepped out cleanly, looking upwards at the tail-fin. There was no sensation of falling. He stayed exactly where he was while the tail-fin disappeared toward the heavens. At the same time, God or the despatcher, whichever one had been detailed off for the task, pulled the parachute off his back like a conjurer producing a string of handkerchiefs from his pocket. First the rigging lines went up, towed by the bag. Then the canopy came out of the bag, filled and blossomed above him. He looked up gratefully, checking its shape. It was perfect. Sheer magic! He was now one of that select band of people who had jumped! A balloon today. Aeroplanes next week. Hands on risers, palms forward, he went through his flight drills in the way he had been taught, assessing his drift, watching the heel of his DMS boot as it drifted slowly over a spot picked on the ground below.

"GO!"

Boult's exit rocked the cage. He leapt at the tail-fin, trying to 'nut' it in mid-air...

CHAPTER 6

The Tall Pines

It was in the early hours of the morning, some months later, whilst mounting up in the four-tonner before driving to their rendezvous with the 'plane for a day's jumping, that Lieutenant Shutbridge broke a piece of bad news to his troop. He slammed the tail-board shut, then stood there looking up at them, illuminated by the arc lights of the company lines.

"A Marine was killed in Belfast last night. It was John Cochran."

Twenty faces froze upon the officer.

"They ambushed the lights at Newington. John got the first round through the head. No-one else was hit."

"We all knew him. A stout, likeable bloke. As you know, he volunteered for an extra tour over there because he was saving to get married. There's no question therefore of a widow's pension, so I suggest a contribution from us would be in order."

Two years ago Taverner had soldiered with John Cochran in Cyprus. Now he was dead.

Sitting on the aircraft as they flew low-level before jumping, Taverner wondered about it. He didn't ask why. He knew *why* he had died. The immediate cause of death was that Johnny Cochran hadn't got his nut out of the way of a speeding bullet which had hit him in the left eye, gouged a groove round the inside of his head and punched out his right eye, leaving it hanging out of its socket on threads. A fairly awful way to die, as death went. That was *why* he had died ...

But what had he actually died for?

For the right of some self-seeking politician to keep himself in the limelight by making political capital out of his death? For the right of the G & T set to show their breeding by sticking their little fingers in the air as they sipped? For the right of the mop-head set to shoot

121

their veins with dope and burn their skulls out with 'acid' in their forlorn search for creativity? For the right of the talking classes to believe that they alone of all the people on God's earth possessed 'higher consciousness?' For the right of the radical trendies to live cocooned in the blissful ignorance of their own illusions, able to turn their faces from the truth for as long as they remained untouched?

'Yeah ...' thought Taverner, 'All that.' That was about it. That was a pretty accurate assessment of all that John Deans Cochran had died for, aged twenty-six, single.

Of course, whenever the windbags and wuffos of the progressive left heard of the death of a soldier, they simply shook their heads and said wisely, "Tough. He shouldn't have joined." That was their stock answer, the instinctive reaction of the dissenting elite of the ruling classes to something they didn't really understand or want to come to terms with—which was that any society worthy of the name required people to defend it. Such people, hog-tied by the false and terrifying assumption that only *they* were intelligent, that only *they* possessed the ability to think, felt that the more 'intelligent' a person was, the more naturally inclined he would be to spend his life as they did, sitting on their backsides, endlessly talking. Doers such as athletes and sportsmen were therefore dumb proles, soldiers dumb fools. So the professional soldier did a job they disdained to do. He was paid to keep the forces of barbarism at bay, to form a hard protective outer rim for civilisation, inside which people could say what they wanted and behave as they pleased. It was ironic that the better he discharged his task, the more out of touch those behind the stockades were liable to become.

Taverner told himself to keep his feelings out of it; that feelings were neither expected nor required of those who served. The progressive wuffos preferred the 'unthinking' image of their servicemen because it saved them from thinking. But it had never stopped the serviceman from thinking. And right now Taverner was thinking something all of them had thought—and said—many times.

"If I ever got my sights on one of those IRA bastards ..."

The thought seemed to warm him. He turned it over in his mind, savouring it for long minutes. Then he filed it away in a place marked 'Accessible' and returned to the present.

The drop zone was short, narrow, stony and full of heather-covered holes conducive to broken legs. Furthermore, it was surrounded by trees and sloped sharply, rising up to a thickly-wooded feature which incorporated the remains of an old castle. It meant, should the first men be released a tiny bit late, or even if anyone behind them didn't leave the 'plane promptly enough, the last men out would find themselves amongst those trees. They would exit in two short sticks of five, jumping simultaneously from both sides of the aircraft, and the precise moment of their release had to be calculated to a nicety by the captain and navigator. Altogether, to land ten men on such a DZ from a 'plane travelling in the region of a hundred and twenty knots was a highly skilful business.

When the troop jumped tactically, Shutbridge and Daffney always went in separate sticks and neither of them at the Number One position. But today being a routine training jump, Daffney had been content to leave his Number Ones to whoever was manifested in those slots. Shutbridge, however, had had a quiet word with the RAF about his. A Number One who hesitated in the doorway could set up a chain reaction right down the stick and this was the first outing for some of his troop since qualifying. So privately, he had volunteered North for the port side and Gerson for the starboard. North was a reliable and experienced jumper, Gerson still very much a novice. But as far as the latter was concerned, Shutbridge hadn't heard a thing about him being scared witless by the balloon jump on his course, far less paid any attention to it. And if it were true that in order to qualify for his 'wings,' the little man had dragged himself a further seven times out of a Hercules, each time with his eyes tightly shut and firmly in the belief he was a goner, then tacitly Shutbridge planned to reward such guts. At his announcement of the present bout of parachute continuation training, he had seen Fear with a capital F bounce into Gerson's eyes like numerals in a cash register and he wanted him—more, he needed him—to stop hating it. Because a man whose actions were governed by nervousness was far more likely to make a mistake than one of the 'nutters,' of which there was a strong element in his troop, whose over-enthusiasm occasionally needed restraining. One blithe display of perfect confidence in Gerson therefore, and his own would soon be restored. Most of the stories about people's performances on the last basic parachute course had—inevitably —reached him via Stevenson's generous mouth, Stevenson himself, of course, being impervious to fear. An examination of his log-book showed that for five out of his eight qualifying jumps he had been a Number One, but as this was currently threatening to inflate his ego beyond manageable proportions, Shutbridge had put him at Number Five today, out of the way, behind him.

"'Captain—Loady;'"

"'*Loady;*'"

"'*Have any of 'em been airsick yet?*'"

"'*Loady, no; one or two are looking a bit green about the gills but no-one's actually spewed yet …*'"

"'*Captain, roger. Okay, we're going to stop rock-polishing now and go up to fifteen hundred feet—that's er, ten minutes, okay?*'"

"'*Loady, roger.*'"

Standing up at the rear of the 'plane, the loadmaster gave the ten-minute signal, flexing the fingers and thumb of one gloved hand to each side twice. Then he nodded to the despatchers who rose. Both first held up a solitary finger to their respective sides, meaning 'first stick only.' Then, using both hands, they made an open-palmed lifting gesture, reminiscent of the conductor of an opera motioning the orchestra to rise and take a bow. The first ten men to jump stood up.

"THE PORT STICK—PREPARE FOR ACTION!"

"STARBOARD STICK—PREPARE FOR ACTION!"

Each man first unhitched his reserve parachute, then lifted his container from the floor in order to attach it to the front of his harness, an act which strongly evoked in him the feeling of hanging a millstone round his own neck. For inside the bulky, padded and cosseted jump-container was nothing more imaginative or useless than a hundred-pound metal jerry-can, topped up to the brim with poured-concrete or sand-and-gravel, such being all that was necessary to simulate the crude weight of a battle load. Struggling to support his load whilst he attached it to the lower pair of D-rings on his harness, he fought with the hooks, twisting them so that the release-levers operated outwards, giving easy access to his thumbs. Once under canopy, he would lower the container to the end of a twenty foot line, thereby allowing it to land independently of him. Failure to lower the container thus meant the start of a new life—in a wheel-chair. Yet such a comparatively simple action could—in mid-air—be complicated not only by fast-approaching ground, but by the now replaced front-mounted reserve parachute which tended to obscure any view of the crucial release-levers.

"HOOK UP!"

Making well sure it ran over his shoulder freely, each man took his static-line, reached up and clicked the metal buckle on the end of it into the gate of a strop hanging near his head from a wire cable. The cable ran down the 'plane from the bulkhead to a strongpoint aft of the doors the troops would exit. Buckles were clicked home and the life-preserving link tugged for re-assurance. After that, each man held it with his inboard hand until the very moment of departure. Another symbolic act, the tying of the umbilical cord to Mother Aircraft...

"CHECK YOUR EQUIPMENT!"

Like everyone else, Shutbridge, in the starboard stick, checked first his own equipment, then that of the man in front of him, 'Ginger' Boult. Then the despatchers worked their way down the lines of men, carrying out for the third time the same checks; reserve pins, static-line, leg-straps, visible break-ties; the fitting of the helmet, the reserve, the container-and-rifle...

"PORT STICK: TELL OFF FOR EQUIPMENT CHECK!"

"Five okay!"

"Four okay!"

"Three okay!"

"Two okay!"

"One okay! Port stick okay!"

From rear to front the cry rippled down the line of standing men —Burns, Phillips, Dickens, Francis, North, each man giving the one in front a confirmatory thump on the shoulder, North holding up a thumb to the port despatcher. Then the starboard stick told off in similar fashion.

"*Loady—Captain*";

The loadmaster's lips moved soundlessly, his voice picked up by a throat-mike over his larynx.

"'*Captain*'";

"'*Troops ready for action;*'"

"'*Captain, roger.*' How many minutes, Nav?"

"Five-and-a-half to Turn-In."

"'*Okay Loady, I'll give you the nod when to open the doors*'";

"'*Loady, roger.*'"

"Okay Co, start to bring her down."

Flying the 'plane from the right-hand seat, the co-pilot glanced at the altimeters, beginning his descent to eight hundred feet above DZ. He glanced up again, and then across at the captain, his lips choosy, like a connoisseur on his subject.

"There's more lift in the air now. Or something."

He made a gesture, as if to tickle the controls. The captain nodded.

"Mmm. But don't forget, she's a different aeroplane to yesterday's. This one's new."

"Well, there's that. Certainly flies better. What's happened to that one? Line servicing?"

The captain sniffed.

"Manufacturer's overhaul, I should hope ..."

Like a beast of burden, Gerson leaned against the side of the aircraft. He sweated with the effort of holding up his container. For something to do, he looked over his shoulder at Taverner. They exchanged glances. Taverner's face betrayed all the interest of a cow in a cattle market waiting to be sold. Behind him stood Boult, big and unconcerned; then Shutbridge, ruminative, his face pursed, his thoughts elsewhere; and last in line, Stevenson, bland, uncaring and playing to some unknown gallery in his head.

'Who's that sucker ...' thought Gerson, turning back to his front, 'standing at the back of the queue? Pardon, Steve? Speak up, I can't hear ya ...'

Privately he assumed that the RAF, not knowing them, had simply pulled their names out of the hat in making up the manifest, putting himself at Number One and Stevenson, to his chagrin, out of the big time at the back. Gerson had been cock-a-hoop. Here was a heaven-sent opportunity to give him some stick back and at the same time show him he had killed any fear he had ever felt about jumping. He wasn't sure if he had or not. But no more, he had decided, was he going to wake up on the morning of a jump with a lead weight called 'fear' on his stomach. All that sweat and tension—it wasn't worth the effort. He had spent a long time lately, thinking about it, rationalising it. All this business was, was a method of delivering recce troops to a place by parachute; and what that boiled down to was this: either the parachute opened, or it didn't. If it did, you were okay; if it didn't—tough. You had dipped out for the day. But no more was he going to have the likes of Stevenson slagging him off because he was a middle-order jumper or overtly apprehensive. Not when *he* was the Number One and Stevenson was at the *back!*

He leaned against the fuselage interior, the unpleasant hand of fear still niggling, as it did with every paratrooper. Nevertheless, in a way he never had before, Gerson was almost looking forward to the opening of the doors. Used before the open doors in the proper manner, he had in his pocket the very thing to make Stevenson look a sucker.

"'Captain—Loady;'"

"'Loady;'"

"'Clear to open doors;'"

"'Loady, wilco.'"

The loadmaster nodded at the despatchers who went to work on their respective doors, bending to grip the wheel-lock with both hands, bracing themselves as they twisted it. Knees bent, they tugged the doors inwards into the guide-rails. With the initial break in the smooth streamlining of the outer fuselage there came a fierce hiss of air like a holed tyre. Faces blanched, brows furrowed.

Some of those sitting nearby watched with rounded eyes as daylight invaded the interior. With the noise of an express train, a howling gale blew into the 'plane, tearing about the place, snatching at things, attacking the lattice-work of the vacated seats, making loose objects fret. The despatchers reached up, securing the curved doors above their heads, before kicking out the jump step from which each man would launch himself into the air. Then the starboard despatcher stood and contemplated the wing, stroking his moustache, whilst the port one went and stood on the step which projected out into the slipstream. He looked at the view to be had from eight hundred feet, gazing about him, sniffing the air, turning his head as though he were a seaside holiday-maker who had just opened the door of his caravan and was seeing what sort of day it was.

The aircraft banked and began a long turn to port, turning in towards the coast on her final run-in to the drop zone. Looking aft through the port door, North watched the estuary below him recede from view, its river lying snake-like between mud-banks exposed at low-tide. Gradually, all his view consisted of was the sea upon which, through the starboard door, Gerson caught sight of a fishing vessel, the faces of its crew upturned, gazing up at the fat belly of the Hercules as the 'plane roared over them, making a swishing-tearing sound through the air, four thin plumes from her exhausts trailing away behind her. Slowly she straightened, resuming straight and level flight after the turn-in, settling in the air, flying steadily, purposefully, deliberately, with studied care and concentration as she picked up her bearing to the drop zone.

"Final dropping checks, Engineer"; the captain glanced behind him.

The engineer flipped open a small booklet at the appropriate page.

"Altimeter";

"Set and compared."

"Flaps";

"Set."

"Air deflectors";

"Clear to open."

"Para doors";

"Para doors open."

"Final dropping checks complete. 'Seven-One-One, Ground, over'"; the captain spoke to the DZ party awaiting the drop.

"'*Ground, Seven-One-One*'";

"'*Seven-One-One, on finals for drop, over*'";

"'*You're clear to drop, Seven-One-One. Out.*'"

As the red sandstone cliffs of Lyme Bay loomed under them, the captain leaned forwards, peering through the cockpit windows.

"Which is the TAP, Nav?"

"Far side of the village, over the river, there's a crossroads. Two-o-clock of that, there's an obelisk. That is the target approach point."

"Got it."

"From there to the plantation there's four miles to run."

"Okay. Come **right**, five degrees, Co. '*Captain—Loady*'";

"*Loady*";

"'*Captain, two minutes. Bring the troops to action stations.*'"

"'*Loady, roger.*'"

"Now **left** five degrees."

Victory-sign fashion, the loadmaster held up two fingers. Again he nodded at the despatchers.

"THE PORT STICK—ACTION STATIONS!"

"STARBOARD STICK—ACTION STATIONS!"

In tribal rhythm, the two sticks tramped down the 'plane, dragging the container-bound leg. The despatchers motioned the leading pair into the open doorways where each put up an arm against the side of the aircraft to steady himself, resting the other arm across his reserve. They stood looking downwards, trying to gauge when the red light would come on. ('Not yet, not yet, God, make it not yet ...!') ('Now! Now! Make it NOW!!') Inches in front of them, the air howled and tore, shimmered and shone, hazy with the fumes from the two engines either side, alternately icy and warm on their faces. A high-octane smell, thin and pungent, wafted over them as they waited, despatchers' restraining hands upon them. The jump lights were unlit.

Gerson glanced at the despatcher on his right, then turned his head the other way, leaning back away from the door, trying to catch Stevenson's eye. Stevenson looked at him. Their eyes met. Poker-faced, Gerson reached into the pocket of his smock, then took out a baby's dummy and put it in his mouth. Daffney's second stick, still sitting down, creased with laughter. Stevenson returned a certain gesture. Then, with the dummy still in place, Gerson looked again at his despatcher, whose face, for several seconds, remained non-plussed, before with a snort, he too broke up laughing. He tapped the loadmaster, pointing at Gerson and grinning. But the loadmaster was not one for frivolity at such a moment. He shut his eyes and prayed for patience. 'Bloody people—why couldn't they

behave properly? Why couldn't they take it seriously like the Paras?'
"Dear Lord," he prayed, "Send me back to a Route Squadron
soonest, I've not long to go till pension ..." To Gerson, he made a
motion as though unzipping himself and urinating on him. Gerson
grinned, delighted at the reaction. Then he himself capped the
comedy of gestures he had inspired by spitting the dummy out into
the slipstream — "Sppoogh!"

"Okay ..." murmured the captain, leaning over onto the left-
hand edge of his seat. He looked vertically down at the ground, his
face a mask of concentration as he studied the gorse, scrub and trees
below, giving corrections to the co-pilot to bring the aircraft exactly
over the release point calculated by the navigator.

"Come two **left** ..."

He waited, studying the ground;

"Now two degrees **right** ..."

The co-pilot's green gloves moved hardly at all — but too much for
the captain who looked up.

"Uh-uh, don't yaw ... bring her back ... wind's from the left,
remember ...

"Good ... hold her there ... that's it ... maintain that heading ..."

The captain glanced at the compass;

"Hold 293 ...

"And steady ...

"Steady ...

"Steady ...

Listening over his headset, the loadmaster glanced left and right
at the two lines of tense faces in front of him. The despatchers stood,
legs apart, braced against the movement of the aircraft, first man's
strop taken, eyes glued to the lights ...

"Overhead now — Red On!"

The red light by each door lit up — 'CAUTION'!

"RED ON!" screamed the despatchers. The two men in the
doorways slapped their supporting arm across their reserve, staring
fixedly outwards, poised ready to jump ...

"Steady ...

"Steady ...

"Steady ...

"Green On!"

The lights glowed green for 'JUMP' and the 'plane exploded into
activity.

"GREEN ON!" yelled the despatchers — "GO!"

"GO!"

North went, then Gerson, despatched a split-second behind him so they wouldn't collide underneath the aircraft. Hard on their heels, the rest followed through the howling doorways, heaving themselves out of each side of the 'plane, winnowing outwards and down ...

Francis
    Taverner
Dickens
    Boult
Phillips
    Shutbridge
Burns
    Stevenson

A heart-stopping glimpse of the step, the fuel-tank and the woods below, then they were through and met by a hurricane blast which tore at them, sending them away like leaves in a gale, beaten and buffeted as though a huge hand were shaking them, rag-dolls, rats in the mouths of terriers, the noise tumultuous, terrifying, obliterating ...

dropping ...

dropping ...

then somewhere behind them a crack of which they were barely conscious, the break-ties snapping, the 'chute parting company with the bag. Freed of the aircraft, stretched out unfilled and propelled by 120 knot slipstream, the canopy and shrouds flew violently over their heads, yanking each one wildly onto his belly, face-to-earth. For brief, horrific moments they watched it on the same level as themselves, waffling, undecided, bending ahead of them like a willow in a gale ...

"TWO!"

"THREE!"

"FOUR!"

"FIVE!"

The despatchers worked furiously, grasping each strop as it was presented, large hands and shoulders assisting the over-burdened and staggering troops through the doors. Behind them, standing serenely amidst the maelstrom, the loadmaster told off to the captain;

"*'Two men gone ... and four ... and six ... and eight ...'*"

"Steady ... steady ... steady ..." intoned the Captain, keeping his eye to the ground, judging the end of his dropping-run.

Two by two in the wake of the 'plane, the 'chutes cracked open with an appalling tug at the legs and shoulders but for which no man was ever less than grateful, each one finally swinging under his canopy as it filled and breathed, suspending him summarily, restoring his ruffled equanimity courtesy of God, the torment over, his relief ecstatic, the peace startling, the quiet uncanny, the 'plane gone ...

"Red on ..."

"RED ON!"

"Red off."

"'*Loady—Captain*'";

"'*Captain*'";

"'*Loady, ten troops despatched, seven seconds, bags coming in now.*'"

"'*Captain, roger.*'"

Like men possessed, the despatchers worked to haul in the bags on the ends of the flailing static-lines where they thrashed and banged against the fuselage in the slipstream.

Shutbridge, following Boult, noticed him off-balance shoulder-charge the side of the door with a force that would have earned him a sending-off from the football field. Briefly he glimpsed him whipped away, spinning in the slipstream, knowing, from the glum look on his face, that the result would be badly twisted rigging-lines. He followed him out, keeping a tight position feet and knees together, eyes open. The slipstream caught him perfectly, turning him neatly at right-angles so he was facing aft. He glanced right and saw Phillips, his opposite number in the port stick, flying through the air with a comical look on his face, waiting for *the moment*, the moment they all hoped would never happen, the moment when they knew nothing *had* happened. Then they were open.

Immediately there came a warning shout.

"STEER AWAY! I'M IN TWISTS!"

Predictably, it was Boult. Shutbridge glanced up at his canopy, checking its shape, then quickly all round him, well practised in the drill, making an instant mental note of the other parachutes; 'Phillips—right, Dickens—half-right, Boult—front, Burns—rear-right.' But as he reached up for the toggles, pulling them out of the velcro in order to steer away from Boult, he heard another shout. Turning his head behind and upwards, he saw another figure in the sky, struggling with a parachute that was twisted up to the periphery. Stevenson! Obscured by his own canopy, he had missed him the first time. He glanced down at the ground to assess his drift and saw with a start that he was directly over the woods. Those in front and to his right were okay, but Jeeze! he would have to work hard to make open ground. He would *just* clear them if he steered off in the shortest line. Stevenson wouldn't though. Behind him, he was right above the thickly-wooded castle feature at the end of the run. And in twists, unable to steer.

Stevenson cursed the packer who had packed his 'chute. Incompetent gett!! He had exited perfectly only to find on opening that the damn thing was twisted up as tight as a hawser! The four lift-webs were one solid object, forcing his head down onto his chest. He kicked violently, swearing aloud, trying to wrench the lift-webs apart behind his head ... damn thing! The bloody container, hanging like a dead-weight, didn't make it any easier to get up a momentum. He kept kicking and pushing back his head, grappling behind him. Trees everywhere. He thought of jettisoning the container altogether but it had the Gimpy* strapped to it and they would accuse him of panicking. The trouble was, he couldn't lower it until he was clear of the trees ...

"Just get the bleedin' twists out ...!" he grunted, kicking like a mule. Slowly, excruciatingly slowly, the 'chute began to untwist.

Shutbridge was clear. With his thumbs he felt for the release-levers to lower his container-and-weapon. Hanging from his 'chute whilst he fiddled, he noticed the port stick release theirs in a beautiful chance cadence in jump order. One after the other in quick, even succession, the containers rippled to the ends of their lines where they bounced and gently swung below each man. He rammed the levers outwards and his own container fell, tugging his harness as it snapped taut the line. 'Yes ...' he thought; there was something distinctly poetic about what he had just witnessed. Military parachuting wasn't all blood and thunder.

"NUMBER FIVE IN THE STARBOARD STICK: LOWER YOUR CONTAINER!"

"Shuddup!" muttered Stevenson angrily.

It was the RAF ground officer who was hailing him over a megaphone. He saw nine containers and wanted ten.

Stevenson kicked out of the final twist, then reached up for the steering toggles and ripped them from the velcro, hauling the parachute viciously round to the right to make for the shortest line of escape from the trees. Tall pines. He could smell them; and hear them. He was coming dangerously close to their tops. Tall pines, reaching up to threaten his life.

"Come on, babe," he muttered, coaxing his 'chute, "Get me there, get me there. Get me out of trouble ..."

He hung passively in his harness, toggles in either hand, studying the ground intently, judging his progress over the trees.

* GPMG—the general purpose machine-gun.

"Come on, come on ..."

Blowing down the line of trees, the wind was of no particular help, and if he lowered his container now, then dangling below him, the GPMG would be certain to catch in the upper branches before he had cleared them, bringing him down out of the sky like a fallen jockey ...

Shutbridge had a choice of landing: the rough, or the track which skirted the wood. In the interests of his ankles, he chose the track. He saw Boult's canopy fold to the ground ahead of him.

"NUMBER *FIVE* IN THE STARBOARD STICK: TAKE YOUR *HANDS* OFF YOUR TOGGLES AND *LOWER* YOUR *CONTAINER*!!"

"Shuddup, I said!" hissed Stevenson through his teeth.

Seconds later he was clear, but on a different side of the wood to Shutbridge, a side skirted by gorse and brambles and small trees. Quickly he burrowed in under his reserve parachute, searching for the vital release-levers with his thumbs. Bloody things. The right one was stiff! Shiiit ...! He tugged in desperation ...

He was level with the tops of the trees he had just cleared when he released one hook but not the other. It was a mistake. The whole weight of the container-and-machine-gun now pivoted about the unreleased hook, twisting it into an impossible position and mashing his thumb in the D-ring. He grunted with pain and withdrew his right hand, thumb bleeding.

With his hands off the steering toggles, the canopy had begun a self-correcting turn downwind, adding the 'chute's own speed to that of the wind and making a broken limb a distinct possibility even without the extra hazard of hard-baked, uneven ground and an unreleased container-and-weapon weighing 120 lbs. In the two or three remaining seconds before he hit, he adopted the best parachute-landing-fall position he could, noticing—without realising why—figures already running across the DZ towards his corner of the wood. His last thought was 'Shoulda took the trees ...' Then he slammed into the ground and stayed there.

"'Seven-One-One—Ground'";
"'Seven-One-One'";
"'Ground, STOP DROP: we've got a blood wagon case, over'";
"'Seven-One-One, roger.'"

The body in the gorse did not get up. There was a large dent in its helmet and blood oozed from its mouth.

"'Captain—Loady'";
The Hercules was on a circuit, preparatory to a second drop.
"'Loady'";
"'Captain, stop drop. Relax the troops; have them sit down again.'"
"'Loady, roger; in that case, could you be at least six minutes before the next action stations—we've got to go through all the blasted checks again'";
"'Captain, will do.' Nav, we'll extend out to sea."
"Roger—how far?"
"Er, Loady wanted six minutes, make is six miles."
The captain sat back and lit a cigarette. He had six minutes.
"Well, it seems like we've bent a bootneck to start the day with. So while they're sorting him out. I'll have a cup of coffee please, Enge; black, one sugar."
"Meanwhile," observed the co-pilot drily, looking down on the captain as he banked the aeroplane, "If we ditch and this lot drown ..."
"My head will be on the line as it always tossing-well is," reflected the captain soberly. He brightened. "But thanks for reminding me, Co, are you sure you want the left-hand seat? And bank the other way, I'm senior to you ..."

Stevenson's eyelids flickered. The clammy sweat of shock poured off his face. He lay still, telling himself he was alright, aghast at the impact. He knew something monumental had happened in the last few seconds but he couldn't think what it was. He seemed to be lying in brambles but he couldn't think how on earth he had got there ... unless ... unless ... he had fallen from a tree. Perhaps that was it. He had been out climbing trees and ... he looked down at his chest. There was a parachute there. Oh yes, he remembered something about that. Perhaps that was how he had got here. In that case, it was important to know if he really was alright. He might have broken his back. *What??* He might have broken ... his ... his ... Raise a leg. Quickly, quickly, find out ... He wasn't sure if he wanted to.

Gingerly, he tried to move his legs. If he could move them, his spinal column was okay—that's what the Doc said. Wasn't it? Move your legs ...

He tried.

And couldn't.

He lay still, digesting the awful enormity of this discovery. He couldn't ... He couldn't move his *legs*. He couldn't even *feel* them! Oh no ... OH NO ... Oh Jesus no ... Oh Sweet Jesus Lord Almighty *no* ... He couldn't move them. He couldn't *move* his legs! He had ... he had ... he *had*! He'd broken his back!

He tried again, panic rising ...

Then he remembered the container. It was lying on top of his legs ...

Frantically, he unclipped the reserve, then fiddled with the unreleased container-hook. He unhitched it from his harness and sat up, pushing the container-and-machine-gun off him. It rolled to one side and where it had been lying on top of him, he massaged. He could feel his fingers and thumbs—Ouch! He examined his right thumb. It was lacerated and sticky with half-congealed blood. Never mind that. He continued exploring his body. So far, so good. Then pain suddenly blared through his torso; he groaned slightly. More pain shot through his head. Jesus, that was some bang! Wasn't it? What happened there??

Bauugh! He sat still, leaning forwards, taking his time. It was beginning to come back, the 'plane, the crowded bit of sky, the kicking and shouting, the trees—then BAM! He was suddenly here on the deck, feebly trying to deflate his canopy with one hand, like a little baby. He looked up at the woods. Years ago he had jumped over woods just like those... and had had a similar accident on landing... yes, that time too, he remembered the noise and smell and vibration of the 'plane; it was all coming back, the blast of the slipstream, fighting with twisted lift-webs, trees below, someone shouting at him from the ground... but all that was very remote, it was all a very long time ago. He could see his boots again now. Ah yes, boots, feet, legs...

Gradually, the disrupted time senses in his brain began to merge.

He tried wriggling his toes. The boots moved. He tried to move a leg. It moved! He tried moving the other leg. It moved too! Both legs moved! He could move both legs!! He offered his guardian angels a prayer of thanks. They must be on overtime today. Slowly, he gathered his legs under him and struggled to his feet. Phauugh!

He undid his harness and let it fall to the ground. As he did so, he heard a rustling in the undergrowth. Damn, the Gimpy was still strapped to the container, he should have got it off by now. Then he remembered, he had landed with the whole thing on, surprising even himself. Quickly he snatched the lowering-line off the back of the container and splayed it about to make it look as though it had been lowered at the last minute.

Two men in RAF blue appeared and stood looking at him, panting.

"You alright, Royal?" enquired one. Evidently an officer.

"Yeh," replied Stevenson, the picture of nonchalance.

They seemed puzzled. People who landed with the container on only did it once. After that, they were invalided out of the Service. Puzzlement gave way to uncertainty. Perhaps this wasn't the right bloke ... but then, if he wasn't what was this blood coming out of his mouth?

"Open your mouth and stick your tongue out."
Stevenson did as he was bid.

"You've bitten your tongue, you know that?"

"It's nothing," said Stevenson dismissively.

The role he had assigned himself for life—that of the 'tough cookie'—began to re-assert itself.

"How many fingers?"

"Five ..."

"What day of the week is it?"

"Day after yesterday?"

"Cut out the jokes, Royal," said the other one, "What day of the week is it?"

"Er, Wednesday, Colours."

It was a Wednesday and Stevenson, to whom three stripes and a crown meant a Colour-Sergeant, was actually trying to be polite. But the Flight-Sergeant, with the speech and countenance of a pugilist, took offence.

"Eh—these stripes-and-crown aren't pretty colours, y'know."
He nodded at the container.

"You ought to have your arse kicked right round the DZ for that ..." he opined.

"Yeah?" queried Stevenson, "Who by? You and your fifteen brothers?"

"Now slow down, pal ..."

"Alright, alright Flight," intervened the officer. "Look Royal, what the Flight means is this: if you want to kill yourself, that's fine with us. But just don't do it in circumstances where we have to attend the court of inquiry, okay? Now, what was the problem?"

"I couldn't get the fuggin' thing off, Sir, could I?"

"And are you hurt?"

Stevenson shook his head and immediately regretted it.

"Alright. If you're not hurt, pack your kit up and make your way over to the RV."

They turned to go.

"Y'know," the officer continued as they walked away, "In all my years in parachuting, I've never seen anybody do that and *get away* with it ..."

"I know," responded the Flight-Sergeant loudly, half-looking over his shoulder, "Some o' these bootnecks are too fuggin' bone to get injured!"

"Cheers, Colours!" shouted Stevenson after him. It was exactly the sort of accolade he would have wished for.

He walked to the apex of his 'chute and began to flip it in a clockwise direction before folding it away into a para-bag, to the handles of which he attached the reserve. Noticing for the first time the scratches on the backs of his hands, he flung his two 'chutes astride his shoulders, then with a 'one-two-six,' heaved the container-and-weapon on top of them. Thus laden, he began to pick his way back to the DZ.

He had not gone far when the RAF officer came back, having had an apparent change of heart.

"Look," he said, eyeing the dent in Stevenson's helmet. "You've had a bit of a bump there, Royal, I think you'd better stay there while the Flight gets the DZ truck over. We'll give you a lift."

"Ah, don't worry about it," shrugged Stevenson, playing his life's role to perfection, "I've crawled twice as far with twice as much."

"'Ground—Seven-One-One'";

"'Ground'";

"'Seven-One-One, are we still on on stop drop, or what's happening, over?'"

"'Ground, cancel stop drop; that was a bootneck who bounced on his head so he's okay, over'";

"'Seven-On-One, in that case finals for drop'";

"'Ground, Seven-One-One, clear drop.'"

Inveterate backer of lame horses and lazy dogs, Stevenson was hopeful of better financial luck during a NATO deployment to mark the 200th anniversary of the United States — the Bi-centennial.

CHAPTER 7

One Night Ashore

AMERICA 1976

The unit was embarked upon the Commando carrier HMS 'Balfour' when, in the spring of 1976, she made her triumphal, majestic and unforgettable entry into Florida's Port Everglades. It was the end of a long haul at sea for her, working up, exercising, extending and integrating the amphibious capabilities of her officers, pilots, seamen and embarked force. Deployments of this nature were infrequent for economic reasons but it was this hard-gleaned experience and long continuity of service of the men who carried them out, together with the assiduous honing, polishing and passing on of their skills in practice that was to pay such dividends in the then distant Falkland's War where, six years later, Britain's servicemen were to put their combined skills into operation with a verve and professionalism that took the British public by surprise no less than the Argentinian junta, leaving both equally open-mouthed with astonishment.

Spruced up for the occasion therefore, like no other in her long and varied career, the 'Balfour' was dressed ceremonially from stem to stern. She looked a picture, her Bosun's pride and joy. Every rust streak had been removed in the days preceding her visit by sailors working from launches with grey-paint-rollers on long poles. Her boot-topping was flawless and her brass-work shone with old fashioned peacetime pride. Yet despite the hyper-critical eye of her First Lieutenant and Bosun, neither of whom missed a trick, she still managed to look like what she was — a ship who earned her living at sea in the remoter places. When finally she secured alongside the quay next to two luxury liners, it was she, not they, who looked like a creature of the ocean. "Their place," she seemed to say, "is in port, not mine." The Floridians knew it and with one accord took her to their hearts. Rarely could a foreign ship have been given a more rapturous welcome. For a week she was a celebrity, her picture appearing daily in the newspapers, and the comment most frequently heard from the hordes who stood smiling upon her decks, being photographed and waving ecstatically, was "Gee, she's like a piece of li'l old England."

Liberated thus from their piece of little old England and from living rough on little-known islands of sparse inhabitation, Marines and sailors swarmed ashore, immaculately dressed in their tropical uniforms. Bronzed by the sun, with shiny cap-badge gleaming in best beret and pay drawn in dollars, they set out like tourists to explore their new surrounds, filling every waiting cab full to the brim, always with the same simple salutary directive—"Downtown please, driver." Car-hire firms, knowing business when they saw it, sent representatives to the dockyard gates, thereby setting the scene for the next few days—big Fords, Pontiacs, Bonnevilles and Buicks cruising around jam-packed with laughing, lolling, sight-seeing, 'having-the-time-of-our-lives' matelots and bootnecks, all believing they were Joe Cool, Jim Rockford and Harry Callaghan rolled into one.

When the ship finished berthing and they first stepped ashore, however, a great many of them stood around in groups on the dockside seeking out their 'grippos,' a term derived from the round of introductory handshakes which denoted Americans who, with the hospitality and generosity for which the southern States are renowned, were keen to adopt two or three visiting servicemen for a couple of days to show them around the country of which they were justly proud. A shoreside agency handled the blind introductions inherent in this wonderfully American institution and rarely had they ever proved to be anything other than outstanding successes. Once in a blue moon, however, the system back-fired.

Haythorne and a fellow mortar-trooper called 'Dolly' Parton—a name which should have gone down well in the southern States—searched the teeming dockside for their hosts.

"There they are, Dolly ..."

A white Lincoln convertible, parked just where they said it would be.

Smilingly, they approached, hands extended in greeting. Parton however, was a third generation Portsmothian black.

"Hi! Mr. and Mrs. Kerdiddlehopper? I'm Phil Haythorne, this is ..."

The man's mouth fell open. He turned to his wife in dismay.

"Oh my gard, Enid," he stammered, "We got us a nigger ...!"

★ ★ ★

1500 Eastern Standard Time.

On the beach at Fort Lauderdale, sand, sea and sky met. Men lay limply half-in, half-out of the water, soaking up the sun and wallowing in the surf which washed over them, shifting their bodies back and forth like pieces of driftwood.

In a strange water-side convention, some former soldiers of one nation and some current ones of another also met. The short back-and-sides of Her Majesty's armed forces mingled with the long bedraggled hair and beads of America's Vietnam veterans. Straightway, perhaps because they had never been accepted back into their own society, it was apparent that the Americans were still fighting a war long finished.

"Where were you guys during 'Nam?" — accusingly.

"Yeah, don't tell me the British were chicken ..." — mockingly.

"Nah, we thought the Viet-Cong was doing okay without us so we didn't bother." Definitely out of order, taking the mick out of the American vets. They only wanted to be around some soldiers again.

The Brits swam and drank with them, listened to them and understood them. Being disowned by America was the final insult. Where was the balm for such embitterment?

1900 EST

After talking about 'the race prablem over there in England' for the better part of three hours, Haythorne and Parton had taken polite leave of their red-neck hosts, excusing themselves on the pretext of duty on board the ship. It was a parting tinged with much mutual relief.

Now they sat in a throbbing bar, a blonde nestling up to Haythorne. An hour ago they were complete strangers. Their mouths met. They kissed freely, luxuriously, French-style, tongues roaming — until Parton jabbed Haythorne in the back with his elbow to indicate his glass was empty.

The lance-jack bought. He was well on the way already.

"You're cute, you know that?" murmured the blonde, dripping flaxen hair across his face. Drowning in her scent, Haythorne moved to accommodate his erection.

"Are you ... are you on vacation?" he asked slowly, studiously, the way men do when alcohol begins to corrode their powers of speech.

"Mmhuh," she nodded scintillatingly, "are you on vacation?"

Haythorne shook his head.

"No ..." he replied in all seriousness, "We're on ner 'Balfour' ..."

Parton spat beer and collapsed.

21·00 EST

Floodlights illuminated the exterior of a Miami hotel. Parked on warm, pliable, palm tree-lined tarmac near a fountain which shot fluorescent green water into the air was a long slinky Bonneville sedan. Reclining, drinks in hand, in the deep plush easy-chairs of the lounge bar, looking for all the world as though they owned the place, were the three people who had it on hire. Smith, Gerson and Dickens.

"Hoh—I can take a week of all this, I can take a week of all this! Can *I*. Ask me if I can take a week of all this, Gerry, ask me ..."

"Can you take a week of all this?"

"I'll do me best, I'll do me best, can't say fairer than that, can I? Ask me if I can take a week of all this, Dickie, go on—ask me, you wanna know, don'tcha?"

"Shuddup."

"Whose round is it?"

"Mine."

"Well, get 'em in, then."

Gerson rose, small, neat, curly-haired, tattoos of his allegiances on both forearms: *Mum-Dad-Sis-Bruv* on one, and *The Elephant-and-Castle* on the other. He picked up their glasses, then turned to the other two, face cracking into a dazzling grin.

"Here, whaja call a boomerang that don't come back?"

"Pass."

"A stick. Good, innit. Whaja call a valley between two mountains?"

"Pass."

"Correct. You're clever you are, Smudge!"

"Sod off and get 'em in."

"So, like I was saying," continued Dickens, "before I was so rudely interrupted. We're all down the London on the vince one night, aren't we—there's George Gillett, Geordie Bromley, Terry North and all the boys, right? Alluva sudden, the door opens and in comes this really tasty bit o' stuff, really tasty she was, y'know—one hundred percent essence! She had some mates with her but they was ... well, a bit on the doggo side, someuvem—you sometimes find that, don't you, one really good one and the rest ... Well, anyway, what should happen—she goes up to the bar and parks herself right next to Geordie. Now you know Geordie, nice bloke, good soldier and all that, but he couldn't trap his fingers in the door, could he? Plukes, bald patch, all that. So after about half-an-hour, he eventually did, he had a go. He plucked up courage, he leaned over to her and he says, 'Fancy a bit o' rough tonight, luv?' 'No thanks,' she says, 'I don't like cider.' 'No,' he says, 'I wasn't talking about cider, I was talking about meself.'"

"Brahmer," chuckled Smith.

2200 EST

In a Fort Lauderdale disco the air pulsed, the floor lit up, people turned different colours every second and the atmosphere vibrated with writhing humanity.

"See ya in a minute," she said.

"'Kay."

Taverner picked his way through the colourful throng of swaying bodies and made his way back to the bar whilst his girl disappeared. He slid onto a barstool alongside North. Burns and Stevenson were still trying to grind the dance floor into oblivion. The place was thick with girls but then the girls didn't pay to get in.

"Well?"

"Nice. Nancy. Makes jewellery for a living. Drink?"

"Ta. Jewellery, eh? Get in there, mate ..."

A man to Taverner's left sought his attention. He touched his arm. Taverner turned. The man was fifty-ish. Lined face. Check shirt. Sagging jowl. Unkempt hair. A loser.

"I find you very attractive," he said.

"Is that so?" responded Taverner playfully, "Well, that's very kind of you to say so, squire, but not now, really, the wife and kids'll be back any minute."

"You're very attractive."

"You're pissed."

"I had a liddle da drink, ya ..." slurred the man, "But I know whad I mean an' when I say I find you attractive, I really mean that. I am a very genuine and sincere person, please believe me."

"Do us a favour, mate ..."

The man leaned closer.

"Thin out."

Taverner turned away. But the man's fingers sought his knee and found it. Slowly Taverner swivelled back to face him. He pointed accusingly at the fingers. Then he grasped the man's thumb and twisted it, forcing him up off his stool.

"Uh, uh, don't!" grunted the man.

"You know," said Taverner evenly, "If I wasn't the perfect gentleman I'd break every one of your fingers. Now *thin out.*"

Resentfully the man moved away, nursing his thumb.

"Beefers," muttered Taverner.

North grinned.

"The last time I were on 'Balfour,'" he confided laughingly, "were four years ago when we did an exercise on Corsica against the Foreign Legion ..."

"They're crap!" interrupted someone with a Scouse accent, reaching between them for his drink. North looked round. Stevenson!

"Mebbe they are, but who asked you, ya snub-nosed brown-skinned baby-faced git?" North's Yorkshire hackles went up at the sight of him.

Stevenson picked up his glass, drained it and set it back down with a thud.

"Nobody," he answered, "Nobody had to. The Royal Marines are the best goddam mob in the world, that's a fact. The rest I wouldn't trust to fight their way out of a three-week old soggy wet paper bag, certainly not a bunch o' tossers like the French Foreign Legion. Bud ..." he ordered, pointing at his glass. "As for the Yanks, dear oh dear oh dear. The Special Farces? 'Airborne Ranger—life of danger—get some!'" he yelled annoyingly at North.

It took all North's self-control just to close his eyes. Had they been anywhere else he would have planted him one straight between the lamps. He fought the temptation. Then a thought struck him. He winked at Taverner.

"What about the Paras then, Steve?" he enquired, poker-faced, "We heard you was a cherry-beret at heart ..."

Stevenson snorted.

"Do us a favour! You tryin' to wind me up? Whose Paras you on about, anyway—ours?"

"Of course," replied North still deadpan but waving the proverbial red rag at the bull, "What others are there?"

Stevenson took his glass and drained it in one. Beer and sweat ran down his cheeks, mingling. He thumped his glass back down on the bar again, then let out a long belch whilst he contemplated his brethren in the Parachute Regiment.

"Their main problem," he finally announced, "is they gob off too much."

With which he turned on his heel and swaggered off back to the dance floor. North watched him go. He noticed that the sleeves of

Stevenson's KD shirt were rolled up as high as possible and that at some stage, to suit his vanity as much as his wiry dimensions, the garment had been taken in at the waist by the Chinese tailor on board so that it now fitted him like a glove. 'Typical,' thought North, shaking his head.

"What the boss sees in him, fukdifino," he muttered, "He's too young to be in the troop." North was twenty-eight.

"He's twenty," asserted Taverner, "It was his birthday last week."

"And didn't we all know about it too!" expostulated the York-shireman, "It were like a pig-pen round his bunk all day and Len never said nowt."

Taverner's girl came back. After continuing to chat with Terry North for a few minutes, they went back to dancing. Seeing them go, the man in the check shirt sidled onto a vacant barstool two away from North.

2215 EST. Miami.

"Nah, you don't get much change out of naval skippers, not in my experience, at least," Gerson was saying, whacking down another beer. "I did a commission on a frigate, right? At the end of eighteen months they'd charged every booty aboard, including the Sar'nt-Major, *bar*—little ole me. They were determined to get me. In the end they did. I went ashore, had a skinful, usual routine, and was a coupla minutes adrift back on board. So, first thing in the morning I'm wheeled up in front of the Captain's table, ain't I. I can see the gleam of satisfaction in the Jossman's* eye as he reads out the charge. First the Skipper has words with the Jimmy. The Jimmy says what a serious offence it is, how it cannot be tolerated of us, all that. Then the boss says his piece, what a good boy I'd been, conscientious, all that. Finally the Skipper passes sentence. 'Seven days restriction of privileges,' he says. 'Seven days, Sir,' I said, bright and breezy like, 'I'll piss that in a week!' 'Course the Skipper had a sense of humour too, didn't he. 'In that case,' he come back, quick as a flash, 'take fourteen and piss it in a fortnight.'"

Smith stubbed out a cigar.

"Are we gonna grow roots in this place or what?"

*Jossman—the Master-at-Arms, head of the Regulating Branch aboard HM ships.

2230 EST. The disco.

The man on North's right slid over one barstool and touched him on the arm.

"I find you very attractive," he said.

North glanced at him.

"I wish I could say the same for you, mate."

His elbows rested on the bar-top, glass between them.

The man didn't get it. He thought North was being modest.

"No, really, I think you're a very attractive person. I'm a very warm, sincere an' genuine human being an' when I say I find you attractive, I really do mean ..."

"Look, mate," interrupted North in the tone of the not-unreasonable-man, "I'm not into your type of scene, okay? I'm not a beefer. You understand?"

"What's a beefer?"

"You are. You're a beefer. A queer."

"You mean 'gay'?"

"Whatever you choose to call it, mate, that's your business. But whatever it is, I'm not one of 'em. Right?"

"I like to suck and fuck," said the man.

"Bloodee hell ..." muttered North, "You're too subtle for me ..."

"Why don't you dance with the girls, then?"

"'Cos I'm married," answered North. "I don't mess about when I'm away from home, it's as simple as that. It doesn't mean to say I'm 'gay' as you call it."

"Oh."

The man shrugged. He sat silently for some minutes, North ignoring him. Then slowly, hopefully, his hand stole towards North's thigh and he began to stroke it. For a second or two North didn't appear to notice.

Then he leaned back slowly, a look of 'Now-you've-done-it' on his face. The hand stopped. The man's eyes opened in alarm, fearful of violence.

"I suppose you think that's gonna get you somewhere," said North.

"Maybe. Maybe not ..."

"Well, let me tell you summut, mate. When I was a kid I came off me pushbike and hurt that leg there quite badly. As a result of which I don't have much feeling in it, so you're wasting your time.

"On the other hand, if you want to come round this side and fondle this leg here, I'll be able to feel ya, just great. And when I do —I'll rip your head off, okay?" he finished pleasantly.

★　★　★

2300 EST. The Fort Lauderdale seafront bar.

Haythorne staggered to the rest-room. Everything was swimming.

"Too much, too much ..." he thought, unzipping himself, "Must slow down. Gotta slow down."

He leaned his head against the flush pipe and studiously directed his flow into the swirling urinal. For long seconds he drained himself, feeling a glorious sense of relief as it flowed out of him.

The girl he had been canoodling came in and stood at the next urinal.

Haythorne smiled at her.

"Hi darling," he smiled, blinking slowly, "Won't be a sec ..."

He gave it a shake and began to zip himself up, frowning slightly. Something was out of place about this. What was she doing in here? Was it the Ladies? Perhaps he'd gone in the wrong one ...

No, it was the Gents, alright. Oh ... perhaps, perhaps she wanted a private thrill of watching him take a leak, or just being there. Or perhaps they were allowed to go into each other's loos over here. After all, this was America, and in America anything went ...

He was in the act of turning towards the hand-basin when the girl began to pee into the urinal, standing up, like himself.

Intrigued, Haythorne took a look. He goggled. The girl was equipped with a miniature three-piece suite, just like a man's. Except the parts were atrophied from disuse. There was a little prick and two miniscule balls.

"Aaaagh!" shouted Haythorne, reaching for the tap, "You're a bloke. Urrgghh!"

Furiously he began to wash his mouth out whilst the transvestite took the wise precaution of disappearing.

★   ★   ★

2330 EST. Miami.

"Nah," exclaimed Smith, "The Corps's going soft. I mean, in the old days the Marines never used the book except for the more serious offences. You take a bloke like Gennelman Jack. He's one o' the old school. Never bothers with charging people. Doesn't believe in it. 'Sides, his fingers wouldn't fit on a typewriter. But cross him — and you'll know all about it. Bang! You're on the deck. Alright, fat lip, coupla loose teeth maybe, but when ya pick yourself up, you know you've done summink wrong and you're not gonna go and do it again, are you? Not only that, there's no messing with paperwork so it doesn't go on your record. But how many are like that nowadays? Nah, the Corps's going soft."

"I dunno," rejoined Gerson tentatively, "Are you going to argue with 'Bung' Haines!"

"No."

"Or Jock Roy?"

"Certainly not."

"Or Pink-Eye Daffney?"

"Definitely not."

"Or—what's that other mean machine in the HQ Company store. 'No-we-ain't-got-none-get-out-wallop!'—that one? George Seward, that's it. Are you gonna argue with him?"

"No," asserted Smith, "I ain't gonna argue with any of 'em. Politeness invariably pays."

Dickens shifted impatiently.

"Now, we're missing the aim of the exercise here, men, which is to drink some fuggin' beer."

"Well, get the bleeders in then."

"Same?"

"Same."

"Right."

He got up and went to the bar, moving in opposite the most delectable barmaid.

"Hi Sandy," he said, reading her name tag, "Three more, please sugar, and take your time, no rush ..."

'White shoes,' thought Dickens, 'They all wear white shoes.'

"Oh gawd," muttered Smith, watching him, "He's trapping. Now we'll never get the wets for a week."

"This beer's gnat's piss," grimaced Gerson, "Whaja say we go up Big Mama's after this and get wired into the Bacardis?"

"Wazzer," assented Smith.

"Fancy coming to a disco later, sweetheart?" enquired Dickens at the bar, "We got a charabanc outside, it'll be no problem. Incidentally, have you ever heard of Charles Dickens, the literary gentleman, 'Pickwick Papers,' 'Christmas Candle,' Scrooge, all that?"

"Sure."

"Well, I am a direct descendant of his, remind me to tell you more about it before the evening's over ..."

"Alright, yes, I agree with you, Gerry," continued Smith, "There is a natural affinity between the bootnecks on the one hand, and the seamen and stokers on the other. But I'm not on about them, am I? I'm on about the greenies, the tiffies, the radar plotters and all those others. *They're* the boys. *They* are highly skilled technical men. The apprenticeship they do nowadays makes Einstein look like a backward child. It's the best in the world. Give one o' those boys a screwdriver, two foot of fuse wire and a set o' spark plugs and he can make an ordinary gunnery computer give out the Greenwich time signal, fry eggs and tell you the name of the next Derby winner all at once ..."

"Hallo," interjected Gerson, "Who's he talkin' to now?"

Smith turned. Dickens was having the drinks bought for him by two Americans. Smart suits. Shoes with snaffles. Early thirties. Somebodies.

They came over.

"Hi there; I'm Jim, this is Larry. We were just talking to your buddy here ..."

"Oh yeah? Well, that's Dickie, this is Gerry and I'm Ken. I'm their manager, I take seventy percent of everything they get. Ken Cash is the name, cash by name and cash by nature. Do siddown."

'Con merchants,' thought Smith, 'Plain as daylight.'

"Thanks. Y'all enjoying America? Well, I can't tell ya how happy I am about that. It's good to see ya around. Now then. We have a little business proposition for ya. How'd ya like to earn yourselves some nice bucks to make your stay in good ole America even more enjoyable, huh? The drinks are on us by the way, fellas."

"Doing what?"

One of the Yanks lowered his voice confidentially.

"We have a totally foolproof way of winning on the slot machines. All you have to do is to cash the tokens for us at the desk."

"And of course, it's all perfectly legal and above board," said Smith.

"Why, yes."

The Americans smiled.

"Percentage?"

"We'll pay ten."

There was a long pressing pause during which Smith's eyes never left those of the two Americans.

"Okay, okay, okay," said Jim at length, "We're reasonable people, we hope you are too, so let's ... let's all be reasonable 'bout this. It's nice to see y'all over here enjoying yourselves, so ..." they looked at one another ..." we'll say fifteen."

"Look, mate," explained Smith settling back, his manner wearily patient and thoroughly condescending, "You may not be pros but we are. We got overheads, airfares, hotels and so on. We pay our taxes, state and federal, we got agent's fees, insurance, kickbacks, protection, all that to pay ..."

"Protection?"

Larry looked at his companion.

"Okay, man," breathed Jim quietly, "We'll pay er, we'll pay twenny percent. But that's the top, man. We can't go no more."

Smith cleared his throat.

"I'm so sorry, I didn't quite catch that last bit. Could you say again?"

"He said that's the top, man," hissed Larry, getting excited, "We *cain't go no higher, man ...!*"

Smith stared about him, an expression of deep contemplation on his face as though somehow he simply hadn't understood. Finally he shook his head.

"I'm sorry, mate, I'm a bit mutt-and-jeff these days and the battery's gone duff on me hearing-aid. Could you say that last figure again? There's just a teeny-weeny chance I may have misunderstood ..."

"*He said twenny percent, man, no more ...!*"

Amateurs, thought Smith. Getting excited over this sort of thing.

"Well, in that case," he said, "we'd better get out the heat ..."

"The heat? You mean the police? Listen limey, you trying to put the screws on us?"

"Let's go, man ..." said Larry, starting to leave.

"Jussa minute," said Smith, "What did you think I said? Did you think I meant the Old Bill? The law? Oh no! What would I wanna do that for? What could I possibly want to do that for? Involving a couple of honest, decent, upright, law-abiding citizens like yourselves with the filth! Ridiculous! Unthinkable! And in the year of your Bicentennial ..."

"Okay, okay everybody," said Jim, "Let's just keep cool, let's just all keep real nice and cool now. There seems to have been some misunderstanding here. I think we should all relax and-and-and just try and keep the lid on this whooole thing."

An ominous silence ensued. The three Royals remained poker-faced.

"You did say thirty percent, did you?" enquired Smith innocently. They looked at him.

"I mean, it's up to you, mate. Like I said, you may not be pros but we are."

"Okay, okay, okay," breathed Jim, "Thirty percent ..."

Smith raised his glass.

"Two for one it is, then, gents. I'll drink to that. Good health."

They drank.

★　★　★

0030 EST

Stevenson walked outside the disco and stood breathing the night air. Phew. That was better. It was like a sauna in there. To his front was a lawn with floodlit palm trees, then a wide boulevard on the far side of which were steak houses, eating places, gas stations and so on. At the front of the disco, cabs came and went. He moved round the corner into some shadows to take a leak.

He was in the act of zipping himself up when a voice behind him said — "Freeze!"

He tried to look round and received a fist in the kidneys for his pains.

"I SAID FREEZE! UP AGAINST THE WALL, MAN! MOVE!"

Slowly Stevenson moved to the wall. As he stopped, fingers alighted on his jugular vein. Something they held made his sweat turn cold.

"THIS HERE'S A BLADE, MAN! YOU WANNA MAKE A MOVE — YOU'RE DEAD! NOW PUTCHOR ARMS *UP!*"

He raised his arms against the wall. 'Black or white', he thought as his assailant searched him. He was holding the blade against his jugular with his right hand and from the manner in which he touched him with his free hand, feeling for the concealed weapon he didn't have, Stevenson figured he was white. He searched for clues. There were two; his voice and his touch. The voice he couldn't really distinguish from that of a negro — it was just American to him; but the fingers ... Something he had unconsciously observed in the past came back to him. Negroes patted. Didn't they? Using the flat of the fingers. Yet this guy was using his fingertips, running them over him, and the difference was somehow discernible. Yes, this guy was white. A fat white Yank. What fun.

The voice of his physical training instructor floated back to him. Unarmed combat, lesson three. One — holds; two — releases; three — defences against. 'Defences against the razor blade', thought Stevenson.

'Right now, this time we're up against a wall with a razor pressed up against the old jugular. Nah then, compared with the ole shotgun or pistol situations, this one's slightly dodgy. Even the minutest act of nervousness on your part or upon that of your assailant will send the blade slicing through your neck, hey presto, we're on the deck bleeding to death. So ... defences against. Now, the commando teaching on this one is that there is no defence against it. So, whaddawe do? What we do is this. Re-assuring your assailant at all times, we reach slowly into the back pocket, or wherever it happens to be, telling him what we're doing *as* we're doing it, and slowly but surely ... we take out the old wallet ... and we give it to him. There we are.

'Loss of a coupla weeks pay, men, somewhat cheaper to the taxpayer than loss of the fully trained bootneck together with all the paperwork that that involves. As with anything, men, we always use the old head. Okay? Any questions on that?'

'Re-assure him,' thought Stevenson.

"Are you a mugger, mate?" he asked, face to the wall.

"SURE I'M A MUGGER, MAN! WHERE IS IT, WHERE IS IT! YOUR MONEY, MAN! WHERE IS IT?"

"My money?" said Stevenson, "I've only got four hundred bucks left on me ..."

He had twenty dollars left and some cents.

"GIMME, GIMME ..."

"Right, right, coming. It's in me shirt pocket, mate; I'll get it out if ya want, no tricks, honest ..."

"NO TRICKS, MAN, OR YOU'RE DEAD!"

"Okay, okay."

With his right arm, he began to reach into his left-hand pocket.

"How many people you mugged tonight, then mate?" he asked.

"SEVEN. YOU'RE THE EIGHTH!"

"Right; I'm undoin' the button, pulling out me wallet .. here y'are."

He handed his wallet behind him. It was snatched away, but the blade stayed on his throat.

'Damn', thought Stevenson.

"Do us a favour, mate ..."

"I AIN'T DOIN' NO FAVOURS, MAN ..."

"... when you got the cash, leave my identity card, will ya; if I lose that I'm in Shit Street ..."

The mugger soon found the twenty dollar bill but not the rest of the money he believed to be there. He was hampered by being able to use only one hand.

"WHERE IS IT? WHERE IS IT, MAN? YOU GETTING SMART, MAN, YOU GONNA DIE!"

"It's there, alright, mate," said Stevenson, matter-of-factly.

"STAY STILL, MAN! DON'T TALK!"

"Look, I don't want me throat slit, mate. Lemme show you. You want the money, then you can sod off and I can go back in the disco. I mean, if you can't find it, whatcha gonna do? Murder me for twenty dollars. You're a flippin' mug if you do ..."

"SHUDDUP, MAN!"

"Give it here and I'll show ya ..."
The blade came away from his neck. Slowly Stevenson turned.
"KEEP YOUR ARMS UP, MAN!"
The blade waved viciously in his face.

The mugger still had the wallet, feeling the lining ...

'As with anything, men', came the instructor's voice, 'we always use the old head. Okay?'

Stevenson crashed his head into the mugger's face. The mugger went reeling backwards, the wallet flew from his grip and the blade scythed lethally upwards, missing Stevenson's face by inches. A second later, the heel of the service pattern shoe crunched solidly into the mugger's cheekbone, cruelly lacerating his skin. Detachedly Stevenson felt the razor bite into his leg below the calf, incising through trouser leg and sock. Blood and battle began to sing in his veins. He kicked again and kept on kicking, vicious blows, always at the skull with the flat of the heel, landing blow after blow with his wounded leg until the mugger's face was a blubbery mess of broken tissue and blood ...

'You or me, baby ...'

Finally he stopped and watched the would-be mugger lie still on the rough ground at the side of the club, breathing noisily through bubbles of blood, his facial features wrecked forever, eyes shut, nose twisted, mouth and jaw distorted out of all recognition.

Taking out his handkerchief, Stevenson made a pad out of it and pushed it inside his sock to staunch the bleeding. The bottom of his trouser was covered with blood, the mugger's as well as his own which was seeping through. His main concern was that because of it he would not be re-admitted to the club, but first he had to retrieve his wallet and identity card. He picked them up, then felt in the man's pockets for his twenty dollars. Upon coming away with a wad of notes, however, he began a systematic search of every pocket and hiding place.

By the time he had lowered the mugger's trousers to around his ankles, he had amassed, he guessed, a sizeable sum of money. There, in his underpants, were a lot more loose notes, probably stuffed away in haste after his last successful mugging of the evening. Stevenson patted the notes together with the rest, then hitching up the trouser of his undamaged leg, slipped the bundle of notes inside his sock.

Lying by the mugger's right hand was his blade. It glinted in the neon lights of the boulevard. Stevenson closed it, then put a heel on it and ground it out of sight. He felt no compunction over what he had done; it might have been him lying there with his life blood pouring out onto the ground through a crimson slash in his neck. He felt no pity or compassion for the man as he watched him lying there, breathing shuddering breaths through his open mouth. From his dress — cheap shirt, trousers and shoes — he recognised that mugging might have been this man's way of supporting a wife and a dozen starving children. Even now they all might be at home, eagerly awaiting his return when they would see what the night's haul had brought in. When he was overdue they would know something had gone wrong. Shame. He had picked on the wrong bloke, that was all. Basic failure to assess his victim. Should have stuck to tourists. They were rich, and insured, and that made them offer less resistance. Whereas a man with only twenty dollars left ...

Stevenson's English sense of propriety made him unwilling to leave his victim with his parts exposed to view, so he pulled up the mugger's underwear and trousers, fastened his shirt again with one button, then turned him over, face down lest he should choke before recovering consciousness. On an impulse he examined the man's socks and shoes to see if he had stashed any notes in them but there was no more to be had. He was alive and that tonight was all Stevenson was ready to grant he deserved to be. It was warm; he wouldn't come to any further harm where he was, so he left him and walked back round the corner with the intention of getting back into the disco.

On his way he passed a sprinkler watering the grass. Cold water. Just what was needed for getting blood out of uniforms. Soaking the stained trouser leg, he washed and rubbed the blood out of it. Understandably they didn't want people who looked as though they had been in a fight to patronise their premises. Not good for the wholesome image of Florida, and the bouncers didn't look the types to brook any argument. Huge men, body-builders, probably all beefers, but it didn't pay to argue with them. Besides, Stevenson had had all the scraps he wanted for one night.

Back in the club he made his way straight to the men's room. Inside a cubicle he shut the door. First, he re-bandaged his leg. The cut was deep and about two inches long, but fortunately, he felt, not serious. He would get it checked out in the morning to make sure it hadn't nicked a tendon or anything, but meanwhile it seemed okay. Next he took out the sheaf of notes from the sock of his other leg. He began to count them, dividing the bills into their respective denominations.

At the end of five minutes and two complete counts he felt almost grateful to the mugger. He wished him well, lying where he was round the back of the club, on rough ground, in the shadows, unconscious. One thousand, one hundred and twenty-eight dollars. A neat haul. Laughing all over his face, he walked back into the disco. It was fifteen minutes since he had gone outside to take a leak.

North, Burns and Taverner were at the bar, the last two canoodling American girls. Stevenson walked up to them in a manner North immediately suspected.

"What's up wi' you?" he asked.

"Guess what," said Stevenson, "I've just mugged a mugger!"

"Geroff ..."

"No ... it's gen!"

Stevenson lifted up his leg and raised the cuff of his trouser, revealing the wad of notes stuffed in his sock.

"How much?"

He told them. He was going to say less but vanity prevented him.

"Bloody hell!" exclaimed North.

"Nice one!" commented Taverner.

"I wish I could get mugged every time I went to the heads," said Burns, "You gonna hand it in?"

"Oh natch!" scoffed Stevenson, "Am I hell ... Spoils o' war, mate. Winner takes all. 'Tcha drinkin' Terry? 'Tcha drinkin', Neil, Nancy? Keith, Laurette? The wets are on me for the rest of the night, lads ...!"

He reached into his sock and pulled out a hundred dollar bill.

06·00 EST

Early morning sun filtered into the room through gaps in the blinds. He looked at his watch and groaned. Oh Jeeze! It couldn't be that time! Panic began to struggle with the cloying blanket of alcohol. He crawled from a large and comfortable bed. His head felt as though it were about to burst. Agonisingly he sat on the bed and pulled on his socks, trousers and shoes. As he did so, a delicate hand smoothed his bare back. Dickens had scored.

He leaned across the bosom of the girl. Her outline showed beneath a satin sheet. Luxury such as he had never known; now immediately to be followed by a day in the grease pit back on board. She ran her fingers through his hair and pulled his face to hers. For long silent moments they roamed each other's mouths until he began to feel his body react again. It was no good—he had to go.

"Whaddareyou going for?" she whispered, her voice sodden with sex.

"I got to. I got to be back on board by seven. I'll see ya tomorrer at ten. Down by the pool, okay?"

Their lips parted.

"You'd better," she said.

Dickens staggered out of the house. He hadn't a clue where he was. Then he remembered. Miami. Oh no! The ship was bloody miles away! He ran through the streets searching for a cab, cursing Smith and Gerson who had thinned out in the car last night. Fine pair o' bleedin' oppos they were ...

0630 Victor—Ship's time

Wrapping a towel round his waist and slipping his feet into flip-flops Gerson sat on the edge of his bunk and held his head, feeling weak, sick and likely to want to throw up any minute. Grasping his washing kit, he staggered towards the heads, lifting his feet uncertainly over the intervening hatch-coamings.

It was early enough for the Burma Way, the central passage that ran the length of the ship, not to be jam-packed with people moving in conflicting directions. He turned off it towards the bathrooms, stepping gingerly down a ladder. Steam poured from showers, water and shampoo swilled back and forth across the floor. People, some in much the same state as himself, stood slumped against the hand-basins, washing, shaving and brushing teeth. Others, now wide awake, congregated, recounting the previous night's adventures.

Feeling restored after his ablutions, the bootneck hauled himself back up the near-vertical companionway, emerging in the Burma Way once more. In the ten minutes that had elapsed, there had been a noticeable increase in traffic along it. He made his way back to the messdeck, skilfully avoiding sailors with buckets and men with mops.

Pulling on olive-green shirt and shorts, socks and chukka boots, he grasped a mug, the black plastic top of his field canteen, then joined the congestion for a third time, heading for'ard for breakfast. Climbing up to join the queue at the cabledeck, he sniffed fresh air and saw sun dancing on the water for the first time that morning. With relief he found that the queue wound once only round the deck. At lunch and supper it was always twice round, but even that was preferable to action messing or rough weather when the cabledeck was out of bounds. Then you joined it outside your messdeck if you could join it at all.

A corporal from the Provost Staff stood in front of the serving hatches, checking personal attire. Those chancing their arm by not shaving before breakfast, by turning up in unlaundered clothing or in flip-flops got turned away. By the time they had rectified the matter the meal was usually over. Gerson helped himself to porridge, kippers and paludrin tablets. Then carrying his tray, he sought out some familiar faces to sit with.

★   ★   ★

0700 V.

The ship towered over the wharf, making the gangways steep. At the top of the middle brow, a petty officer of the regulating branch looked down at the quay, watching taxis being paid off as the last remaining libertymen scurried aboard to collect their station cards from the rack by the ceremonial life-buoy stand. Two minutes to seven. Some walked aboard feigning disinterest, others were clearly relieved to have made it. Confined-to-ship in Florida? Unthinkable ...

On the stroke of seven he pounced on the uncollected station cards. A solitary green one caught his eye first. Great! A Marine from the Support Company. A bootneck! He hated bootnecks. No more shore leave for Marine Dickens. Ha bloody ha!

★   ★   ★

When he had finished eating, Gerson filled up his mug of tea a second time before starting back to the messdeck. Dickie would need the tea if he was going to make colours on time.

The messdeck was alive when he got back, swarming with be-towelled figures clambering over one another in their efforts to dress in the confined space. Gradually the bedlam diminished. Kit became stowed, bunks were racked up and the hundred or more occupants of the messdeck began to filter up top, to the flight-deck for the ceremony of colours, leaving only the messdeck dodgers below to sweep up and polish in their twice daily ritual. Gerson drank the tea he had brought for Dickens for the simple reason Dickens wasn't there.

Companies of Marines lined the flight-deck of the 'Balfour' facing to starboard, the Support Company nearest the stern. At five minutes to eight exactly, Sergeant-Major Roy brought the company to attention and turned them right, facing aft. At intervals along the flight-deck other company sergeants-major did the same. The public address system crackled.

"Attention! Face aft and salute! Colours."

Onlookers ashore and aboard the nearby cruise liners watched with a mixture of curiosity, fascination and envy as the centuries-old

naval ceremony of colours took place; the bugler sounded the
general salute and the white ensign was broken out on the stern and
hoisted close up. The companies of Marines stood motionless at the
salute whilst a seaman secured the halyards. The flag of Nelson and
the 'Victory' fluttered in the breeze.

"Carry-on."

Saluting arms returned to the seam of the trousers ...

'With the speed and co-ordination of a striking slug,' thought
Sergeant-Major Roy. He turned his company left and faced them.

"The front rank will take four paces! The centre rank two paces!
The rear rank stand fast—OP-ENN OR-DAH—MARCH!"

Taking with him the senior corporal present, he toured the ranks,
critically scrutinising the dumbfounded bootnecks at close range.
'Inspection?' they thought resentfully, staring at infinity as he passed
under their noses, glaring at each one, 'Nobody said anything about
an inspection ...' The Sergeant-Major took his time, going up and
down the front and back of each rank. When he had finished there
were three names in the corporal's book.

"CLOSE OR-DAH—MARCH!"

He stepped back and surveyed them through narrowed eyes.

"Ye weren't expecting that, were ye? No? No, I know ye weren't.
One night ashore—and look at yous! *One night!* We've got five more
days and nights in this place ... for those of you who *get* shore leave.
And if your present attitude is anything to go by, I wouldnae be too
optimistic about any of ye getting ANY further shore leave—AT ALL!
If you want bringing down from the clouds—I'll bring ye down! And
I'll do it if I think you need it! If you want to carry on the way you're
going—you're going to suffer for it! Do I make myself clear?

"Right, the following are charged. North, Stevenson and
Taverner. You're all charged with being incorrectly shaven. *I know
ye've shaved* this morning! I didnae say you had *not* shaved, I said
you're incorrectly shaven. You know what the answer to that is as
well as I do. Get up five minutes fuppin' earlier and do the job
properly!

"And Dickens, you're charged as well. Yes, Dickens?"

"What am I charged for, Sar'nt-Major?" asked Dickens
indignantly.

"Dickens, if I can find three people in this company to charge,
you're always going to be the fourth! Right?" answered the Sergeant-
Major, having himself a little joke.

The Marine choked back his words. First the reggie, now the
stripey-major. It wasn't his day.

"I've got eyes in my fuppin' arse, Dickens. If you think I didnae see you creeping into the rear rank during colours, you're *wrong*!

"So the message, friends, is this", continued the Sar'nt-Major, addressing the entire company again; "Any twat who decides to get up my snot-box between now and when we disembark is going tae pay for the privilege heavily. And for anyone who can *afford* to pay —keep on doin' it! *Don't* shave, *dress* like a scran bag, *keep on* turning up adrift! Because today it'll cost ye a tenner! Tomorrow twenty! Thursday thirty and so on! Are there any questions on that?"

Dickens put up his hand.

"Yes, Dickens?"

"Can I open an account please, Sar'nt-Major?"

Lt. Col. Jeffrey Tarlton RM closed the file on NATO's **Westlant** deployment and considered again the dry phrases of his next directive. The fun in the sun was over. America's allies were homeward bound.

'*... relieve 3rd Battalion, the Parachute Regiment on the Irish border ...*'

'*... continue the unrelenting attrition of terrorism in your area of responsibility.*'

Notwithstanding the outstanding morale of his unit, nor the even higher regard in which he himself was held by every man in it, the CO was painfully aware that the odds were not in his favour. True, he had the summer months in which to train the Commando for the task ahead exactingly, even remorselessly, if need be; but to leave that region without having had one or more killed was a feat yet to be accomplished by any unit in the **entire** British Army.

Etched against a flawless mid-Atlantic sky, there grew a vapour trail. On board the jet, a man with delicate hands sat gazing down at the dot that was the Devonport-bound 'Balfour'. Of a small group of Commandos who watched from near the stern, he had neither idea nor concern which ones would be amongst his next victims, far less any premonition that he might be theirs.

CHAPTER 8

Operation Roulade

SOUTH ARMAGH, late November 1976

Slowly they worked their way up a steeply inclining field in the dark, keeping a discreet distance from the hedgerow, slipping occasionally in the mud. It was bitterly cold and a strong wind blew, masking the all-important sounds of the night so crucial to the infantryman's instincts. It discomfited all of them and it rendered vocal —whispered— communication useless. Visual communication too, was unusually hampered by the intensity of the dark, making it necessary for each man to follow closely behind the one in front in order to stay in touch and to avoid losing each other. Daffney disliked it. They were too close. Working as they were, an improvised explosive device would take out the lot of them. It was wrong, but like it or lump it, there was nothing he could do about it. The cloud was down. The wind was up. They were weathered in.

It was midnight and the first hour of their insertion had gone according to plan. After the mortar attack, his men had helped their undaunted mates in piling the wreckage outside the police post from where it would be choppered away. Then Daffney had told them to rest up. At half-ten, they were shaken and on the stroke of eleven, the six men stole out of the battered camp with its emergency lighting and its atmosphere of nervous stress underlying forced heartiness, out into the open fields to a tension of a different kind. Now they were alone in the night, picking their way across the trip-wire-sewn countryside of South Armagh. Sergeant Daffney's section. Himself plus four. This time plus five.

Snow lay on the high ground and the wind was a strong south-westerly, yet before long, inside their stout combat-jackets they were

159

drenched with the sweat of their exertions. North led the way, feeling rather than seeing his way forwards. From his wrist there hung a thin green birch stick, about two feet long. Occasionally, near trees or shrubbery, he ghost-walked, groping the air at arm's length in front of his face with his free hand. In his other hand, he held his camouflaged rifle, keeping it across his body or down by his side when feeling for something. He trod with care, searching the ground as best he could before taking each step, feeling his footfalls into place. Behind him came Daffney, the patrol commander, the gap between them varying according to whether or not he expected to see his lead scout disappear with a bang and a flash. Taverner came next, carrying the bulky camera gear, then Stevenson, barely less laden with the radio set, closed down for the move in. Both carried in addition to rations, ammunition and extra clothing, spare batteries for their particular piece of equipment. After Stevenson came Private Challice, the Army man, and last was Gerson with the Bren.

Something about the patrol was making Daffney nervous. Something was out of line and he, as patrol commander, was at the centre of the thing, whatever it was. He was the 'wheel' but he couldn't pin it down. Prior to setting out, he had mulled it over in his mind again, lying on the floor amongst the others, head resting against his bergen. Was it the mission? Or the wires and booby-traps they knew they were going to have to encounter? Was it the unknown quantity of an outsider who had been suddenly foisted upon him? Or was it the fact that he had been thoroughly shaken at seeing an entire company of Marines, many of his best friends amongst them, come within a whisker of being wiped out? He tried to put his finger on it and couldn't. Maybe it was just him. Maybe he had become unnaturally jumpy. Maybe he was getting uptight because the end of the tour was coming up but it wasn't quite in sight. No; he was used to pressure, to pacing himself, to seeing things through. In the end, he had put it down to an unusual extension of pre-patrol nerves that would disappear when they got going properly. But they had been going an hour and now, dammit, he was still worried.

For inside every commander was a finely calibrated pair of mental scales used for weighing up the means against the end. And any good team of planners, which he and the OC were, took careful account of those scales in the making out of their appreciations and orders. Nothing was wholly without risk; the rule was simply to minimise risk by thorough planning and preparation beforehand. And though the time had been short, that they had surely done. Nevertheless, something was upsetting his equilibrium tonight, either his own or that of this well-tried and balanced section. Something was out of line, something was making him uptight. It was the old 'unforeseen, the overlooked, the taken-for-granted' once again. Or perhaps it was a feeling they were on a wild goose chase this time. And wild goose chases had an unpleasant habit of ending ...

North suddenly stopped.

A hedge loomed in front of him, blocking their progress. It was the top of the field and the wind fairly howled. Daffney knelt, and as the lead scout came back towards him, he unzipped his smock and took out the map. Together they perused it, checking bearing and position in the red glow of a torch as the others slunk into all-round-defence. After a second, he touched North's arm and pointed. North nodded and walked back towards the hedge. Trees shivered, boughs heaved.

Winter had come to South Armagh. On still days, ribbons of hoary, soaking mist lay across low-lying areas of the undulating countryside. Near-freezing droplets of water hung suspended in the air and heavy skies pressed down on what a few months ago had been a picturesque patchwork of tiny fields, allotments and dwellings, covered by a network of stone walls and thorn hedgerows. Now men trod the sodden turfs of a landscape where damp chill air, pregnant with half-frozen moisture, pressed into their lungs with every breath they took. For this was that part of Northern Ireland that journalists liked to call 'Bandit Country', where people killed other people because they somehow differed, and where the security forces, soldiers, policemen and UDR-men alike, were fairer than fair game. Here, lawlessness had been a way of life for centuries. Violence was endemic. Cattle-rustlers and sheep-stealers had turned terrorist, plying their trade from across the border, keeping the troubles forever simmering, sometimes making the pot boil over, sometimes erupt altogether. Killing was excitement, excitement was enjoyment and the cause mattered not. To people whose lives were otherwise hard mundane existences, lawlessness was the very stuff of life. With sanctuary so close to hand, banks and post offices were easy meat. The open countryside lent itself to the planting of mines and devices in culverts and drains to catch a vehicle or men on foot. For everyone in the town of Newry, daily shootings, a bomb once a week. For soldiers at Forkhill near to the Belfast-Dublin railway, the constant threat of the hijacking of a train and the massacre of its passengers. For those at Crossmaglen and Bessbrook as for all, suspicion, even open hostility, whilst they struggled to prevent a repetition of incidents such as the Kingsmills massacre where, earlier in the year, gunmen had murdered workmen, slowly and methodically pumping bullets into them one by one as they stepped from the back of a mini-bus, until no less than ten bodies lay in the roadway, dead.

The Marines' answer to the cunning and effective killers of the region was alert, meticulous and ceaseless patrolling on foot. Helicopters too played an important part in inserting and extracting patrols as well as in the cargoing of provisions from headquarters at Bessbrook down to Forkhill and Crossmaglen, for the roads of the region were impassable owing to mines and booby-traps. Able to start and to finish their patrols in unlikely places in this way, and to appear out of the blue en route, became for them the best method of deterring the activities of the gunman who, nervously looking over his shoulder, never quite knew where they would turn up next or who was looking at him down the sights of a rifle. From Warren-point up the east side of Carlingford Lough to Newry, west over the mountainous area to the pretty little fishing village of Forkhill, where in summer the odd holidaymaker or two was still to be found, down onto the flat farmland round Crossmaglen and up to the rolling hills that surrounded Camlough, Belleek, Bessbrook and Whitecross, they patrolled with constant vigilance, ever seeking to outwit their opponents who sewed trip-wires and booby-traps among the walls, gateways and hedgerows—to kill THEM.

For their part, the IRA twisted and turned, pulling every trick in the book, trying everything they knew to lure a gravel-belly to his death, poking and probing for weaknesses in his organisation and leadership, searching for a chink in his armour of vigilance. They studied him, set him up with car bombs and lured him towards 'IEDs' or improvised explosive devices ... but still they were denied. It became a battle of wits. From across the border, the Marines heard shots and explosions indicating that training of some sort was taking place. They cocked an ear and looked at one another quizzically. No prizes were being handed out for guessing against whom it was going to be directed. None at all. Not one. Not a single one.

The door of Colonel Tarlton's briefing room stood slightly ajar. Inside was the CO himself and the military intelligence officer, a Major from Brigade.

"Of course," the Colonel went on, "much of our time down here is taken up with the clearance of improvised explosive devices. Which are a nuisance. And finding out where they are after they've gone off and killed somebody is hardly the best way of dealing with them. The Paras unfortunately lost two chaps like that. One blown up by a device concealed in the saddle-bag of a bicycle in the middle of Crossmaglen; the other by a device in a hedge in the middle of nowhere."

"How did that happen?" asked the MIO.

"It was a radio-controlled device. Somebody with a transmitter was watching the movements of a foot patrol and when one of its members walked close enough to where the mine was hidden, he detonated it. Poor chap lived for two days afterwards. Of course, all those that we find, we make a careful note of."

The CO pointed to a map covered with a rash of red dots and circles.

"We've cleared twenty-eight so far. But we've had to go carefully — some may be intended for our finding in order to draw us into an area where others are concealed."

"Are all these radio-controlled devices?" asked the MIO.

"No, some of them are plain trip-wires. Which are no easier to find than the aerial on a McGregor device, in most cases. We had one of the trip variety which was found and 'cleared' in the same instant by a horse."

"Which didn't do the horse any good, presumably."

"I was amazed at what a horse could live through. We had to shoot it in the end. It was still alive when we got to it."

There was a knock at the door. It was the Special Branch man. Soft-soled shoes. Harris-tweed jacket. Late thirties. Slightly corpulent. He put his head round the door.

"Could I just have a wee word with you there a minute, Sir," he said, addressing the Colonel in a pleasant Northern Irish brogue.

"Certainly," the CO, gestured towards a chair. "Have a seat."

"That's quite all right, Sir," the Special Branch man reassured him. "But I'll just shut this door here if I may ..." He walked into the centre of the room.

"Right, Sir. This concerns an old friend of ours, a man we've been interested in for some time ... he's a particularly unsavoury character from anybody's point of view ... he's been responsible for a murder in Belfast and another in Magherafelt, and of late he's been taking a break down South for a wee while. Anyway, it so happens we've received a tit-bit of information that suggests he may show his face in the North, by crossing the border at a certain time, on a certain day, at a certain place. And that place is ..."

The Special Branch man drew a sharpened pencil from his jacket pocket. It hovered over a series of photographs on the wall depicting the nebulous border countryside taken from the air.

"... Er ... I'm not quite such a hot shot with these aerial photographs as you military fellas ... but ... ah, yes ... there we are." The pencil came to rest.

"Now before I ask you for your help ... or, at any rate, your opinion, I'll just tell you the rest of the story. Our man ..."

The men of the Royal Ulster Constabulary, both those in uniform and those in plain clothes, kept the real picture of the community in which they both worked and lived, and to which they belonged. Unlike the soldier, who took the brunt of the violence for four months and then was relieved by others, the policeman could never be relieved. He lived in constant apprehension of every knock on the door, fearful for the safety of his wife and children when he was at work, never able to relax his guard even when having a drink; and all the while knowing that there could never be any public acknowledgement of his worth — for to receive any form of acclaim would be to imperil his life.

After seven years continuous violence, the RUC numbered amongst its members some of the most adept and experienced policemen in the world. They had struggled to combat the rising tide of violence as it soared from the beginning of 1968 to a horrific peak in 1972. All the while they had sought to break out of the steadily enmeshing web of mindless murder, bombing and shooting which was engulfing Ulster, by bringing the perpetrators to justice. Now they watched the statistics as the year of 1976 challenged that of four years earlier for the distinction of becoming the bloodiest in the province's recent history.

Lieutenant Shutbridge closed the door and sat down at his desk. His brow was furrowed. On the outside of the door of his troop operations room was a note for the members of his troop. It read 'keep out' in his handwriting. The OC stared at the partition which partly divided the small room and against which his desk was situated. Around the walls, the usual maps and air photographs. On the desk, the usual grey blanket together with aide-memoires, wanted-men lists, papers, pens and pencils. In front of him, a roster, a state-board, astronomical data and so on. In one corner of the room, two high-powered radio-sets hissed quietly. There was one other person present. The on-watch signaller who sat listening out. Silence. On the other side of the room the water-boiler sighed.

"Cuppa coffee, Sir?"

"No thanks."

The CO had just dropped another job into his lap. It was one that had to be fitted in between his other observation tasks. Flexibility was what was required as always but it didn't make things any easier to have such short notice. The CO had tasked him, the unit intelligence officer across the corridor had briefed him. Now it was up to him. Special Branch wanted the missing link on 'our man' as they called him; whom he met, and where he went. There were the mugshots, together with the description on his desk.

'Our Man'; a Provisional IRA killer who had risen to 'officer' status within his organisation. Rather than picking him up just yet, the Special Branch were for that reason more interested in establishing or confirming his contacts in the North at the moment. He was thought to be a 'training officer' down South. It seemed likely, a former member of an active service unit teaching people his old tricks. In other words, thought Shutbridge, a vicious bastard who had earned his promotion by knocking people off. He thought back to his very first tour in 1970. At that time it had been all riots and civil disturbances in Belfast and there had been no shortage of would-be heroes lobbing bricks and petrol-bombs at the troops. 'Our man' was probably one of those; let's see, yes, he was about the right age to have been a stone-thrower six years ago. In the meantime, he had graduated as an assassin and now he was passing on his trade to others. The irony of having to put men's lives at risk simply to obtain pictures of someone like that occurred to Shutbridge more than forcibly. But he didn't dwell on it. His job was to carry out the task given to him by the CO, nothing more, nothing less.

According to Special Branch, the political wing of the PIRA, the Provisional Sinn Fein, were holding a meeting in the border village of Cory at two pm on Saturday, the day after tomorrow. That much was already known to him, having seen it advertised. Also known to him was the fact that, with the advent of the Women's Peace Movement, the Provisional Sinn Fein weren't doing too well at their rallies these days. In fact, at their last two meetings they had mustered barely a couple of hundred on each occasion and these had been held in sizeable towns. By contrast, Cory was nothing more than a hamlet a few hundred yards from the border in a most unpopulated part of the region. And in view of their falling attendance figures of late, it really was a most unlikely place for a Sinn Fein rally. Unless... unless its purpose was more practical than political. Unless, as Special Branch held, it was to enable someone to slip over the fields, into the crowd, into a car and away. And that was where Shutbridge came in.

His job was to send a section to monitor the event, to get video, good clear video-pictures of what took place. Faces at the rally, car numbers, 'our man' as he sneaked over, and especially the car, *above all* the car he got into. Special Branch had the big picture. They just wanted the missing part of the jigsaw.

Well, that he could readily provide. The job was simple reconnaissance work with one man recording on camera what he saw whilst it was happening. Once it was 'in the can', Special Branch could scrutinise it endlessly, if they so wished, until they had extracted every possible piece of information useful to them. That was alright. But then Brigade had to go and complicate it all by wanting to send a man with a microphone so they could know what was said at the rally. Marvellous. Not only did he have to produce a movie, but it also had to be a talkie. Why didn't Brigade also stipulate music, lights, dancing? Then they could put the whole thing on general release and make their fortunes. He fancied sitting in a chair with the words 'Bob Shutbridge — producer' on the back of it, surrounded by dolly-birds instead of sitting at a grey-blanketed desk surrounded by pencils. He grabbed one and wrote four headings down the left-hand side of a pad, leaving plenty of room between each.

An hour later, he had just about cracked it. His plan was, they would go in tomorrow, Friday, and do the job on Saturday, coming out the same night. To complete his planning, he noted down the times of sunset and moonrise on the relevant days and then ran a finger along the table of astro-data on the wall in front of him. It had been compiled by himself from various sources and he stopped opposite the date in the column entitled 'Lunar State'. He clucked with annoyance. The moon would be full on both nights. Marvellous! Just what was needed ... The 'met' or meteorological conditions were clearly going to be crucial to this operation. Aldergrove gave the flying forecast for the next 48 hours as first fog and rain, with three-to-five kilometres visibility during daylight hours and snow on high ground; followed by, on Saturday, the wind, a south-westerly, increasing from force 6 to 8 to severe gale Force 9. Getting them in would be one thing; getting them out another.

He didn't want to use Daffney for the job but he had no alternative. He and his section had been brought out of the field only that morning, filthy, wet-through, haggard and shivering and they deserved some rest. Besides, as Troop Sergeant, Daffney had responsibilities over and above those of section commander. He wanted him to get abreast of the stores situation over the next couple of days; start 'proffing' back (at which he was past-master) all the items the troop was missing before there was an outcry over them due to the impending arrival of the incoming unit. But his was the only section available at present. All the rest were either committed to other observation tasks or were about to relieve those which were. And all Daffney's attempts — after he had been woken up with a warning order for this latest operation — to persuade his OC to take his section into the field and do the job himself whilst he remained behind in the warm-dry of Bessbrook Mill, running the ops. room and doing the stores, had fallen on stony ground. Sometimes it took Shutbridge all his powers to resist the sort of good-natured bulldozering of which his troop sergeant was capable but on this occasion he managed it.

Then he ran up the stairs to his room in search of a pamphlet on the subject of 'Aerial Reconnaissance'. Something he had seen in the air photographs during his planning had rung a warning bell and he wanted to know more. It was in the area where the section, or at least one of them, would have to go to observe and record the movements of the mystical figure 'our man'. Privately, Shutbridge had doubts as to whether Special Branch hadn't simply started him on a wild goose chase. It wouldn't be the first time such a thing had happened, he felt sure.

On his way, he passed Major Perrier, now the unit second-in-command. Even after an interval of seven years, it seemed they still had little enough to say to each other. Perrier had arrived in the unit at a time when, after jumping ship in America, Daffney was still awaiting trial for desertion; and he had scarcely been able to conceal his disbelief, first at the verdict of the court-martial and second, at the commanding officer's decision to re-instate Daffney as Shutbridge's troop sergeant following it. It was his not-altogether-private opinion that any troop which had two such people as Shutbridge and Daffney in charge of it was little more than a

cowboy outfit, and sooner or later, because of what to him was its
'operationally vague and shadowy nature', that troop would be
bound to involve the unit in a highly controversial incident with the
civilian population in South Armagh, over which the press and the
IRA propaganda-machine would have a field day. 'Long-haired
private armies' were far too unaccountable in the Major's book, and
he wanted no truck with it. The fact that he wasn't required to, he
seemed to have overlooked, thought Shutbridge. Clearly, Perrier's
opinion of him hadn't changed.

'Notes On The Interpretation of Aerial Reconnaissance' lay on
the up-ended suitcase which served the lieutenant as a bedside
table. On top of it too, was a framed photo of his beloved wife,
Claire, suitably endorsed by her. He picked it up, kissed it and set it
back down again. Yes, it was true, he thought looking at it, that as a
silent reproach for having been associated with a certain troop
sergeant who had disappeared in Florida back in the spring, the
Corps Gazette, listing promotions and appointments, had been
conspicuously free of his name all year. Which was disturbing to one
who had recently assumed marital responsibilites, especially as he
was now fast approaching the end of the time-zone for making it to
Captain. Either he made it in the Christmas Gazette or he didn't
make it at all. In which case, he would remain a lieutenant forever.
Or rather, up to the day someone quietly said to him, "Sorry, Bob,
this is as far as it goes. It's time for you to carve out a new niche for
yourself. Go and see the resettlement officer and he will give you
advice on behalf of a 'grateful nation.'" He caught sight of his
reflection in the glass and picked the photo up again, using it as a
mirror. The lines on his face were no longer just wind and rain.
There was age in there too, now. For several long seconds he stared
at himself and tried to gauge why it was he always seemed to differ
so vastly from the average twenty-nine-year-old grammar school
educated villain.

In ten years he thought he would have stopped being at odds with
people over things. Ten years ago he had been busy crossing swords
with his first company commander, Captain Malcolm Blantyre. Not
a good man to cross. A veteran of fearsome battles in Korea, he had
spent a lot of time up the sharp end and was one man who did not
tolerate fools gladly. He would never forget the rollocking he got
from him in Aden for not handling his first contact correctly. That
was the sort of man he was. A stormy bastard. He had been a bit
taken aback by him. Reputed to be chicken-farming in Sussex now.
He wondered if he ran his chicken-farm the same way he had run his
company in Aden. God help the chickens if he did.

He snapped his fingers. Daffney! He was there! He had been on that very patrol! Yes, of course. Of all the hundreds of patrols you did, how could he have forgotten? He smiled at the memory of the tall sunburned youth who had shyly grinned at him when, as a young officer straight from training, he had met the men of his very first command. Men? They were boys, all of them, teenagers like he himself was at the time, yet he had thought of them all as being such veterans! Daffney? Twenty, a big raw-boned bootneck with that terrifying-looking eye which always served to distinguish him. And on that very foot patrol, he had stepped into a side street somewhere near Grenade Steps and had all but got his head blown off. But he had survived. He had survived that and a thousand other incidents because he was a survivor by nature. No, he was more than that. With his enormous strength and powers of endurance, he was a winner, a legend, immortal, indestructible ...

And now it was time to go and put his indestructibility to the test again. He picked up 'Notes On The Interpretation Of Aerial Reconnaissance' and made his way back down the stairs.

In silence, the Sergeant and his section studied the air photographs of the fields they would have to cross to obtain video-tape of Our Man—if he showed, which they very much doubted. In particular, their firm base and final position they examined in the minutest detail. Their lives depended upon their ability to interpret in advance every scrap of information the photos contained.

Two small fields, rising in a whale-back feature, overlooked the hamlet. The hedgerow running along the top of the feature was the best, perhaps the only, place from which the job could be done. It contained a gateway.

There was a telegraph pole next to the gateway. At the foot of which was something ... logs, stones perhaps, a pile of something? Dung?

The surrounding fields had contained animals when the photos were taken, but the two fields on the whale-back feature had not. The photos were taken a week ago.

Tractor tyre-marks, which showed up easily where frost had turned into slush, were visible in most fields, especially at the gateways. But not in the gateway adjacent to the telegraph pole ...

The minutes ticked by, getting longer between each discovery. Then one of them nudged the man next to him.

"Look at the pole."

On the oblique photographs, with the aid of a stereoscope could be seen two whitish objects sticking out either side of the pole near the top. The insulators, designed to carry the lines.

"It's a two-line pole, right?"

Daffney grunted, following the man's reasoning.

But there were no actual wires. The telegraph line was defunct. They examined the poles next to it. True, it was an old telephone line, and the poles carried nothing.

"Now look again. At the one by the gate. There *is* a line on it, leading to the South."

The photos had been taken from a moving aircraft on a camera run in indifferent winter light; yet very faintly discernible, dark where the background was lighter, a thin line stretched from the pole by the gate into the South. Only one line and that they could only make out intermittently. But they could see it ran for six more poles, enough to take it a couple of hundred yards into the South. Not only that, as it ran from pole to pole, it switched insulators. For the first three poles it ran on the left, but it ran to the right of the fourth pole before switching back again. No telephone linesman would have rigged it like that.

Daffney breathed out.

"It's a command wire they've rigged up. That pile of something at the foot of the pole is an IED."

So there it was. An improvised explosive device only metres from where the close-observation group would have to crawl.

"What's this?" asked the Sergeant, picking up another photo. This one had been taken not from the air, but from a hand-held camera on the ground. It depicted a tree-stump in a gap in a hedgerow. Upon closer inspection, it depicted a taut strand of wire strung across the gap.

"Trip-wire," said North, whose job as lead scout was to find all such wires before he blew himself up on them. On another air photo, he pointed out the hedgerow where it was thought to be. One, naturally, they had to cross.

Daffney's face was a picture of suppressed violence.

"That's two we know about," he breathed, the tension beginning to get to him as it had already reached the others. "How many more?"

They would be hanging their lives by the slender thread of whether or not they would be seen crossing those final fields. The odds were ludicrous in view of what was to be obtained. They were all thinking it, yet it was the Sergeant himself who finally voiced their misgivings. Six lives were at stake—for what?

"All this," he said, shifting uncomfortably, "just to get five minutes video on a wanted criminal who isn't wanted just yet. A known killer of innocent people. Be different if there was some ... some purpose to it. Like we were going to lay an ambush to knock him off."

There was a silence. Then someone said:

"Well, why don't we? I mean, if we've *got* to pick our way through that lot, we might as well make it worth our while ..."

"There's only one place from which the job can be done," said the fair-haired section commander, addressing his five charges. "And that's been IED'd. Which means," he continued matter-of-factly, "that in order to carry out the task, we have to get in, do the job and get out again WITHOUT being observed. If we are ... you won't know nothing about it, you'll just be blown up." He watched their eyes.

It was after 11 am the following morning. In the quiet of the briefing room, facing the Sergeant, sat the patrol in their order of move. On the right sat North, the lead scout; between him and Taverner, a gap represented Daffney's position in the patrol, the man himself standing up giving them the briefing. Next to Taverner sat Stevenson, these middle two being the most heavily burdened members of the patrol. Next to Stevenson sat Private Challice of the Intelligence Corps, and at the left-hand end of the row sat Gerson, whose job was that of rear scout.

Daffney had slept badly that night. Even in the security of a comfortable bed in a room he shared with two other Senior NCOs, deep in the heart of Bessbrook Mill, his sleep had been shallow and fitful and dream-ridden. It was the same old dream which had been recurring a lot lately. Dreaming there was an emergency and he couldn't wake up to react to it. Knowing in his dream that he was asleep and that it was only a dream, but dreaming that sleep would kill him, he would die unless he awoke. Groaning and tossing and turning, trying to force himself awake, desperately trying to break out of the cloying web of unconsciousness, almost sobbing with the effort, panicking from the fear of not making it, of going under because he wasn't able to flash into instant consciousness, to flood his limbs with adrenalin, to act and move and react ... Till finally, he would sit bolt upright in confused consciousness, perversely startled at the lack of crisis about him, staring at the darkened room harbouring the huddled and slumbering shapes of the other two sergeants. Once, returning from the showers at the dead of night a room-mate had caught him like that, wide-eyed and sweating, and he had put on his bedside light and simply winked at Daffney without saying a word; and had then gone off in search of a wet of tea for him, dressed as he was in towel and flip-flops. And Daffney, who hated any fuss like that, had nevertheless accepted it from him with gratitude. Because he knew he would say nothing. Parkesy, the signals sergeant, whose world was power outputs, frequency ranges and rebro units but who nonetheless recognised the signs and symptoms of nervous stress and emotional fatigue when he saw it. And who knew or sensed that what was required was not words, but a simple casual gesture of almost unconcerned re-assurance; a grin, a wink, a wet of tea. Some small token of normality.

"Any questions?" said Daffney at the end of his briefing. There was only one. The same one that was on everybody's mind but no-one cared to voice it. They would know the answer to it soon enough.

"Right," said the Sergeant, picking up his papers. "Remember, stay in the tracks of the man in front. We'll have to pick the trips up as we go. It's going to be a nerve-wracking twenty-four hours ... so screw the nut and stay switched-on. That way we'll all get home for Christmas."

He moved to the door.

"A quarter past five, then. On the helipad. Ready to go."

Alone in his cabin, Daffney was possessed by a welter of pre-patrol nerves. It had begun whilst he was eating a light lunch; his intention had been to have a good meal but his stomach tightened and before he had eaten much his appetite fell away. Every soldier experienced nerves in anticipation of action. Actors called it stage fright and became overcome by it but soldiers learned how to exploit it. For Daffney though, to have this amount, was unnatural. He had gone through his preparations after lunch, slowly, painstakingly, laying out his kit and stores with a tense humility kept rigidly under control by concentrating on what he was doing. Two or three times he had gone through it all, selecting the right clothes, comfortable against the skin, to prevent chafing and to preserve warmth; leaving out every unnecessary item, judgement on which only came with experience. No letters or personal documents to be taken. Just his identity card as per standing orders. And so on.

Then he had sat on his bed and had gone over it all in his mind, right from the beginning. The task, the boss's appreciation of it, his own planning and preparation for it, the writing of his orders, the briefing of his men, the nomination of special equipment to be carried, the order of move and so on. At length it was time to get rigged, so he had taken a last shower, shave and shampoo, it being of psychological importance for a man to at least start out clean, no matter how much he might purposefully dirty himself in the course of his preparations. Ritually, he anointed feet, crutch and armpits with powder, applied vaseline to hands, face and neck for protection from the cold and wet. As he thrust his naked limbs into the thermal underwear, he ruthlessly dismissed the morbid thought which every time flickered across his mind at that juncture—"How would this body come back from this one, this time ...? Wet, cold, exhausted but ALIVE? Or smashed, broken and bloodied, in different plastic bags ...'

He built up the layers of clothing against the cold, putting on last his combat-jacket and tying the drawstrings before zipping it up, feeling neat and functional inside it. His boots and denims he fussed with, adjusting them till they looked and felt right; doing the same with his bergen, balancing its contents so it sat evenly upon his back. Maps, signals instructions, notebook, pencils ... he checked his pockets were secure. He checked in his locker; on the shelf lay his good-luck charm; round his neck were his dog-tags. Not in the Radfan, not in Aden, not in the East or in the Arctic had he ever worn a good luck charm on patrol. Not in Belfast in '72. Nor now, in South Armagh, in 1976. Luck ran away from those who relied upon it.

Fitting his belt-order around his waist, he straightened the counterpane of the bed and tidied up his part of the room, at the same time noticing with an acute pang the framed pictures of the other two sergeants' wives which stood on their bedside tables. Physically bigger than ever in his bulky uniform and kit, now he suddenly felt small, humble and in need of protection. Familiar things now assumed a poignancy bordering on the sentimental. At this moment, his own estranged wife seemed utterly dear to him, faced as he was with the unknown in which he might perish. He pulled on his beret, took a last look around the room, then picking up his weapon and shouldering his bergen, closed the door and walked off down the corridor, experiencing a sense of relief, as once again, foreboding was translated into action.

In the shadows cast by floodlights, the six men waited at the edge of the helipad. Opposite them, in total silence, pilot and co-pilot aboard, stood a Royal Air Force Puma helicopter. Impatiently, Daffney looked at his watch, unbuttoning and buttoning the leather face-piece. Another unaccountable hold-up. They were meant to depart at half-past five. That was ten minutes ago. It was about fifteen minutes' flying time to 'A' Company's location, which meant that in another five minutes they should have been there. What the hell was the RAF playing at? Waiting on Aldergrove a hundred miles away to give them permission to start up? He wouldn't put it past them ... He heaved an impatient sigh and was on the point of going over to have words with the pilot when there came the rising whistle of twin turboshafts winding themselves up. Hot air began to dance out of the exhaust apertures, shimmering over the turbine cowlings on either side. The whistling gave way to a strident sucking sound, and the sucking to a throaty roar which rose to a screaming howl. High-octane fumes, a sharp penetrating tang, assailed the nostrils of onlookers. The pilot engaged the rotors. Standing on the damp concrete, supported by double tyres and retractable undercarriage, the big fuselage wagged from side to side with the first few revolutions of the four-bladed main rotor. The blades sliced into the cold air in front of and above the heads of the waiting men who, all hearing obliterated by the noise, braced themselves bareheaded in the icy blast, observing the pilot. At a signal from him, they scurried to the doorway, heaving themselves and their bergens aboard and raising a thumb to indicate they were strapped in and ready.

Sitting inside a stationary chopper which had its rotors twirling did nothing for Daffney. He had seen in Aden how a few rounds of small arms fire could reduce one of these things to a twisted heap of tortured metal that marked the grave of the men inside it. He glanced forward to where a red night-vision light illuminated the two pilots. Seconds later the undercarriage stiffened as the rotors took purchase, cleaving them into the air. The fuselage gave a succession of little upward jerks, tugging in defiance of gravity. Then rapidly, the ground receded. For a couple of seconds, the big animal hovered whilst the pilot orientated her, seeming to point her nose towards a distant prey in the glowering, rain-laden skies. Then they dipped and banked, downdraught flattening the leafless trees at the south-east corner of the mill, pitching forwards until the lights of Bessbrook disappeared from view, swallowed up in the murky night. Daffney checked his watch again. Nineteen minutes adrift. At the moment he had no idea of the significance of those minutes. The men sat clutching their weapons, staring at nothing in the dark. Up front, the pilot spoke briefly with HQ telling them he was airborne and en-route; the acknowledgement was perfunctory. Down the corridor in the Troop Operations Room, their exchange was monitored by the on-watch Marine listening out on his sets. Taking up a ballpoint, he duly made a note in the radio log:

'1749: Callsign Ten-Zero-Alpha airborne for Crossmaglen — Operation Roulade.'

★   ★   ★

Just south of Culloville, pulled up at the side of the L14 road inside the Republic, sat four men in a car, listening, the windows wound down. Hearts beating fast in eager anticipation, they looked at their watches and assessed the chances of their lorry being discovered, parked as it was out of sight behind Crossmaglen Square in the centre of the town. On its back, a multi-barrelled mortar was aimed at the police station, where lived some of the Marines they so dearly wished to kill and whose death and destruction they had long and assiduously sought to bring about. The device was set to go off at six o'clock. Each of the ten barrels contained a gas cylinder packed with explosives equal in effect to a 105mm howitzer shell. Ten direct hits would obliterate the police post. As six pm approached they could barely contain themselves. They were proud of the fact that of the 275 British soldiers who had been killed in their pernicious little conflict over the past seven years, no less than 27 of them had been shot to death or blown to pieces in Crossmaglen. Tonight that score would be doubled at least. They licked their lips in anticipation of glorious carnage.

The minute hand edged past six. What was wrong? Was their circuitry faulty? Was the wind obscuring their hearing? They got out of the car to look. Two miles away, on slightly higher ground stood Crossmaglen. Hearts in mouths, hardly daring to breathe, the 'freedom fighters' strained their eyes. Two minutes past six ...

There was a flash. Then another. Then another. Faintly, the sound was borne to them. They shouted and screamed in triumph, jumping up and down hugging and kissing each other like footballers, each death a goal, hoping that what was taking place during the half-minute of mayhem would far exceed their wildest expectations ... hoping beyond hope for an orgy of annihilation.

"KILL ... ! KILL ...! KILL ...!" they screamed and sobbed, almost beside themselves at the moment of supreme climax, of psychological orgasm, weeks of pent-up violence finding release. In the cold, they sweated, tears of joy running down their faces at witnessing the fulfilment of their work. The grass was the greener for it.

When it was over and there was no more to be seen or heard, they got back in the car and drove to Dundalk in ecstatic mood, jubilantly laughing and singing, hugging and cheering. They could barely wait for the morrow, for the media to tell them how many. Ten, twenty, fifty ... a hundred? Anything was possible! Tonight they would drink and drink and drink ...

★   ★   ★

As the first bomb left its barrel, a hollow tubular crack, caused by the exploding propellant charge, gave a couple of seconds warning of the attack. Fast asleep in his troop hut, a young Marine instinctively rolled off his top bunk and fell to the floor. A second later came another crack. That was the last thing he heard. The first bomb struck.

It hit the protective wire netting directly above his hut and exploded before he had time to crawl completely to cover underneath the bottom bunk. The explosion blew in the roof, downwards. Bent and mangled by the explosion and the weight of falling beams and timber, the beds crashed down upon him, inexorably crushing the life out of him. A second blast lacerated one arm poking out from under the debris ...

A Sergeant, lying awake on his bed in the Senior NCOs hut, decided seconds beforehand to move. Even as he did so, the room was blown to bits ...

Blood spattered the command post. A man screamed repeatedly in agony. His left forearm ended in a bloody stump, the wrist and hand missing ...

A direct hit obliterated the Company Quartermaster's store, in which he slept. He was in it.

The Marine in the sangar nearest to the square, searched in the gloomy night for a target. 'Hit back! Hit back!' was all he could think. He took the machine-gun and cocked it.

The Pakistani employee of the Naafi, who sold coffees and teas to off-watch Marines in the tiny television room, squealed in terror and ducked behind his plywood counter. Men rammed themselves behind their seats, every second expecting the hit that would blow them limb from limb, carelessly strewing about their balls and brains, legs and arms and bloodied intestines. Elsewhere, as everywhere, men went white, taking cover as best they could, behind anything, tables, chairs, walls, whatever, hauling themselves into themselves, curling up to protect head, spine, legs, genitals ...

The young bootneck who had rolled off his bunk as the first bomb went off was caught half under the bottom bunk when the bomb exploded. Immediately the world went black and he found himself being crushed ... crushed to death. God ... oh God, he couldn't breathe ... he had no thoughts of dying, but an enormous weight was squeezing the breath out of him ... he choked ... he struggled ... he tried to fight himself free of the debris, summoning all his willpower for the one enormous heave that would clear him, but he couldn't budge. He couldn't move his feet or pelvis; his chest was being pushed into the floor. He tried again and again but each time he was weaker ... unable to breathe in. Oh God no! He tried to fight his panic ... surely someone would come around and see his arm sticking out and know he was there. But they were all taking cover! There was no-one! Let the bombing stop ... LET IT STOP! Another blast blew debris into his free arm, lacerating it, destroying all feeling in it. Oh Christ, he had lost his arm ... he was dying ... no, please, oh God ...

His arm twisted, the back of the hand flattening against the floor. Involuntarily, the fingers curled up, pathetically grasping a chunk of plasterboard that lay in the palm, searching for reassurance that help was at hand. All around him, bombs were still bursting ... four ... five ... six ... His breathing stopped and he lay still.

One man cowered under a table in the galley with others, his anger mounting. No one could do this to them without being punished ... NO ONE ...

He was big and solidly built. A West Countryman, loud-mouthed, humorous, punchy, uncaring, perennially at odds with authority, and aware of his own size and strength. He had been promoted to Lance-Corporal and reverted more times, he claimed, than the CO had had mess dinners. Right now, the stripe was on his arm. As he took cover from the exploding bombs, he knew which huts were empty because the men were out on patrol and he knew that the first bomb had hit a hut where men were sleeping, resting in between their patrol programme as best they could. Even as the bombs continued to fall, he got out from under the table in the galley and charged past the communications centre where someone was already applying first-field dressing to the stump of the screaming man's arm. Down the corridor, through dust and debris he ran, till he came to the hut he was looking for. It had ceased to exist. He found himself standing underneath a gaping hole in the chicken-wire which gave onto the sky. At his feet, a heap of debris. Another bomb plummeted onto the chicken-wire, now an entangled mess affording scant protection. It blew apart an empty hut further

down the corridor. He hardly flinched. He was mad; white-hot-
seething-mad. He waded into the wreckage, lifting bits of it,
flinging it aside, tearing at it in the manner of King-Kong. With the
strength of a madman, he lifted a huge expanse of asphalted
timber, the roof. Underneath were broken trusses, crumpled
plasterboard, mangled ironwork. Just poking out, curled upwards,
feebly gripping some wreckage were the fingertips of a human hand.
It belonged to the arm of the young Marine who had rolled off his
bunk and that was all there was to be seen of him.

The Marine manning the sangar nearest the square whence the
mortaring came was a youngster who had only signed up for three
years. They had been expecting a second mortar attack ever since
the first one failed, but it was impossible to predict what form it
would take or when it would happen. At dusk was the obvious time,
so that the opposition could get away. He always kept a damn good
look-out when he was in the sangar. It was a responsibility he
enjoyed, for behind him were the company to which he belonged,
where the feeling of mutual protection and kinship had reached
such a pitch of intensity that it entirely outshone the desire of the
opposition to have them wiped out. Which meant that if the Provos
thought that he was going to just stand there and pick his nose whilst
they connived at the destruction of half or more of 'his family', they
were wrong. As the bombs started to burst behind him, he peered
out of the sangar, searching for a target. But finding none, he fired
at the *sound* of the bombs as they left the hidden lorry. He fired off a
belt of fifty rounds in one burst and had just taken down the gun to
reload it when the bombing stopped. He slapped another belt across
the feed-tray, slammed the top-cover shut and remounted the gun,
looking out expectantly, hoping for a target. He anticipated at least
to be reprimanded for what he had done, if not charged with any
number of offences ranging from conduct-prejudicial to murder,
because it was the sort of war where you had to take it without giving
any back — officially. But that would never happen so long as men
possessed initiative and the ability to think for themselves. Which
this Liverpool-kiddy did. No-one told him to fire. No-one needed
to. He had the practical philosophy of the Scouser. 'What the hell'.
In six months' time he would be out. Right now he supposed that
half his company was dead but at least someone had fired back. At
least, *someone* had done *something*. He remained at his post,
watching intently ...

The last bomb fell, like several of its predecessors, amongst the
sergeants' accommodation, blowing off more of the roof, ripping
apart the pressed-board walls, spattering the metal springs and

horse-hair stuffing of easy chairs and sofas in every direction, spewing the transistorised innards of radios and televisions round about and destroying everything else in sight; bedding, kit, personal possessions. Even as it did so, down the corridor a short distance away, the big lance-jack was clawing at the wreckage burying his comrade.

"Get him out!" he raged. "GET HIM OUT! GET THE BASTARD OUT!"

He uncovered the Marine's arm and saw in the dim light that it was a bloodied mass, like a lump of horsemeat. Oblivious to everything, he grasped one end of the buckled bedframe, and bracing himself like a weight-lifter, using the massive strength in his arms and back and thighs, he drove the chaotic twisted mess upwards, grunting as he did so, dipping his shoulders inside and under so that the whole crushing mass of the wreckage bore down upon him. Crouching, supporting the debris on his back and neck, momentarily he reached down and fished for the lifeless Marine with one arm, grabbing him by the seat of his pants and pulling him towards him till he was by his feet. Then feeling he was in danger of collapsing under his horrific burden, he sought to steady it with both hands. The body at his feet he hooked backwards rugby-style, 'heeling' it out from under the debris until it was clear. Somehow he manoeuvered himself to the edge, fighting the wreckage on top of him every inch of the way. With a final effort, he heaved it up a fraction, face contorted in disbelief at the agony; then he shoved himself out and away, just clear enough of the whole heap of splintered timber and twisted metal as it crashed once more to the floor. He had lifted the better part of a ton.

Torchlights flashed in the black. Willing hands were on the scene at once, grabbing the body, turning it onto its back and lifting it clear of the mayhem into a piece of open corridor. The face was white with dust. The head was tilted back and an air passage cleared through mouth and throat. Another head bent to the limp Marine's lips, breathing life-giving air into his lungs. The pulse was felt for, found to be missing and the heart re-started by a series of controlled jolts applied to the centre of the chest. Slowly, agonisingly slowly, life flickered back into him. Calmly, the medical attendant bandaged his shattered arm, watching with relief the involuntary rise and fall of the chest as the young man came back from the dead.

Even as they circled the football pitch at the back of the police station, Daffney sensed something was wrong. He slid the door open and stared out. The location was not lit as it normally was and from what he could see there were holes in the protective wire over it. The pilot too was ill at ease when he saw there was no reception party standing at the back gate. As they hovered nose-on to the gate, gently coming down to earth, they all saw the pall of smoke, the broken glass, the torn and shattered walls and the smashed framework of the netting, scaffolding poles crazy. The time was 1804.

For a moment, as he left the port-hand door of the Puma, Daffney had the impression he had come too late to relieve a beleaguered fort. The men followed him inside the high corrugated iron gates, part of the anti-sniper screen that surrounded the camp. In the sombre half-light cast by the one remaining flood-light at the front, the picture that greeted them was like something from the trenches of World War One. Stumbling across duck boards were the first of the shocked casualties needing immediate evacuation. One, whose denims were tattered and blood-stained, walked purposefully but in obvious pain towards the back gate, half trying to break into a run. He was bareheaded but wore a flak-jacket and carried a loaded rifle. It was the Quartermaster Sergeant, the same man who having been wounded in a previous mortar attack, had now survived a direct hit on his store in which he had been taking cover at the time. His legs were lacerated; nevertheless he walked. His eyes were wide open with shock and his face bore the fixed expression of one whose sole aim is vengeance. In the same moment that he saw him, Daffney recognised what he was about.

"STOP HIM!" he roared against the noise of the chopper; "STOP HIM ...!"

A second later, a maddened teenage Marine dressed in shirt-sleeves and carrying an SLR, rushed out of the ruins shouting, almost sobbing, crying in a high-pitched hysterical voice. "I'm gonna blow some fucker's head off for this ... I'M GONNA KILL SOME BASTARD FOR THIS!!"

Mercilessly Daffney chopped him down. The Marine fell dazed into the mud. Viciously he snatched the rifle away from the youngster and tossed it to Stevenson who unloaded it.

"GET UP!!" he shouted at the man, their faces barely an inch apart. The bootneck obeyed, his eyes wide with a new fear.

"IF I HEAR ANOTHER WORD, I'LL BEAT THE LIVING SHIT OUT OF YOU!! NOW GET BACK IN THERE AND REPORT TO YOUR TROOP SERGEANT! DOUBLE!"

The man grabbed his rifle and ran.

Between them they supported the wounded Quartermaster Sergeant out of the gate and onto the chopper. He sagged against them, the fierce venom that had sustained him thus far leaving him as swiftly as water from a bucket, shock and lassitude being all that remained.

Around the devastated compound the men mustered; NCOs picked their way through the wreckage looking for dead and wounded, counting the casualties and reporting in. Working parties were formed to rig lighting, to clear the wreckage and debris from the operations room and galley, to make an immediate start on getting the place habitable again.

Within ten minutes the burned, the blasted, and the shocked were casevacked on the Puma to the military wing of Musgrave Park Hospital in Belfast. As each report came in from his NCOs, the Company Sergeant-Major held his breath. Finally, he reported to his company commander:

"Dead: nil. Wounded: six, three seriously."

The company commander could hardly believe his ears. He offered a silent prayer of thanks to the Almighty, to the manufacturers of the wire netting and to the Army Engineers who had erected it. It was little short of a miracle.

Among the ruins of what had been their home they stood, forming a line for the evening meal to be served in sittings. After an attack, for the survivors as always, euphoria. Metal food trays clanked, banter filled the air, emergency lighting lit their beaming faces.

"Supper will be a bit late tonight, lads," announced a chef.

"Just 'cos of a poxy mortar attack?" Laughter.

"One other thing."

"What?"

"There'll be no film show tonight."

"*Why not?*" mocked someone. More laughter.

As they waited in line for stew-with-shrapnel to be served, some even started to brag.

"I was there," said one.

"So was I," said a second.

Instant veterans. The idea caught on.

"We were there," said a third leaning out of line to catch his oppo's eye. "Weren't we, Scouse?"

"Too right, mate," came the reply. "'A' Company, tour of '76. We were there."

Behind them, in the middle of one of the tables, stood the cheese plate. Over it, a metal combat helmet bore the inscription, 'In case of mortar attack,'please cover the Stilton.'

At the top of a long ridge, they paused and went down flat into all-round-defence, whilst again North and Daffney conferred over the map. The wind was biting, bending the uncut blackthorn hedgerows nearby. Gerson watched the six o'clock, tapping gloved fingers on the stock of the Bren, the bipod standing on a mound of long wet grass. Near him lay Challice, distastefully feeling the wet soak into him as he lay at full length on the ground. Challice was discovering what his companions had learned by hard experience; the tiny techniques of the field soldier, such as angling yourself off the wind so you could hear with one ear and the wind didn't blow straight in your face or up your anus; lying on one hip so only one side got wet; drawing up one knee to find purchase with that boot so you didn't get left floundering on the ground when the order to move came; and so on. Little things, almost insignificant in themselves, but they were the stock-in-trade of those required to operate in the open in any part of the world, living out of what they carried on their back. They maintained a man's morale and efficiency, but Challice, knowing little of such minutiae because of his normal clerical employment, got wet the first time he went to ground, thought 'Ugh!' and exposing his face to the wind, soon began to shiver.

They upped and moved off once more, along the ridge, moving in the lee of the high ground, careful not to be silhouetted. Slowly and gently, they squelched over the sodden turfs, nagged by thorn bushes and hampered by stone walls. The fields were the size of pocket handkerchiefs here. It made for laborious going.

Soon, they were slipping off the spur, literally in some cases, and making their way down into a vague and shadowy re-entrant. The ground was no longer walled but rough open ground and it was for the far side of the re-entrant that Daffney was making, heading for a piece of ground where they would lie up. It was a game of chess, keeping their opponents guessing as to their route to the king.

As they descended they moved slowly, joltingly, a few steps at a time, knee ligaments resisting the impulse of their loads to rush them forwards. It became exceptionally dark. Daffney had just thought he heard the sound of running water, which would indicate the stream at the bottom of the re-entrant, when North came back very cautiously and pointed to an L formed by two open gateways, through which they would have to pass. Daffney knelt, flicked his torch onto the map and checked. Then he nodded to North and got down flat, giving the signal for all-round-defence. The lead scout walked forward again a matter of metres, until he reached as far as he had gone before. Daffney stayed down, watching him.

North put his rifle in his left hand, holding it so the butt was uppermost, the barrel pointing at the ground alongside his left leg. Then he grasped the stick which was loosely looped around his right wrist, holding it delicately between finger and thumb so that the tip of it touched the ground. He held it vertically and slackly, and began to sweep in front of him, feeling ... feeling for anything it might snag against. The gateways were on a slight rise, an undulation in the ground at the bottom of the re-entrant. The sniper walked forward ... sweeping ... one step at a time ... sweeping, gently, carefully, methodically, with studied concentration. The first gateway was where the wire would be.

An open gate. No cattle in the fields, then, thought North. Thorough training grafted onto natural canniness; he let the picture come to him. A thick thorn hedge, channelling them, tempting them to use the gateway. Bluff ... or double bluff? An open gateway, creating suspicion, prompting a detour ... onto a killing ground? Or through the hedge which had been wired? Be easier to find a wire here, if there was one. He was level with the gateposts, up-ended railway sleepers. The metal gate hung open ... not held back ... it simply hung that way. He stopped, heart beating fast. Underneath his woollen jersey, his chest was sticky with sweat. His face was set, tongue between slightly parted lips, eyes crinkled like a man concentrating, doing something tricky. In North's case, trying to keep himself alive.

Slowly, he switched the birch. No wire. He turned to his left. No wire. Then to his right. No wire. He moved the stick in front of him, back and forth a few times, then took a pace behind it, sliding his foot just an inch off the ground. Same again. No wire. He felt all around him, reaching out as far as he could to the side, careful not to lose his balance. Still no wire. Where was it? It had to be here, didn't it? The evil you found was the better ... The blind man's stick probed again ... he shuffled on, bending over, leaning forwards, waiting for the tiny tell-tale jar that would come up the stick, pass through his finger and thumb and signal his brain that he was a metre or two away from a charge that would spread his Yorkshire entrails amongst the ancient thorn bushes of Erin.

Daffney watched, brows knitted. As North progressed through the first open gateway past a small piece of hedge only three or four metres in length, and turned into the second gateway, he shifted his position slightly, so he could observe his lead scout the better. The others stayed put, lying flat and still in a rough circle, moving only their head or raising a finger to wipe the drips from their nose as they watched their arcs of fire. Trained animals, outlined by their humps. Their sweat had run cold now. They shivered yet it mattered not. Terry North was doing a job about which it was impossible to be impatient. Minesweeping was what they called it. In the Navy, it meant picking someone else's mines out of the sea. In the Marines, it meant picking up someone else's beer, time-honoured tactic of the skint bootneck. Or doing what Terry was doing now. Either way, life was pretty cheap.

The radio pressed heavily but somehow comfortingly upon Stevenson's back. He sniffed and gazed steadfastly around his arc, senses channelled like the beam of a lamp in whatever direction he looked.

He was abreast of the second gate now. Though the wind had dropped in the re-entrant, it was still uncomfortable; but while the others shivered, North sweated. Then he was through, the gateposts behind him. The wire would run across each gateway, if there. Well, he had swept them both. Nothing. Not a thing. The gates were clear; wires ran in straight lines, didn't they? So they must be clear. Wiring the gaps was standard practice for the setter. Wasn't it? Through the gap, kick the wire and wumpeter! That was their idea. Unless ... unless ... he shuffled forward, guarding against the tendency to relax, yet sweeping in bolder strokes ...

Well through the gate now. No. Nothing here. But he didn't really expect there would be. Six or seven metres inside the field now. No. No wire. There wasn't a wire. Turning to his left, he walked outwards a little way, towards the centre of the field, treading in small steps and still sweeping in front of him. His right boot was swinging forward ... CHRIST!

He froze.

It was a wire.

His face contorted in agony as he looked down ... Slowly, he bent to examine what it was that the stick had fetched up against. It was a wire all right. And it was brushing his puttee! His foot had touched it fractionally *before* the stick. The bastards! It was coming in from behind him at an angle. Another inch and he would have tripped it. Perhaps even now he had! If it went off on pull ... then he hadn't tripped it. But if went off on release ... Oh Christ! then he might have done ... and he would only find out when he took his leg away. He didn't even know if the charge was in front or behind him. OH

GOD! Bloody hell! He had to be sure before he moved he wasn't going to snag another wire. What a mess! What a fuck up! Get yourself out of this, snipes ...

"Terry!" It was Daffney.

North stood stock still, petrified. It was so bloody dark. 'Oh come on God, give us a break, will you? Get the moon out so I can see what the hell I'm doing!'

There was silence, strange and tension-ridden. Suddenly, the cold was forgotten, trees seemed to stop swaying, time stood still. The men sensed the predicament of their lead scout. Without moving, all their senses became focussed on what was taking place inside that field. Our Terry was in lumber.

"Terry!"

"SHUDDUP!" he hissed, stressed beyond limit. The words came out in a hoarse whisper.

Slowly, keeping both eyes wide open, he moved so he could see the wire running in both directions, in front and behind him. Was it straight? Or was it being pushed out of line by his ankle? Yes. No. Yes. No. Oh shiiiiit ...! No. It was straight. He couldn't tell. There was only one way to find out. That was to remove his ankle. Slowly, making sure he moved the offending ankle not a millimetre, he crouched down, the better to escape the inevitable blast. He breathed in and out deliberately before making the decision to take his leg off the wire, conscious with each lungful of night air that were he to decide to act that might be the last breath he ever took.

He put down his rifle and curling up as near to the ground as possible, wrapped his head in his arms, flinching against the explosion he knew must come, bracing himself and wondering how on earth his flesh and bones could stand up to the blast ...

He rolled away from the wire.

Nothing happened.

Quaking with surprise, North stood up. Carefully, he picked up his rifle. Then, still fearful of an explosion, he began to sweep his way with huge deliberation back towards the gate. Shaken by his encounter and suspicious of his earlier findings, he swept his way through both gates again, this time from the other direction. Once he was through, he began to swear. He swore all the way back to where Daffney lay.

"What's up?"

"There's a wire ... running in at an odd angle about eight, ten metres through the second gate ... we'll 'av to go round ..."

North was breathing hard.

"Sure it's not electric fence?"

"Course it's not a fucking electric fence! I had me leg against it for about five minutes ...!"

"It might have been switched off then ..."

"You're the one that's switched off ... I was touching it with me bloody leg!" Normally, North didn't swear much.

"All right, keep your shirt on. How high is it off the deck?"

"About six inches; I nearly tripped it with me ankle!"

"Christ ..."

"That's what I thought ..."

"Hold up. I'll come and have look with you."

The big man signalled Taverner 'WIRE ... RECCE' and went forward with North, who began to unsheath a white flashlight. Daffney nudged him, shaking his head.

"No. Put it away till we've had a good look; it might be light-sensitive. No point in taking a chance."

Creeping forwards, Daffney following, they refound the wire with the aid of the blind-man's stick approximately where North had touched it. It was running across their path at 45°. Puzzled, Daffney motioned North to act as his reference point in the dark by staying still. Then taking the birch from him, very slowly on hands and knees, he followed the wire away from North, into the field. He had gone a fair distance when he came under the shadow of the hedge, which was tall and uncut. The wire went on.

Daffney unclipped his torch, making very sure its beam was on red. Red was neither so conspicuous as white nor did it disturb the ability to see at night. He pressed it to the ground and flicked it on, gradually allowing the light to spread outwards as he raised it and shone it into the hedge. The wire went in some way, until it met the stout trunk of a young tree round which it was wound numerous times and knotted. It might have been a ploy to deceive the casual onlooker, with the wire going on further, but Daffney examined it hard and eventually found the loose end hanging down after the knot. It was knotted in the manner of 'a dozen round-turns and two half-hitches'. He recognised that this must be the beginning of the wire. Here it was anchored, and robustly so, and its height off the ground was still six to nine inches.

He examined the wire itself. It was new; the galvanisation was still on it and it was stranded, not the type of solid wire used for fencing. He followed it back past North, moving with great care, running the back of his hand along it, feeling with his fingers for any clues that might lie underneath it.

He wasn't far past North—four or five metres perhaps—when something made him stop. He remained exactly where he was, tensed up, crouching on one knee in the mud. Slowly, he looked to his right and stared, moving his head to catch a glimpse of something he thought he had seen. Taking the birch, he extended a steady hand ... and probed ... in long delicate upward strokes, like an artist putting the finishing touches to a canvas. His arm came forward a little. Ping! The birch alighted on a wire.

It was another wire, running in, converging upon the one North had found and Daffney was following. Had he gone on tracing the first wire with all his concentration focussed upon it, he might well have snagged this new one where it got closer to him. And North, when he rolled away from the first wire, had been unaware of the presence of this second one.

For a moment he thought, then centering himself between the two wires so he could touch them both, Daffney lay down full length and crawled forwards, thumbs sliding along both at the same time. Sure enough, they converged; within a few metres, his arms were directly in front of him. The two wires obviously met. Intrigued, he took out his torch again.

There, in front of him, was a peg. The peg was metal and was driven into the ground hard, on a slight mound. It had an eye through which the wires ran. His own eyes studied the wire, a half-smile faintly pulling at his mouth. It was not two wires but one. The first wire ran through the eye, doubling almost back upon itself through something like 120° to its original direction. Careful to touch neither side, he leant forward again to confirm that the peg merely acted as a guide. It was true; the wire ran continuously through it. It was not a stake to which two wires were fastened. The peg simply turned the one wire off in a new direction. In that instant, Daffney knew what he was looking at.

He sat up on his haunches and grinned ... Pantai Ridge, Malaysia; visual trackers' course on which he had got a 'distinguished'. He breathed out long and hard, whistling through his teeth.

"The cunning bastards ... so somebody's taught 'em that one, eh?" He grinned to himself again; "Of all the fucking ... Terry!"

"Yeah?"

"Come towards me ... very, very carefully ..."

Instead of setting the wire straight across either of the gaps where it might be detected by the method North had used, whoever had set it had done so in a manner designed to catch the unwary. It had been set in an inverted V-shape and set big and wide, so that the lead scout, making a perfunctory search of the gateposts and the area immediately inside each field, would find nothing—as North nearly had. He would then unwittingly call the patrol through and when all of them were inside the killing ground — and it would be all of them with a V this size — someone would snag the trip-wire, thereby wreaking death and destruction upon themselves. Had not Terry North pursued his search so far into the second field, they would have fallen for it. To all of which Daffney had only one thing to say. "Tough." They hadn't fallen for it. It didn't work. 'Arrd bloody luck. One up to Royal.

The Sergeant edged back a little as his lead scout loomed out of the dark.

"It's a V-shape wire," whispered Daffney. "That end's the anchor, this here's the crutch. Stop here. I'm going down this leg of it. This is where the charges'll be. Don't fall in a dead faint across the wire while I'm down there, will ya ..."

North grinned at Daffney's apparent enthusiasm. He watched the big NCO disappear into the dark, going about a job a ballet dancer under floodlights would disdain. Here they were in the pitch black, the pair of them, searching for an explosive device on uneven slippery ground with heavy muddy boots on, in nail-biting proximity to a trip-wire the slightest tweak on which would blow them both straight out of this world.

Daffney traced the wire from where it doubled back through the eye, a distance of ten or fifteen metres to a point in the hedge a few metres inside the gatepost. Here the hedge grew out of an embankment and the bank had been revetted in places with a stone wall. He used his torch, heart beating fast, feeling like a naked cave man approaching a sleeping monster, hoping to get a good look without rousing it. Being as close as this somehow made it easier, for there would be no time to realise anything, yet at the same time he took tremendous pains to check his nervous impulses by doing everything with the maximum deliberation, thinking every move through in advance. Slowly, he raised the torch.

The wire ran into an old tin water trough, the size of the average bath, which lay canted over amongst the fern and briars growing by the bank. For a second he was nonplussed; then he realised; that was it. The trough contained 'shipyard confetti': nuts, bolts, bits of old ploughshare and broken hand implements, all swimming in oily water. Precisely the sort of thing you would expect to find on a farm somewhere and at which you wouldn't glance a second time. But here, in a field, with a wire running to it ...

He bent underneath it. Sure enough, he could see plastic fertiliser sacks dug into the bank behind it. Four of them. About a 400lb charge, he reckoned. Phew! An elaborately set-up Claymore device.

The charge alone would take out an armoured vehicle, but the Army never used vehicles down here and everyone knew it. No, this was aimed at reducing the luckless half-dozen Poor Bloody Infantry, caught in that killing ground, to Meccano-men, nuts and bolts through every joint. And those who didn't get the confetti would be spattered around and about by the blast.

He sat there looking at it, almost relaxed, face to face with the lethal device, inches away from the evil every soldier hated and feared. And rightly so, because he was ignorant of them — unlike the ATO and his bomb disposal team, who knew about them and understood them, but whose knowledge and understanding only made their matchless courage in dealing with them seem that much the greater in the eyes of the ordinary soldier. For a few seconds more, Daffney lingered. It was evidently quite new. Maybe they were hoping to get a patrol with it tonight. Tough. They were out of luck. Even as he thought that, he experienced the oddly gratifying feeling of deliberately taking on and beating fate. His men had found it by their own skill. By their own skill, they would evade its evil. And if it went off now while he was looking at it, then just like his father in Germany in 1946, he wouldn't know a thing about it. On that occasion, the opposition had triumphed, succeeding in blowing to bits Warrant Officer John Daffney long after the cessation of hostilities, as he stooped and sweated, carrying out his duty to King and Country in a dusty suburb of Dortmund. But now, on this occasion, his son had the feeling that this time at least, he had got the better of the opposition.

Standing astride the wire, North and Daffney checked the rest of the section over it, steadying the men under their loads as they crossed. When they were all safely over the obstacle, they moved on a little way, then paused whilst Daffney marked the position of the device on his map. The trap set for them offered counter-ambush possibilities. At the last count, the unit had found and cleared with the help of the Ammunition Technical Officer a total of twenty-eight improvised explosive devices. Thirteen more were at this moment 'soaking', lying untouched but not ignored. Add that one, fourteen. You never knew who you might catch sneaking down to inspect his charges. For the 'peacetime' soldier, it was about the only time that all was fair in love and war. Any volunteers? 'Yes. Six of us, right here.'

He sniffed and folded away the fablon-ed map, slipping it inside his combat-jacket and zipping up the garment. They shook out into formation again, crossed the stream and began to ascend the far side, working their way along and up till they came to more walled-in fields.

★   ★   ★

One second they were asleep, the next awake. Not moving, not breathing. Tense. Aware. Listening. Hands curled round rifles. Inside his sleeping bag, head resting on his belt-order, the patrol commander lay rigid. What ...? Something ...

He swivelled his eyes, taking it all in; trees, bare branches, stone wall, hoar-frost on the steeply rising ground behind them ... something was different ... something was *wrong*.

Eighteen inches from his face was the face of another man, likewise. He listened. Nothing. No measured breathing. All the men suddenly awake, listening. Searching for an explanation, his eyes alighted on the face of the man next to him. Taverner; sleep-laden eyes wide open with alarm, black camouflage-cream mingling with his moustache. Taverner looked at Daffney, whose rugged skin seemed suddenly very pale against the black cream applied at random to distort the outline of his face. Why had they all awoken in the same instant, rigid with tense expectancy? Why could they see each other so clearly?

Then they knew ... The answer was one and the same.

Taverner rolled his eyes towards the moon and back. The big man nodded and tilted his head, looking up. The clouds had suddenly parted and there was the moon, full, illuminating them as though it were daytime. He raised his head looking for the shadow of the sentry. He might have known he wouldn't find it. The man was masking his own shadow with that of a tree. As for the rest of them, their instincts, honed to a razor's edge by use, had seen to it that they were aroused when the moon came out.

"Ssst!"

A head bent round a tree. He was just standing there.

"What."

"That you Steve?" He knew by the single word.

"Yeh."

"All right?"

"Yeh."

"Who's on next?"

"Les."

"'Kay."

Daffney glanced at the huddled forms of the other four. A man turned quietly inside his bag; his breathing was long. He pulled his belt-order down into his shoulder, snuggling his head onto it like a pillow. The next second he was asleep.

Stevenson leant against the tree, watching his breaths condense in front of his face. The frosty grass showed white in the moonlight. He glanced at the shapes of the men he was guarding over, up against the wall amongst nettles and brambles. Then he glanced at his watch and thought of his month-old daughter, all 6¾lbs of her at birth. Suzanne. She would keep her father's heart warm on a freezing night.

Suzanne Stevenson. Dark eyes like her mother so his wife said. Rubbish, they were like her father's; he could see it in the photograph. She had his face too. Of course she did. Everyone said he had a baby face and she was a baby. So she must have his face. She would grow up to be a raver all right. A beauty queen, a model, an actress. Earn a lot of money to keep her old man when he'd finished serving Her Majesty. Serving Her Majesty? That didn't sound right. A year ago he had been busy serving the daughter of a Warrant Officer in the RAF. Hence the marriage. Hence Suzanne. Nearly the other way round. Five months gone at the altar. Father-in-law doing his nut. Not good for an RAF Warrant Officer's image to have his daughter marry a bootneck with one so flagrantly in the oven. He had nearly flipped his lid at Stevenson's facetious suggestion that if he was so hard up he couldn't throw a reception big enough to accommodate the entire troop, they had better economise by having the wedding and the christening on the same day. He had called him a randy Scouse git, silly old bugger.

Stevenson confused everyone who set store by it because he spoke like a Scouser, but he wasn't one. He came from the other side of the river. The Wirral. It was nice there but he wanted away. "I wouldn't join that rough lot", his father had said when he came home and announced he was off to join the Marines. But that had just made him more determined. And look what happened. He had taken to soldiering like a duck to water. He had a nine-year contract and now a young wife and daughter. Five weeks old. Five weeks yesterday, or was it six? Or four? Be about two months old anyway by the time she first saw her dad. Two months ... two months old ... Suzanne Stevenson ... he liked the name. He couldn't wait to see her.

Thinly, the chill wintry sun shone on them as they lay up, resting inside their sleeping bags to preserve body heat, energy, alertness. A few feet away, another stone wall, built by a feudal landowner for the protection of his estate. Centuries old, now symbolically crumbling. Which suited Daffney fine. He had found a place where there was a hole in it through which they could observe the ground over which they would move to their final position. Crumbling stone walls; just what the doctor ordered. Cover from fire, cover from view. Well done that man! Take a make-and-mend.

Shortly before dawn, they had upped and moved on, having rested for about three hours in the place where the moon had woken them up. Now they had found this place and they settled in quietly until it was time to make the next move across the chess board.

The morning wore on. They passed it in the same way they had passed a hundred others and would pass a hundred more. Mornings, evenings, daytimes, nightimes, dawns, dusks. Once they had familiarised themselves with their new position, checking out likely approaches, fields of view and so on, so that it became defensible, they ate and drank. Food from the ration pack and a hot drink. Instant restorers of morale and energy. From then on, it was a question of staying as warm and as comfortable as possible until it was their turn on watch. Some dozed; some read a book; most passed the time in the traditional manner of the British soldier — contemplating. Contemplating his surroundings, his circumstances, the heavens over him, the earth underneath him, the future, the past and so on back to his surroundings again. At which point, he would usually stir in order to make some new and positive contribution to the security of the position. To be lying up like this, killing a few hours in daylight and reasonable safety, was a holiday. It was the dusks that were bad. Failing light always dropped a soldier's morale, made him nervous. By the same token, the dawn always raised his morale. Simply because he could see again. No longer did he have to rely upon hyper-extended hearing and sixth-sense. How many times, having agonised through a never-ending night, waiting for a dawn they thought would never come, had the words 'safely delivered through the night' sprung to a soldier's lips. Every dusk brought with it an act of faith, a silent unspoken unformed prayer that that deliverance would take place. Against which circumstances, the present phase of Operation Roulade was pure vacation.

The Sergeant unzipped his bag and crawled out. His turn on watch. He slipped a pair of duvet trousers over his combats. Tightly hugging, they gave him the appearance of a ballet dancer in leotards. Then he crawled over to Gerson who was studying their final position through field glasses. He lowered the binoculars when he felt the presence of the Sergeant beside him.

"See anything? Any thoughts on the route?" asked Daffney.

"There's a blue poly-bag in the second field. In the hedge on the right-hand side. Looks a bit suss to me. Could be summink ..."

"Or nothing."

"Yeah. Maybe an empty plastic fertiliser bag innocently stuffed into the hedge."

"Innocently designed to go innocently bang when you're innocently looking at it," said Daffney. "What else?"

"Pile o' stones. Farther up, beyond the blue bag. See?"

Daffney grunted.

"Why a fresh pile of stone crammed into an ordinary thorn hedge?" he asked, almost rhetorically.

"Because the hedge isn't so ordinary," grinned Gerson.

"Hmmmm," mused Daffney, working it out. "A new or newish pile of stones—dumped into a hedge—for no good reason I can see—except it's there to disguise or conceal something. Perhaps there's a wire running into it. Or maybe it's a radio-controlled device. Flying stones—at fifteen hundred feet per second, they could do your health a lot of good. Mmmmm, there's probably a McGregor device stashed away there somewhere. There's not a bad line of sight to it, 'specially from that hill over there."

He nodded towards a hill in the South. Now, on the ground, it seemed to overlook the whale-back feature far more dramatically than the mere contours on the map or the bird's eye view offered by aerial photography had suggested.

"Well, I don't go much on the right-hand route," he breathed, "What about the left?"

The left-hand side of the second field was not so readily visible from where they were. But its chief merit was it provided slightly more cover from view from the hill in the South. Its chief demerit was the presence of the known IED at the foot of the telegraph pole, which was on the left at the top. They would have to go uncomfortably close to that to stay in cover. Once again, he found himself thinking how ridiculous it was to go to all these lengths for such a paltry objective.

"No cows?" he asked Gerson.

"No."

"Is that a good sign or a bad sign for us?"

"Well, if they're not there, they're not gonna stand around dropping turds on you, are they?" grinned Gerson, ever the optimist. "I'm gonna make love to a bacon grill," he announced and crawled off.

"That the full extent of your love life these days, is it, Gerry?" asked Daffney absently, "It is mine."

Wives and lovers alike, all were distant memories from here, some cherished, others not.

Once, after his court-martial, he had written to his American millionairess just as he said he would, but had received no reply. Which was just as well, he reflected as he crouched by the wall, wallowing in his own stale sweat. They belonged to two totally different worlds. *Had he really done that*? Had he really jumped ship to pursue the American dream? It seemed incredible from where he was now. He smelled himself. He was already beginning to stink.

He examined the fields, looking for the tell-tale signs of disarranged grass, the unnatural shape of a man-made object, anything that didn't fit in with the random symmetry of nature. Slowly and methodically, he swept the glasses from side to side, S-bending his view up the fields between the two hedgerows so that the lower part of his binocular vision covered again what had been in the upper part on the previous traverse.

He paused at the extremity of each steady sweep — left to right — right to left — left to right — allowing the brain time to understand what the eyes had seen. Locate. Examine. Identify. From training and experience he knew that the brain would often not register some tiny clue until it had digested the picture sent to it by the eyes. He wove his way upwards, searching in parallel lines until he was at the top hedge. He examined every blade of grass along it, searching for the one that was metallic, straight, different. For a minute he rested. Then slowly he worked his way down again to the bottom hedge. Somewhere down there was the tree-stump with the trip-wire. The question was, where? He sucked his teeth. These two fields on the whale-back feature were nothing less than a death-trap, yet he was about to lead his men into them. But what was the alternative?

He lowered the binos and rested his eyes. He had been in some tight situations in his time but this one about seemed the most heavily stacked against him. This was not men versus men; this was men versus explosive devices set for them by men, and against which men could only lose. What it amounted to was this. The only leeway, as far as Daffney could see, was the element of double bluff. The IRA had discovered what they considered to be a likely place for an OP overlooking the hamlet of Cory. A solitary ration-pack wrapper or tin dropped by some unprofessional unit in the past had probably confirmed it in their minds. So they had proceeded to land-mine it. However, they had *possibly* got tired of waiting for someone to come back and use it. And if they didn't know or didn't *think* anyone was ...

That was about the only let-out Daffney could see. 'So,' he sighed to himself, 'Who dares wins ...' They bloody-well better had do. He cleaned the finger-nails of his left hand with the thumb-nail of the right. 'Fuck it,' he thought; 'Who cares who wins.' There weren't going to be any winners this afternoon. Only losers. If he got this job done without loss of life, that was victory enough.

Up top was the final position where Challice and Taverner would do their thing. He would put Gerson with the Bren up there with them for protection, keeping an HQ element of himself, Stevenson and North down the bottom end of the field with the radio set up all the time they did the job. He raised the field-glasses once again and began to scrutinise the left-hand hedge, examining it for 'nasties'. Not much could be seen of it until it began to crest the rise. Just poking into view there, sure enough, was that pile of logs ... right at the top. Not twenty metres away, perhaps not even ten from the final position. Well, final it would be if they got pinged. And he was going to have to sit and watch them all the time they were up there; all the time waiting for the crump ... the mushrooming earth ... and the spattered remains of his men to fall around him.

So there you are, Sergeant Daffney. There you have it. You have drawn the short straw. And now you've opened the envelope, you know what's required. That's your command task for the day. Get your men in and out of that one. Alive. Anything less than 100% — brackets F.

And of course, there are others watching you too, Sergeant; as always, from afar. The politicians, the churchmen, the media-men. All of them with a ready moral judgement. (Ah, but Sergeant, they sit in comfortable chairs and sleep in warm beds at night. Not like you ...) Well, you know what they say? 'If you can't take a joke, you shouldn't have joined.' And it's *true*. Because today's joke is, you're about to see three of your blokes blown to bits before your very eyes. And then, *then*, they will try *you*. They will judge and condemn *you*. Not just for that; but for the brutal, vicious and callous 'murder' of a murderer. For taking the life of a life-taker. What would they have done in your place?

He sat there and rubbed the stubble on his chin, ruefully thinking 'So this is what it amounts to.' Lives ... for what? The Corps never bartered away the lives of its personnel to gain an end in 'peacetime'. In conventional war it was different. Losses had to be planned, projected, taken account of in advance. But even in 'peacetime' there was no shortage of risks. And to a sergeant like Daffney, when it was your head that was on the line, there was only one rule in the end, and that was 'an eye for an eye'. If you *had* to lose a life, the only possible justification for doing so was to take one. And now, he thought gloomily, if he lost the life of a single one of his men this afternoon, all they would have to show for it would be some video, and possibly not even that. The scales were tipping heavily to one side. We no longer take terrorists out of our midst. We just leap about photographing them and interviewing them on prime time.

He checked his watch and looked back at the men resting behind him, heaving a kind of sigh.

"Two hours to adrenalin-time," he announced.

They were all awake, Taverner squeezing margarine and jam onto a biscuit, Gerson reading '365 Days' with a mug of tea in his hand, North sitting half out of his bag, back against the wall, binding hessian onto the stock of his rifle; Challice contemplating the ten-foot radio antenna which Stevenson had poked up a tree, Stevenson himself reading 'Devil's Guard', earphones that were slung over his bergen exuding a persistent mush. Occasionally he glanced up, looking out past his feet through the cover of brambles and bushes at the fields beyond. The readers' choices of literature were standard reading matter for bootnecks, in or out of the field. But one who never read on operations was North. Of all of them, he found the interim hours of idleness the hardest to bear. Most of them, if they read, did so simply to pass the off-watch hours; a book was like a companion, a means of shedding boredom. Yet once, arriving to take up a long sojourn on an OP, they discovered they only had one book between them. It was Zeno's 'Cauldron', a book about the Arnhem landings. It did the rounds. Everyone read it. Finally North picked it up. And threw it down in disgust when he got to page twenty-four, the page on which the platoon in the book took its first casualty.

North was a happily married family man, with a three-year-old son and like all of them, he had great attachment and loyalty to the unit. It was his fifth tour of active duty in Ulster and he had promised his wife that it would be his last — but only for the time being, he meant, he hoped he hadn't spoken prophetically. He was due promotion and a draft to a training establishment. For the Corps constantly required instructors to train the new material entering its portals and North now had more than the requisite experience. He would be sorry to leave the unit though, for the unit was more than just a numerical name. It was a family, people, friends, characters, attitudes, kindred spirits, shared experiences, a tangible atmosphere of spirit, unity, raw energy, common purpose, all of which — and more, much more that could never quite be put into words — added up to the unique 'esprit' of the Commando, the body of men, the brotherhood, the *thing*. The atmosphere of a training establishment was entirely different, but it was time to move on. Nothing lasted for ever.

Daffney sat by the hole in the wall, watching the day, the sky, the fields. Sometimes, he thought, these moments were the best in a man's whole life — the sharing, the comradeship, the almost spiritual companionship and feeling of mutual dependence with those behind him, the living in the very moment of the present with no before and no after. Sometimes, he committed these thoughts to paper in the form of poetry which he typed on the ops. room typewriter. Once, thinking he was typing a patrol report, Shutbridge had leaned over his shoulder ... but finding him typing a poem had asked if he could read it, thereby revealing a side of themselves neither knew existed in the other. The boss savoured it.

Back in the mill, he had an old anthology of poetry. It was yellowed and had badly cut pages and he had bought it for fifty pence in a second-hand bookshop. But in it there was a stanza he especially liked. For him, it neatly summarised the attitude and beliefs of the professional soldier, his own attitude and beliefs.

> *'Their shoulders held the sky suspended;*
> *They stood, and earth's foundations stay;*
> *What God abandoned, these defended*
> *And saved the sum of things for pay.'*

One hour to go. "Terry ...!"

North looked up to find Daffney beckoning him. Wiping crumbs and jam off his mouth with the back of his hand, the sniper crawled over to him. Daffney then showed him the route they would take, describing the parts they could not see, with the help of the map. It was more a conference than a briefing, an exchange of confidences and fears in the traditionally close relationship between lead scout and patrol commander. Because to Terry North fell the job of leading the last move across the chess board, of exploiting the ground to its natural advantage, of utilising the minutest scraps of cover and of finding the hidden jokes. Pawn to king seven — check.

A generation or so ago, British servicemen had stood alone in the defence of the free world against tyranny and oppression. Today their job was to keep the peace, to stop the spread of a civil war into something bigger. Tomorrow it might be to resist the unprovoked aggression of a totalitarian regime in the far corners of the earth. A group of islands in the South Atlantic, a neck of land in the Arctic, some small country somewhere with a jealous and more powerful neighbour. For the island race of Britain took its democracy and its freedoms and its security very much for granted. But not everyone in the free world did and there were those who still looked — and would always look — to the Old Country for their protection. And whatever the parliamentarians at home said, be they hawks or doves, peacemongers or warmongers or whatever, it would not be they who would be doing the fighting, if fighting it was that needed to be done. It would be that breed of men, following their calling, who had done it before and who would do it again. They were the same one hundred years ago, they would be the same in a hundred years time. Technology would change, weapons would change, but one thing that would not change would be the man, with his skill, his resource, his determination to endure, his humour in the face of adversity, his general idiosyncracies. Causes and wars came and went, but soldiers soldiered on, keeping the peace no less than fighting the wars. People from the same mould as these six had fought the last war, and they would fight the next. Maybe even this self-same six would be there ... Edward 'Pink-Eye' Daffney, 30, married with two children and in the process of getting himself unmarried again; Terry North, 29, married with one son; Neil Taverner, 27, single; 'Steve' Stevenson, 20, married with a newborn daughter; Les Challice, 23, single — but in love; Gerry Gerson, 25, single, one child — to the mother of whom he sent money, sometimes.

It was the same type of men as these, possessing the same faults and qualities and the same type of skills, who had bailed out the free world before and if they had to do it again, they would. For that reason, the recruitment and retention of such men was, in the words of one constitutional theorist, 'in the national interest'. It was they who enabled people to go about their everyday business.

He walked away from the wall.

"Saddle up!"

Bergens were heaved on and personal camouflage touched up with the aid of a diamond-shaped tube of black cream. Gerson held Stevenson's bergen whilst the radio operator struggled into the straps. Taverner got into his on the ground and North pulled him up. Others strained one strap — always the same one, they noticed — by slinging the bergen over one shoulder, bending forwards at the waist to counteract the weight before fidgeting the free arm through the other loop. They checked for tell-tale signs of their brief sojourn, then, one at a time, slipped through the hole in the wall, each man taking up a defensive position until they were all through.

They shook out into staggered-file, and North led off down the track to their right, some of them flexing the stiffness out of their muscles after the hours of lying up, feeling the weight of the bergen

bite once more into their shoulders. The Yorkshireman walked first
with the instincts of a thoroughbred, his retroussé nose seeming to
scent for danger. Behind him came the big man, the width of his
shoulders contriving to make the bergen he wore look like a school
kid's satchel. Then came Taverner, whose combats still held a
certain sartorial air even after being slept in; and Stevenson, supple
and unconcerned and probably hoping for a fire-fight to liven
things up. After him was Challice, looking slightly weedy amongst
present company, and last, turning and weaving at the rear, was
chief-humourist and furphy-teller, Gerson. Being on the move
again, their spirits rose. The watching and waiting were over for the
moment. Now it was time to do again, and they felt the grim, bland,
clear-eyed satisfaction of being on a collision course with fate.

North stopped to examine a place where they might cross a deep
overgrown ditch to gain access to the first field. He slid down the
bank and grimaced as he entered icy cold water and slime at the
bottom. Quietly, he slooshed across and hauled himself up the other
side, crawling out between some young birch trees. The field was
neither cultivated nor grazed. One by one, the others followed,
heaving each other up. Again, they lay in fire-positions, along the
hedgerows either side of their point of entry into the field, until the
crossing was complete. Then they rose.

Conscious now that they had nearly broken into line of sight of the
hill in the South, they moved cautiously round the perimeter of the
field, keeping low. The grass was long, withered and tufty like
elephant grass. Slowly and methodically, they worked at five-metre
intervals, bending under the weight of their packs, frequently taking
one hand off the weapon to use as a paw. The ground was uneven,
with awkward gaps between the tufts. North searched for wires. He
kept close into the hedge, for the grass was nearly white, making
their dark personal camouflage stand out. Something about the
field, however, comforted him now that he was in it. It was low-lying
between the track and the second field which sloped up to the crest
along which the defunct telephone line ran. Maybe it was the grass,
or the way it was rutted and broken up, but it seemed the wrong sort
of field in which to find a wire or a device. He went steadily but all
the time feeling the field was safe. It was a feeling he couldn't
explain, just a hunch; nothing to do with optimism, but the result of
months on end of this type of work. He drew comfort too, from the
fact that the others were following in his exact path. They were
taking no chances today.

It was maddening on occasions, especially at night, suddenly to
find that whilst he had been picking his way forward, straining his

eyes and nerves and senses, there was 'fucking Pinky' sauntering along out to his flank. That got North's Yorkshire hackles up. Just as on two occasions this tour, having deliberately ignored a gate because of the obvious danger, having dragged himself through a tiny gap in the hedge, getting himself scratched to bits in the process, he had found Daffney already on the other side, smirking at his efforts, having himself gone through the gate. That made him mad. And whilst Taverner and Gerson, being switched on, would follow him through the hedge, Stevenson would follow Daffney through the gate. Because he was a twat. He always had to do things for bravado, governed by what was 'flash' instead of using his head. So he stood alongside Daffney, laughing at the other three. They had only done it a couple of times, but that was twice more than was necessary. And each time they got back to Bessbrook, North had thoroughly taken them to task over it, exploding with exasperation, "Bloody hell, Sergeant, I've told you before, you'll get yourself blown up one of these days!" Whereupon Daffney, grinning mischievously and patting a big hand onto North's shoulders, would re-assure him, "All right, Terry, keep your shirt on, mate. I won't do it again if it upsets you." To which North would laugh hollowly, "It don't bloody upset me, mate. I don't give a monkey's."

The others all wanted North's job for its prestige but he held it against all comers. He was the lead scout, he had the specialist qualification; the others were GD Marines—general duty. And now it was paying off, just look how. The competition for his job and the genial abuse he had received at first, needling him to prove himself, had long fallen off as grudgingly, over the tour, they began to acknowledge his superior instincts and training. Like that time they had encountered the abandoned car on an isolated bend in the road. That had shut Stevenson up; that had definitely got him off his back. Daffney had motioned him to go forward and recce it. North had gone a little way, then stopped. Something about it didn't look right. He came back. Daffney told him to go forward again, closer. He did and he knew there was something wrong. As he neared the car he stopped and looked over his shoulder. The rest of them were nowhere to be seen, the bastards. They had all gone to cover including Daffney, expecting the big flash and bang. He had edged on a bit but the 'dangerometer' in his brain was in a state of alarm. Sod it! They made a three-field detour round that one—and wasn't he right to do so? The next day a loose horse got blown up by it. He had known all right and how he had enjoyed rubbing that one in! Before then they had been prone to 'dripping' about how he made detours for no good reason. Not a murmur after the poor old horse bought it. After that they stopped trying to make out they could do better and just let him get on with his job.

As they completed two sides of the low-lying field, North noticed in the corner of the two hedgerows a plastic fertiliser bag. He signalled it to Daffney, who immediately led the rest away from it by cutting the corner, sacrificing cover from view to keep away from a suspicious object. Stevenson took a good look at it, turning and pausing as he went past, even approaching it a little, but he couldn't make out anything that would confirm it as an explosive device. The problem was, it was in the bottom hedge of the sloping field and in the same hedge there was the trip wire by the tree stump of which they had seen a photograph. Until they found that, they were stuck between the two. They went to ground as North began to search.

Thirty metres away at the rear of the patrol, Gerson was still uncomfortably close to the bag in the corner of the field. He faced it, far enough away from it not to be killed by the explosion, he hoped, yet wondering what life would be like without a face... He pressed himself into the ground.

The ditch was shallower than the first one. North worked his way down it, groping along in amongst the wet and mud and undergrowth. He had to use the ditch because it ran next to the hedge in which the wire was meant to be. He hadn't gone far when he came to a place where the hedge was broken down, affording easy access to the next field. Gingerly, he put one foot in the bank, stepped up carefully and had a look. Sure enough, there was the stump, inviting a hand-hold by which he could pull himself up and out of the ditch ... and there, six inches away the other side of it, nice and taut, was the wire. Easy enough to spot during daylight. But at night ...

He followed the wire along its length with his eyes. It was only about six feet long and he could see the end without the charge. Carefully, he reached with his hand for the other end of it, pushing aside some undergrowth—and there it was. A thing about the size of a beer can, with a dull and jagged surface, designed to fragment so everybody got a bit when it went off. He recognised the make. A POMZ-2. Russian. 'Sorry, comrades—that'll not beat Yorkshire.' Two up to Royal.

The lead scout signalled Daffney a thumbs-up indicating he had found the wire. At the same time he motioned with an open palm and a flex of the forearm that they were to cross where the section commander was. He went back, keeping to the ditch, until he found Daffney pushing his way through the prickly barrier at ground level.

Thanks to the Russian grenade, it took them a good ten minutes to push their way through the hedge into the second field on the whale-back feature. Once through, however, they went left, away from the side with the obvious traps and lures, crawling, pressing themselves into the long, cold, wet grass, aiming for the bottom left-hand corner of the field, which sloped down into a very watery bog. For several metres at its edge, it was reedy and marshy and tall bulrushes grew, affording them cover. At a hand-signal from Daffney as they approached, they entered one by one and again adopted all-round-defence. 'This,' thought Gerson, as he sank knee-deep into freezing mud and water, 'is why the fuzz don't go leaping around the rural areas, they like to leave it to the squaddies.' He didn't blame them. An hour of this and he'd have nuts like a brass monkey's. His teeth began to chatter.

Near a tree on the hill in the South, was a man with a sack. He put down the sack and out of it, took an object. The object was a radio transmitter, the aerial of which he began to extend. Then like a gun in a hide anticipating the incoming duck, he settled down to wait.

"Stay put," the Sergeant told the rest of them, "We're gonna check it out. Steve, tell 'em we're in."

He waited for Stevenson to send the appropriate codeword to Lieutenant Shutbridge over the air, watching with an uncomfortable sense of apprehension as the signaller pressed the presser-switch and began to transmit. But there were no loud bangs from nearby—which didn't mean to say there were no radio-controlled bombs in the area, only that they weren't on that particular frequency.

Daffney crawled off, going nearest the hedge, snaking through the grass up the slope towards the crest. Abreast of him, about five metres to his right, moved North. Flat upon their bellies, they wriggled, levering themselves forwards with the flat of the forearm and the inside of the leg. Each drew his weapon with him, grasping it by the stock, taking the weight of it across one forearm. Moving in front of them was the free hand, searching the earth among the acid wet grass for the trip wires they feared to be there ... feeling for it with the fingertips ... the wet beginning to wear their fingers raw ... each move reaching forwards cannily, searching to live ... trying to tickle the wire into existence, the only guarantee of a future.

A quarter of the way up. Sweat poured from their faces inside their heavy camouflage headgear. For Daffney, a moral obligation and he knew it. His men didn't expect it of him though, he knew that too.

But it wasn't on. He could have stayed down at the bottom; the operation required only Taverner and Challice to go up, but that wasn't the way he worked. He had a thing about leaders who couldn't lead from the front. It was times like this when it counted. When the chips were down. Other times, as any old soldier knew, you could relax the rules, play around a bit and it was okay. But you could never fool the men for long. They knew. They knew what sort of a bloke you were. So when the pressure was on, you had to produce the goods ... or get found out. And if you tried flannelling, it would get remembered. Because that was why you had the stripes, drew more pay, and as a Sergeant had membership of the mess. You were tried, proven and found 'not wanting' ... it was on your documents. That was why he was crawling. Crawling up a field with his lead scout, searching for wires. Besides, for as much as he would readily trust his men with his own life, he couldn't bear the suspense of watching someone else do it ...

Terry North crawled. He was the lead scout. He had the specialist qualification. That was why he crawled. What was his superior training about if it wasn't fieldcraft, crawling and observation... and that meant doing it yourself. If anyone could find the wire it would be him. Wasn't that his job? He would show them. Just as he had done before, finding other wires, like the one last night, like the one a half-hour ago. Keeping the men alive, that was his job; that was what he drew an extra bob a week for. He wasn't going to have someone else do it, certainly not Stevenson. Stevenson would most likely blow himself up, crawling over the damn thing. Then how would he, North, feel about that? Bad. Awful. About as bad as he felt now looking for the bastard. Worse. He couldn't bear watching someone else doing his job; he would feel he was shirking it. Worst of all would be if Stevenson found it. The sneering look on his face as he said, "All right, snipes, *I* found that fucker ..." He wasn't going to have that from him. No way. North sweated; to stay alive, to find a wire, to keep a cocky youngster in his place. He crawled, he searched, sifting the grass through his fingertips. Crawl, search ... search, crawl ...

★ ★ ★

In the troop ops. room, Shutbridge sat scowling. The constant mush of the high powered radio-sets suddenly went quiet, the prelude to a transmission. They listened. The sender was whispering.

"*Hello Ten, Hello Ten ...*"

The radio operator picked up the handset and spoke into it with the standard signaller's voice; bland, clear and so utterly normal and lacking in emotion that operators in the field, knowing it to come from the secure confines of HQ, somehow found it immensely re-assuring.

"*Ten, send, over.*"

He scribbled the whispered words onto a piece of paper, acknowledged the message, then set about decoding it. Finally, he pointed to the map.

"Just there ... that's their position, Sir."

Shutbridge grunted, then got up and walked out. 'Well, don't look so bloody happy about it,' thought the signaller.

★　★　★

At the other end of the ether, crouching in the bulrushes, Stevenson switched his radio to 'mute' to cut down the sound of the mush. Then he lay on his stomach, feeling the wet nauseatingly soak into him. Nothing for it. They couldn't lie around in the open. He watched the two figures worming their way up the field without envy. The others would be going up in a bit. He was in for a boring afternoon lying in amongst the bulrushes, watching and waiting. Most of this business was watching and waiting, combatting the cold, slyly making a wet of tea to keep your spirits up, encoding and decoding, moving from A to B and sending 'locstats' to the boss. And generally having what passed for a 'good time' until you could get that bergen off your shoulders. And tip out the empty tins and the torn biscuit-wrappers and the used radio batteries and the bits of fern and grass and mud which contrived to get in amongst everything; and strip off your sodden clothes and stand under a hot shower and stop shivering. And put some clean dry clothes on and oil up your weapon and service your kit and have a can of beer down the goffer-wallah's and a game of darts and watch some television and 'phone your young bride of six months. And prepare for the next one. Always one more; not long now ... nearly cracked it ... nearly cracked it ...

Daffney's breath came in short bursts. Sweat poured down his throat into his combat-jacket. He began to move away from the left-hand hedgerow as they approached the crest, giving the telegraph pole and the pile of logs as wide a berth as possible. Feel ... search ... crawl ... heave the body over the earth. Mother earth. Crawl ... heave ... search ... crawl. Fingers raw and painful from parting the sodden grass. The smell of earth. Grey. Grey substance. Grey-brown. Little insects at the bottom of the blades of grass. Tiny twigs. Mother earth. Swallow me up. Like a whore. Grind the pelvis into the earth. Like it was a whore's pelvis. Feeling every contour. There's one for the hip bones. Another for the leg. Giving purchase to the next push, the next coital thrust, the next grunting slide forwards, flattening the grass they had minutely searched. No wire. Where was that bloody wire? No mistakes. The situation is black and white, men. This one's for real; it won't spray dye all over you which you can scrub off in the shower. This one's a different type of die. Lose concentration. Crawl over the wire. Bang! That type of die. Both of them. Claimed by Mother Earth's volcanic eruption, sprinkling the field with their intestines and spleen. Swallowing them up. Like a whore. Breath. Sweat. Nose dripping ...

"Stop!"

They paused.

"Stay there, Terry. I'm gonna take a glimp at that pile of logs."

"Eh ...?"

Inches at a time, Daffney crawled towards the logs, drawn by its evil ... He had to *know* ...

North wriggled backwards till he found a hollow. He pressed himself downwards, toes out, heels flat, flattening himself hard down into the ground. It was about twelve metres away from him; if it went up there was just a chance. Anatomy of an explosion. It would go up in a V. He hoped. And miss him. He hoped. It wouldn't Pinky though.

Daffney crawled closer, shielding his face and head with his arms against the anticipated explosion, shying from it each time he stopped to look up—grimacing—at the stack of logs. He *had* to know ... He got to within a few feet of them. The were oldish, wet, the bark peeling off some. Obviously been there for a while; grass growing up around them. Must have been stacked up in the summer. But why there? It *was*, wasn't it? It was to look innocent, to conceal a bloody great bomb, to lure the unsuspecting through that gate. He lowered his head, inching his way round the side of the heap towards the gate ... Holy Shit! It was gonna come. IT HAD TO. God Almighty. There was the command wire, just as he thought, running down the lichen-covered pole, straight into the logs. In through the long grass there. His face was only a metre away from where it went in! Right on top of it now! Jesus Christ! These things were impersonal. He was only flesh and blood. It would rip him apart. The bastard. He tried to think clearly, fighting the almost unconquerable desire to get up and run away. His heart pounded, his blood coursed, his nervous impulses twitched. To do that was certain death. Someone somewhere was watching. If they saw him, they would press the tit. It was barely conceivable he hadn't already been seen. They must have seen him crawl right up to it. What did they want him to do? Sit on top of it and wave? GO ON! BLOW IT NOW, YOU BASTARDS!. BLOW IT! I'M HERE, RIGHT BLOODY-WELL BY IT! IF YOU'RE THERE—BLOW IT! YOU'VE SEEN ME!

Quickly, he looked at the command wire, fighting the impulse to raise his head. This one was designed to catch a patrol going through the gate. But—a tiny surge of hope seeped into his brain—perhaps more from the other direction. Maybe, just maybe, their line of approach and fieldcraft had caused them not to be seen ... maybe ... 'Get out of here ...'

You couldn't help it. However carefully you tried to move away from a sitting explosive device, the impulse was to run. Daffney backed off, guts churning. He crawled swiftly away from it, gritting his teeth, clenching his buttocks. The explosion would cleave him in two, ripping right up his unprotected anus. North looked at the Sergeant's face as he crawled back towards him. It was that of a boxer who had just endured a round of sheer bloody toe-to-toe attrition. The expression on it was 'KILL'. He wanted to kill someone for putting them through this.

"That one's set up for the gate", breathed Daffney heavily. "But it'll clear anything round here. Go along a bit, we'll take a look further along."

They moved away from the gate in the corner of the field with its carefully concealed device, along the top hedgerow which, after about fifteen metres, became a mess of bushes and uncut thorn trees. This was better, this was where the close-observation party should go. Swiftly, they examined the undergrowth for signs of digging or disruption of the ground but found none. Time was getting short. Daffney motioned North to start back down, then followed him.

They crawled slowly but easily over their previous tracks, resisting the temptation to rush, bodies brushing the grass the other way, until they were down by the bulrushes once more. They were soaking, with wet, sweat, adrenalin ... It was several moments before the Sergeant could speak. He drew a huge breath and exhaled.

"Okay, Neil, off you go. Use *Terry's* path. Pick your position when you get up there as best you can ... but there's not a lot of choice. You go in next to him Les, Gerry'll cover you both from the rear. You'll all only be about fifteen, twenny metres from those logs ... which is a definite IED by the way. Can't be helped. Just concentrate on the job and forget about it. If it goes up, you're close enough not to know nothing about it. We'll pick up the bits. Soon as you've got what you need, pack up and come back down. Don't hang about, all right?"

They nodded.

Taverner crawled off, his bergen swaying with the movement of his hips. Challice followed in similar manner, imitating the Marine's movements, staring at the design on his boots as they twisted from side to side, looking ahead directly up the disruptive-pattern crutch-piece in front of him. Writhing limbs, propulsion. Elbow and leg, elbow and leg, elbow and leg ... methodical painstaking work, a far cry from collating intelligence in a nice cosy office. His thoughts became turbulent as the sweat began to run, the effort became agony. This was further than he had crawled in his life ...! Christ ... hairy-arsed Marines ... must ... must have ... special kind ... special kind of ... devotion ... to duty ... need it ... Instant ... instant Commando ... for the duration ... Christ ... knackered ... chest muscles hurt ... They'd lent him a Green Beret ... instant bootneck ... crawl, ya bastard ... crawl.

Behind him crawled Gerson, easily, with the muscular suppleness of the snake, sliding effortlessly over the surface of the earth, unencumbered by anything except his belt-order and his beloved Bren. He loved the feel of it, the precision of it, the neatness of its workmanship, and he cradled it the way a musician cradled his instrument, a gangster did his violin case.

Daffney's breathing returned to normal. He watched the three of them grinding their way up the steep slope. Two camels and a snake, headgear masking their faces. He could have sent them up straightaway with the simple admonishment "Don't bump the wire, lads," but that wasn't him. He had seen how they felt it was their job to go up, not his. They had to get into the OP to do the task, not him, and what their faces had said as he was about to crawl off was, "Don't go, Pinky, we'll do it. It's our turn. You've taken your chances in the past, there's no point in pushing your luck any more. You're the stripey, we're the blokes, we'll do it. You stay at the bottom." Which was why he had gone. To return that love. The kind of love six human beings felt for one another in a totally non-human situation. Because of that, he had gone, to at least clear a crawl-path for them. Everyone was shit-scared of explosive devices, and no-one more so than him. He had been in a dream by that pile of logs, living his own death second by second, psychologically tormented almost beyond sanity. In the half-minute he had spent by it, he had aged a complete decade, yet his blokes were going to have to stay not so far away from it for God only knew how long.

Taverner rolled his bergen off his shoulders and gently, carefully, eased himself into the undergrowth, pulling his pack after him as quietly as possible. Panting, he undid the buckles and took out the camera. Onto the front of it, he screwed a lens the size of a coffee flask. A lens of this magnification required to be rock steady, a condition unlikely to be met in the circumstances. The slightest tremor and the subject would disappear from the film. He set up the tripod and mounted the camera. The floor was soft earth, he was squatting in total discomfort surrounded by thorns, and there was a wind. Altogether the sort of studio conditions that would send a BBC floor manager into early retirement. But—the law wanted film on Our Man and that was what they were gonna get. How come they never went to these lengths on the 'Sweeney' though? It was softly bloody softly, alright.

'The film "Our Man"; camera by Marine Taverner, sound by Private Challice', thought Taverner. 'An everyday story of country folk, simple rustic terrorists who liked knocking people off ... Act one, scene one, one take only. In which Our Man, out for an afternoon stroll—if he shows up and we haven't been made to look right suckers—saunters over to the charming little hamlet of Cory, there to swop a tale or two, down a pint or two and plan a thing or two. Such as the blowing off of some luckless fucker's head with his little Armalite, generously donated to the set by Noraid-Kremlin-Gadaffi Enterprises Incorporated; parental guidance required for junior ministers of state; on release from IED Films Ltd. Now showing at your local cinema.'

He settled as comfortably as he could upon his rolled sleeping bag. Nearby, Challice lay at full length resting his mike on some stones in the bottom of the hedge, the recording machine to one side inside his bergen. They settled down to wait.

Gerson set up the Bren in rear of them. He lay behind it, looking about him slowly, wiping the sweat from his eyes and nose with a gloved finger. His breathing slowed down.

Down the bottom, Stevenson began to shiver. This bog was *cold*.

Daffney gazed vengefully at the top end of the field. He could no longer see his men ...

North sniffed.

The minutes went by. The observation party waited, motionless, looking down on the scene, heaving the odd long breath. At two o'clock, the advertised time of the rally, there were only about fifty people present. Maybe they had all joined the Peace Movement.

Eventually someone began to address the crowd.

The longest half-hour Gerry Gerson had ever spent had just dragged itself by. Dragged itself by like a wounded man. There was something about this place he knew to be wrong. He sensed it as soon as he had crawled in. As the minutes ticked by, his nerves unaccountably tautened until they were like violin strings. Danger. The logs were one thing but there was another danger around here somewhere, carrying with it an even more immediate threat of death, if that were possible. He drummed his fingers on the butt, hauling it more securely into his shoulder. Good ole Bren gun. Curved magazine. Offset sights. Lovely working parts. It was better than a guitar to a lad from the Elephant and Castle. It was what a bloke needed at a moment like this. He kept looking all round his arc, trying to 'suss out' the danger, tapping his fingers silently, brow knitted.

The Army weren't the only people to use notebooks, as the man on the hill in the South knew. He too had one. He felt in his pocket for it and drew it out, opening it at a certain page. The page listed the frequencies of four bombs in the area immediately across the border. Each one he had planted himself. There were others he knew of, such as the one by the telegraph pole over there, but that was someone else's and it was a command wire. His were all radio-controlled. The trouble was the troops kept a low-profile these days; he'd had a couple of juicy successes in the past. He knew the Tommies sometimes used the gate in that field there, which was why he had helped his friend leave a little surprise for them at the foot of the pole. That had been good fun! They had concealed it with logs and used the poles to carry the wire. Brazen, eh? Shame they hadn't fallen for it yet. But whilst they were doing that, he had found a wee thing in the bushes about half-way along the top hedge there. It was a button, a green button. An Army button. Something told him it was a good place for another little surprise. So they had dug one of *his* in this time, in the late spring, and now it was nicely overgrown.

Gerson glanced to his left. Then back to his front. Then quickly to his left again. He stared at what he saw. There, two metres away, poking up out of the withered fern was a metal blade of grass, an instrument capable of receiving a radio signal he recognised as a McGregor device. Everything about Gerson seemed to stop, held in terrifying suspense. He hardly dare breathe. It could only mean one thing. This place had been *mined* ... and they were lying on top of the *bomb!* For seconds on end he remained frozen solid, rigid with fear as he digested the enormity of his discovery. Then, slowly, he turned and glanced at the other two, their backs to him, blissfully unaware ... Christ, what to do? ... If they made a break for it they wouldn't get two yards before it blew up. Icy with apprehension, he sank back into the scrub, slipping gently backwards, pulling the Bren delicately after him, an inch at a time. He'd better tell somebody. They'd better know ...

Taverner waited. No sign of our man. He began to think what a waste it would be if those logs were to go up now, killing them all, wiping them out for a man who didn't turn up. Frittered away over a futile mission. The Corps had lost precious few in the seven years of the conflict so far; they could be counted on one hand, but each one was a brother to the rest and everyone knew the exact circumstances of every one of those deaths. One of them, Johnny Cochran, had been a close oppo. He was a good soldier. He had been engaged when he died. Saving up to get married, he had returned to Belfast with a neighbouring unit and there had been killed. Death stalked the professional Marine from the time he first walked in those gates—not that that had ever stopped anyone joining. It was part of the way of life and regarded as just a hazard of the livelihood, though that was something the public could never quite understand—why there were people who *wanted* to share those risks. For until a relative died of old age, the average person was spared the experience of death. But in the Services, Taverner mused, you learned it happened to YOU—*unless* you prevented it.

Gerson had a small pocket-phone radio inside his smock, with which to communicate with Daffney. It was switched on, at low volume, but so far they had had no need to converse. It was his job to keep Daffney abreast of any developments up top and certainly, with the discovery that they were lying on top of an explosive device, there had been one. The information must immediately be passed, therefore, to Daffney, in whose hands lay the power to abort the mission. But Gerson was afraid that to transmit over the pocket-phone might set off the bomb. He shut his eyes for a second or two before he pressed the presser-switch, every muscle tensed ...

He relaxed.

He couldn't bring himself to do it. The chances against the McGregor device having the same frequency as the pocket-phone he at first calculated to be about a million-to-one. Then he speculated that the setter probably knew the military's radio frequency range. That brought the odds down to a thousand-to-one in one go. Then he remembered that a pocket-phone was rumoured to have been lost in Belfast. They had only three fixed channels on them, so by now — that was supposed to have happened three years ago — all the bomb-setters in the entire province would know all three frequencies. The chances against the McGregor device being set on the same frequency as his pocket-phone was now only THREE TO ONE! Gerson set his face against transmitting. He just wouldn't. He felt a damn sight safer with it switched off, too. Abruptly, he reached inside his smock and turned the switch. It meant — if he was right — that Daffney could still blow up his own men by transmitting himself. Gerson tried telepathy.

'Don't call me up. Don't call me up, Pinky ... Don't call me up. Don't ... don't ... don't ... 'cos one way or another you're not going to get a reply ...'

Johnny Cochran, thought Taverner, watching the fields for Our Man. He had been killed at night, shot through the head while on mobile patrol in the Antrim Road. Those with him had told how, once they had got him to cover, they had lain him down and he had died clenching and unclenching his fists, willing his heart to go on working for him, trying desperately to pump his own blood. A typical damn bootneck, never giving up to the bitter end, determined to go out through life's front door, fighting every inch of the way. Taverner recalled their friendship. He remembered hoofing him out of bed in Cyprus and he remembered the good times together, the bars, the laughs, the girls, the monumental runs-ashore. He recalled how, in Belfast, Cochran had made him an 'egg-banjo' one night after a foot patrol which had left them all physically and emotionally drained. And how, another time, having drawn straws for the very last patrol of the tour, the Scot had said to him, "Pity, I could have done with you on this one." Which had prompted Taverner, after agonising over it, to return the compliment by changing places with a bootneck who had drawn a short straw. They had shaken hands at the end of that one, all of them. Then, sooner than go on a NATO exercise, Cochran had volunteered to go back to Belfast out of turn, with another unit. Within a month he was dead. Taverner's mind filled with resentment. What if it had been Haythorne? What if it had been

Kenny Smith? He pondered the sheer futility of pussy-footing about video-ing the sort of man who was the killer of good men like that. Mates, muckers, oppos ... Something had to be done to balance the score sheet, to justify their deaths. Something the puerile politicians at home would never know about. Something right here in 'bandit country' where the rule of law was by bomb and by bullet.

★ ★ ★

They were about to die. Actually be blown to bits. Gerson could feel it in his bones. His body was rigid; he took little short breaths. He had always envisaged going down fighting to the last in the way he had been trained. He wouldn't mind that so much, but *this* ... this wasn't dying; this was being exterminated like a rat in a trap. The damnedest part was that there was nothing he could do about it. Except tell the others; they ought to know since they were going to die too.

"Neil ..."

"*Neil*!!"

The second time Taverner turned sharply away from the fields, appalled by the urgency in Gerson's voice. The face looking at him was a mask of dread, eyes wide like moons. What the hell ...???

He followed Gerson's outstretched arm.

"It's a McGregor device ...! There ...!

Challice too was watching. Gerson saw the colour drain from Taverner's face and Challice's gaze switch between the two Marines, knowing something was disastrously wrong but not fully comprehending what.

"Turn the radio off!!" whispered Taverner.

"I have!"

"Just stay still!"

Taverner's heart was thumping. He tried to think, his breath coming in shallow waves.

"If they see us," he said, "it'll go up ... but they might not have seen us ... but if we start to pull out they will do ..."

Horrified, he turned back to the task, to the people to his front now so *normal* as to be vaguely of comfort. After a minute or two of digesting the fact that they were sitting on top of a bomb, his brain began to slow down. Taverner turned again to Gerson.

"We'll have to stop here till it's dark enough to leave without being seen ..."

"Oh Jeeze!" fretted Gerson. "If we wait that long Pinky'll try getting in touch over the *radio* ... and ya know what that can do to *this* ...!!"

Taverner looked at him. He was right. Whatever they did ... they were going to have to ... all they could do was to ... shiiit! ... He forced himself to think straight. The tension inside him was so great he felt almost remote from the situation, as though someone else were involved, he was just an onlooker ...

"I'll get the film first," he said, looking scared at Gerson who was looking scared back at him; "When I've done that we'll see about it ... if we're still around!" He tried for a smile that didn't even get off the ground.

The two of them turned away from each other. Three-quarters of an hour had elapsed from the advertised time of the rally.

Gerson moved his head very slowly, trying to watch the hill that overlooked them, staring intently at a small clump of trees he could see on it. His view was obscured by the brambles and fern into which he had instinctively shrunk more deeply upon the discovery of the McGregor device. Was there somebody up there? Was there? Looking at him? Not sure if there was anybody in this patch of scrub? Both trying to figure the other out; one with a chance to kill, the other with an equal chance of dying. Gerson's muscles were in knots. He couldn't relax and philosophically accept the outcome of the situation. The man who could would not be real. By the same token, the demand upon his mental strength, forcing himself to lie still on top of a bomb, believing that to be his best chance of survival, was nothing less than staggering. His teeth started to chatter. He clamped his jaw shut.

Taverner concentrated on his front. It was the only thing he could do. Just carry on with the job. In the century that had passed since their traumatic discovery, he was curiously aware of each thought as it occurred, as if grateful for still being able to think, magnificently conscious that in the last second he had been alive, totally disregarding the next, disregarding time altogether, the minutes on his watch-face being too long to bear thinking about. Challice had looked at him a couple of times; in search of re-assurance, he knew. The first time he tried a simple wink; the second a cheesy grin, both gestures utterly unconvincing, pathetically betraying his innermost feelings instead of masking them as he had wished. Nevertheless, from those same gestures, Challice had somehow drawn the reassurance he sought.

Tension at snapping point ...
'Come on ...'

Gerson let out a long shivering sigh ...

One hour had· passed.

He had him. One second he wasn't there, the next he breasted a small rise and was obligingly walking towards them. It was Our Man. Taverner got the camera onto him early in case he turned off, but he carried on walking a curiously circular route towards the hamlet. At this rate he would pass much closer to them than expected.

Despite the light, which was beginning to fail, the camera was managing to reproduce remarkable detail. Taverner studied the face in the viewpiece. Longish mousey hair and sideburns. A not very remarkable face, slightly fatter than in the photos—the legacy of good easy living down South, of sleeping a full eight hours without fear of a knock at the door. A diffident sort of walk ... The magnification made him seem much closer than he was. He took his eyes from the camera and looked over the top of it. Yes, good. He was still coming towards them, and this was what Special Branch wanted, they wanted to know it *was* their flipping man before he got in the car. He could make out his eyes now, and his hands. Delicate hands, not the hands of a drawer of water or hewer of wood, but those of an artist. Maybe he only killed people part time, the rest of the day was spent painting, composing music and writing books. 'Nice jacket you've got there, mate, (buttoned against the cold) jeans and sweater a bit scruffy but the jacket's definitely what Gerry would call "a nice bit o' schmutter". Who would have thought you were a killer of other human beings? (But then, what did a killer *look* like?) Say "Cheese ..." Danny boy, you're on candid camera.'

Taverner had never thought of himself as a killer either. Until this moment. When suddenly, he knew he was going to do it. How many times had they said if they were gonna go down, they'd take some bastard with them. How many times had they said, 'What I'd give to get one of those IRA bastards in my sights ...' He'd never *known* he had been as close as this to a terrorist before. You never *knew* who terrorists were. But now he did. Here was the heaven-sent opportunity to claim one back before he perished, before *all three* of them perished as they were about to any second now; ('You won't know nothing about it—we'll pick up the bits.') It was to do with his mate, Johnny Cochran; it was to do with every soldier who had perished in Ulster; but more than anything, it was to do with *taking one of those Provisional bastards out.*

'I'll kill him,' thought Taverner, 'I'll take him out! A head shot. At 100 metres. You can do it with your eyes shut. One round to stop him in his tracks before he brings about someone else's death! Drive a slot through his skull like they did to Johnny Cochran!'

His rifle lay by his side. Twenty rounds in the magazine. He had only to pick it up ...

The camera faltered. His eyes flickered onto the readied rifle ... Kill him ...

Orders, loyalties, the CO ... discipline, democracy, all that shit ... *Kill him* ...

Tarlton ... Shutbridge ... Daffney ... Johnny Cochran ... KILL HIM!

His heart beat fast with the impulse ... Slowly, he swung the camera as the man walked by.

★　★　★

Daffney kept his eyes fixed on where his men were. No movement up there. Jesus. He looked at his watch. Ten-past-three. One hour and ten minutes since H-hour. They had been up there over an hour-and-a-half. He fought the temptation to get on the blower and ask Gerson for a sitrep. It was obvious they hadn't finished but inwardly he swore. He was only human. He had nerves and weaknesses as well as strengths. He just wanted some re-assurance, that was all. Just tell me, boys, what's going on up there? The old troop stripey wants to know?

OLD? Christ, he was only thirty! He felt about fifty today, rubbing his fingers over his grizzly chin. The patrol commander's litany came to him; 'Get them in; do the job; get them out again.' Well, he had got them in. HE had got them in. All right, it was a team effort but ultimately his was the responsibility and the achievement. Now they were doing the job. His blokes. His Marines. Whom he had picked. As soon as it was over—get 'em out. GET THEM BACK. All his enormous physical and mental resources would be channelled to that one end. To make the RV with the chopper and get them out of it. Once they were aboard the chopper, it was up to the pilot. He would have done his job. He lay there, staring belligerently, impatiently at the miserable overcast sky. Come on. The light was fading. How much longer?

Stevenson and North shivered, watching their arcs.

The first drops of rain fell. That was all they needed. Thank you God, thought Daffney. So bloody much. Quite unconsciously, he found himself muttering the words of the creed.

'I believe in one God, Almighty Father,
Maker of Heaven and Earth
Maker of all things visible and invisible ...'

Everyone had their God. Protestants and Catholics, Moslems and Hindus, Arabs and Jews. So did Daffney. It said 'RC' on his dog-tags.

> *'I believe in One Lord Jesus Christ, only begotten Son of God,*
> *Born of the Father before time began*
> *God from God, Light from Light*
> *True God from True God*
> *Begotten not made ...'*

He believed. He didn't practise, but he believed. He believed privately and fervently that the Lord would take what the Lord had given and give Him half a chance He would. Pray. Pray all you like. Pray for strength, for skill, for guile, for good judgement ... But don't rely on praying. God helped those who helped themselves. Ultimately, it was down to you. But right now he was praying. Now that it hung in the balance, he was praying. Oh Christ, was he praying ...

> *'One substance with the Father*
> *and through Him all things were made.*
> *For us men and for our salvation*
> *He came down from Heaven;*
> *Was incarnate of the Virgin Mary*
> *by the power of the Holy Spirit*
> *And was made man ...'*

Man. There you have it. That's where the trouble starts. Good old Mankind. Made in his Maker's image. Possessing the same weaknesses. And quite possibly the same strengths ... 'Give me the strength, the skill, the guile, the judgement ...' prayed Daffney, 'to get these blokes out alive. If You can help a simple Sergeant, God ... if You can help me out ... in any way at all ...'

> *'For our sake under Pontius Pilate*
> *He was crucified, suffered death*
> *and was buried.*
> *The third day He rose from the dead*
> *as the scriptures had foretold;*
> *He ascended into Heaven*
> *where He is seated at the right hand of the Father.*
> *He will come again in Glory*
> *to judge the living and the dead.*
> *And His Kingdom hath no end ...*

'Sometimes you need a little help, God. You know what I mean. It

happens, doesn't it? You get yourself in a situation and ... it don't
look too promising ... you know, you can't seem to see your way out
of it and you need a helping hand. I mean, I'm a bootneck Sergeant,
I've got broad shoulders and an unbreakable back. I can hack it,
I've done the courses, but sometimes you need someone to turn to ...
and you can't let the blokes see that ... not if you're the boss, you
can't. Not when you're leading ...'

> *'I believe in the Holy Spirit*
> *The Lord and giver of life*
> *who proceeds from the Father and the Son*
> *Together with the Father and the Son*
> *He is adored and glorified*
> *He it was who spake through the prophets ...'*

'Look, I've never forgotten a word of thanks yet, have I? Once a
year at least, come Remembrance Sunday. At the Cenotaph or on
the Hoe. Stood to attention during the Two Minutes' Silence; and
when they read the roll of the poor sods who've copped it that year.
Most of whom I know. I always say a little thanks for me and my
muckers who are still around. I never forget to give You that thanks.
Do I? Every year the same. And other times too. Even during the
days when I was a bit young and godless, when life never ended and
death only happened to other people. Even then I said a word of
thanks for getting me out of the tight corners in Aden and up
country and out East and in Belfast and up the Arctic and *every*
time I jump, wherever it is. And here, this tour ...

> *'I believe in one Holy Catholic and Apostolic Church*
> *I profess one baptism for the remission of sins*
> *And I look forward to the resurrection of the dead*
> *And the life of the world to come.'*

'*Amen,*' thought Daffney. 'But not yet! The world to come ... NOT
YET! NOT WHILE THERE'S BLOOD IN MY BODY ...!'
He gripped the pocket-phone.

> *"'At the going down of the sun and in the morning*
> *We will remember them.'"*

'Don't let the sun go down on these bastards yet. Just hold it right
there while I get 'em out.'
He stopped. Something, *something* — said 'don't.'
The wind was getting up. Large drops began to splash the trees.
"Hello Two, this is One ..." he muttered. But he didn't press the
button. Clouds had collected, lowering, gloomy and pregnant with

rain, barely holding off. Somehow he sensed there was a predicament up there which he could make worse. What the hell had happened ...?

The sun had gone down ...

It was nearly dark now, dammit; why would they stay put so long? They *couldn't* be filming all *this* time.

Then he knew. He knew that the length of time was something to do with their *safety*. It was the *dark* they were after, they needed the cover of darkness to get out! There was the hill—they must've stumbled on another IED.

He strained his eyes into the twilight. And then suddenly, he saw one of them crawling down towards him.

One?? Only one?? What the Jesus ...

It was Challice. And something was so wrong, he could hardly speak.

"Where are the others?" snapped Daffney.

Challice jerked his head over his shoulder, gasping for breath.

"Coming," he heaved.

Then Gerson and Taverner arrived. They looked crucified; panting, sweating ...

"IED?"

"Sitting on the fucker ..."

"Get the film?"

Taverner nodded.

"Got him, the van he got into, the plates, everything ..."

But somehow, with the heavens suddenly cracking open upon them in a prelude to the storm, he felt it wasn't going to matter. And as the others broke out of the bulrushes, they began to crawl, following North, retracing their tracks past the Russian grenade to the elephant-grass field, the torrential downpour their staunchest ally in making good their escape.

Into the clearing swept the drenching rain, borne on a ranting wind that twisted and heaved and battered the bare branches of the trees of the countryside, buffeting the hedges and bushes that grew out of stone walls. The little group huddled close together, red torch shining on the radio in frustration, rivulets of water running down inside their cagoules, sodden Green Berets cramped on heads. The static hiss of the set rose and fell as the ten-foot aerial bowed before another squall.

"'... *Hello unknown Whisky callsign, unknown Whisky callsign* ...'"

A mile to the north of them hovered a Wessex helicopter, high up, its red tail-light flashing, watching a smaller Scout chopper below it search the fields for them with a powerful beam projected downwards. In the storm, the RAF pilot held his Wessex steady whilst below him, an Army Air Corps warrant officer turned his machine this way and that, pounded by the severe south-westerly gale, probing the ground with his incandescent 'nitesun'. His wipers made scant impression on the rain-lashed windshield. Fully preoccupied with the taxing conditions, neither pilot saw the tiny strobe-light on the ground a mile behind them to the south.

The big man squatted by the radio.

"'... *Hello unknown ROMEO callsign, unknown ROMEO callsign, this is Ten Zero Alpha ... Romeo Victor—one mile; bearing one niner zero degrees; one mile on bearing one niner zero degrees ...'"*

Exposed in the middle of the field for endless minutes, Stevenson held the strobe-light aloft to indicate the landing site, every second anticipating the sniper's bullet ...

"'*Hello TEN! Hello TEN! relay to Whisky and Romeo callsigns to come SOUTH, one mile, on bearing ONE NINER ZERO degrees for Lima Sierra ...'"*

"Come on boss, get a grip of these fly boys, will you."

Abruptly the swaying nitesun went off. The heart of each man on the ground leapt in torment, all thinking alike that the chopper had been downed. Then their mouths dropped open in speechless agony as they saw the muted red lights of the helicopters begin to disappear into the night.

Howling wind and rain stung their faces. The radio crackled incomprehensibly ...

"'... *say again, over ...'"*

"'... *you are difficult; say again SLOWLY, over ...'"*

Frustration at breaking point.

"'... *you are extremely difficult, say again slowly, over ...'"*

Rain lashing the crouching figures; headset pressed up against the big Sergeant's ear, trying to decipher a message both faint and garbled, wind screaming at him, patience tearing like calico.

"'... *TEN ZERO ALPHA, UNWORKABLE—OUT.'"*

Violently, he flung the handset and cable back into Stevenson's bergen. Nobody voiced the question but he answered it just the same, venting his spleen at the storm and the night ...

"Out of flying hours! Out of avgas! Unsuitable flying conditions! Don't like the storm! Can't get comms! Can't see a bloody strobe-light! Gotta phone their bloody wives! They're blind, deaf and fucking dumb ...! How the hell do I know? SADDLE UP AND SHAKE OUT!!"

It was twenty-six miles back through the trip-wire sewn countryside of South Armagh. They set off, North sweeping ...

★ ★ ★

'When panoramic view is nil
And dark conceals what us can kill
When frost and mist all silent glisten
To every shape and shine and shadow—listen!

'We lurk with cudgels by a tree
Then flit across the fields so free
With belt of link 'neath stars so bright
Aren't WE the terrors of the night?'

Pink-Eye Daffney
Mountain Leader 1

November 1976

THE END

CHAPTER 9

Epilogue

PLYMOUTH

Gently Smith took the tiny infant from his wife and looked down at him, experiencing the flood of emotions a father feels when he holds his first-born for the very first time.

"You," he said, "are my son and your name is Neil. You are son and heir to the Baron of Cockney du Flash and I'm gonna give you the lot. By the time you're three, you'll be wearing a three-piece suit with a gold pocket-watch and chain. And by the time you're four — you'll be smoking a cigar *so big,* it'll take a team of men with brooms just to sweep up the ash."

Then he passed the baby boy back to Gina and continued to sit by her bedside, chatting. His son was one day old.

★　★　★

The previous day he had left South Armagh with the rest of the unit, travelling first to Belfast docks. No matter how many tours of active service were behind them, the relief that poured off them as they made the boat on this occasion was nothing less than palpable. They were the first unit in seven long years to complete a tour of duty in the region without a fatality. And as the screws of the LSL began to turn and the CO addressed them all for the first time in months, they experienced a feeling that would stay with them for the rest of their lives. It was unbridled elitism and they revelled in it.

Then, high enough on euphoria alone, they sat and lounged around the ship during the night at sea, recounting the past, anticipating the future now that they had one again, laughing,

221

gossiping, boozing and burbling over one another. Beer cans pished and frothed, fizzed and clanked, piles of empties threatening to submerge the drinkers. In the teeming galley flat Haythorne and Parton held centre stage, presiding over the hugely noisy celebration of Mortar Troop's survival in general and that of a wounded mate in particular, his leg having been drilled through by an Armalite round. Away from the throng, RSM Haines, Jock Roy, Gentleman Jack and the other Senior Non-Commissioned Officers and Warrant Officers quietly looked forward to hearth and home again, whilst squashed into a corner with Smith and Taverner was Mazzi, whose particular experience it had been to have twice sheltered in his company location from IRA bombs bursting only feet above his head. Crammed into the starboard recreation space too, were Stevenson, Gerson and Dickens, all downing ale like they hadn't seen it for four months and swopping ideas on their personal futures. They thought of putting in for a draft to a place called the Falkland Islands, a small group of windswept isles and inlets in the barren South Atlantic where there were no improvised explosive devices, just a simple hardy all-weather way of life revolving around peat, sheep, kelpers and five pubs. Gerson said it was a good run, that the beauty of the place was its openness, its space, its freedom from rules and regulations. But Stevenson remained non-committal. Then he heard Dickens say the place might get invaded.

"Who by?" he asked.

"The Argies," they told him, "Could happen any time."

Stevenson sipped his beer thoughtfully. For years the islands' only regular defence force had been but a handful of Royal Marines, no more than forty in all. Now, if he happened to be one of them when it happened ...

And that settled it.

Then a mortar-trooper, his shirt soaking in beer, stood up on a table and opened his lungs:

> "'I was walking through the dockyard in a panic
> When I saw this matelot o-ld and grey ...'"

"Siddown!"
"Shuddup!"
"Fuck off!"
"Nice one!"
"Carry on, Buster!"

> "'He was carrying his kitbag and his hammick
> And this is what he had to say:'

With the collective intake of breath, bulkheads began to sag and
heave;

> *'OH I WONDER, YES I WONDER, DID THE JOSS-MAN*
> *   MAKE A BLUNDER*
> *WHEN HE MADE THIS DRAFT CHIT OUT FOR ME*
> *WELL I'VE BEEN A BARRACK STANCHION*
> *AND I'VE BEEN TO JAGO'S MANSION*
> *BUT I'VE NEVER EVER BEEN TO SEA ... OH*
> *YES I LOVE MY TIDDY-OGGY AND I LOVE MY FIGGY-DUFF*
> *AND I ALWAYS SAY GOOD MORNING TO THE CHIEF—*
> *   "***GOOD MORNING, CHIEF!***"*
> *I'VE BEEN TWENTY YEARS ASHORE*
> *BUT THERE'LL BE NONE OF THAT NO MORE*
> *'COS I'M FINALLY REPORTING TO THE FLEET—*
> *TO THE FLEET!'"*

Behind the wheel-house windows, the Chinese helmsman stared
out at the dim stern light of the fleet auxiliary ahead of him, and
thought of his next plateful of chop-suey. 'Troops vehy happy
tonight, Sir. Hoh! Vehy good, vehy good!'

> *"'THERE ONCE WAS A LAD CALLED ALADDIN*
> *   WHO HAD A MAGIC LAMP*
> *HE BOUGHT IT FROM A BOOTNECK*
> *   WHO WAS STATIONED UP THE CAMP*
> *HE BOUGHT IT FROM A BOOTNECK*
> *   TO SEE WHAT HE COULD GET*
> *SO HE RUBBED AND HE RUBBED AND HE RUBBED*
> *   AND HE RUBBED*
> *BUT HE AIN'T GOT FUCK-ALL YET! OHH ...'"*

Rivets started working loose;

> *"'AND WE'LL ALL GO BACK TO OGGY-LAND,*
> *   TO OGGY-LAND, TO OGGY-LAND*
> *AND WE'LL ALL GO BACK TO OGGY-LAND,*
> *   WHERE THEY CAN'T TELL IT FROM*
> *TISSUE PAPER*
> *TISSUE-PAPER*
> ***MARMALADE AND JAM!!'"***

★　★　★

On Thursday, 16th December, 1976, the Commando completed
a tour of internal security duty in South Armagh, bruised, battered,
burned and with a few chunks missing — but complement complete.

During its period of residence there had been no massacres of the civil population, no murders and no maimings and the crime statistics for the region reflected the overall lowest level of terrorist activity for seven years.

★   ★   ★

The night after the unit's return to Plymouth, waiters served winecup and handed round drinks from silver trays at the Officers' Mess Christmas Ball in Plumer Barracks. People were greeted in the hallway by an ebony baby elephant grasping in its trunk a balloon bearing the words 'Merry Christmas' whilst one attached to its tail wished those leaving the cloakrooms a 'Happy New Year.' Ivy, mistletoe, cotton-wool snow and holly bright with red berries abounded.

All the officers were present, the CO being congratulated by a guest upon the difficult feat of bringing his unit through a tour of duty in South Armagh without suffering a single fatality. The fact that he was the first commanding officer in seven years to be congratulated thus was some indication of the odds.

Lieutenant and Mrs. Robert Shutbridge stood in a group which included the two padres whilst all around, borne upon a flood tide of gin and rosé, the shrill conversation and shrieks of laughter of the wives and female guests rose by the octave and doubled in decibels.

"I think," one of the padres was saying, "that the whole Northern Irish thing can best be summed up in the memorable words of Lucretius: 'Tantum religio potuit suadere malorum.'" He turned towards Shutbridge. "What do you think, Robert?"

"I think," answered Shutbridge, taking his wife's glass, draining his own, proferring them both and being no Latin scholar, "You ought to get the wets in, vicar."

At which moment he felt his elbow being taken. He turned. It was Major Perrier.

"Would you and your charming lady care for a drink, Robert?"

"Well, that's awfully kind of you, Sir," replied Shutbridge, completely taken aback. "By the way, have you met my wife Claire, Sir? Claire, this is Major Perrier, the second-in-command."

The Major extended his hand.

"Neville Perrier," he gushed, oozing charm, "Absolutely delighted ..." He took their glasses and summoned a waiter.

"Now then, what are your particular poisons? Allow me to buy you a drink from the bar. I'm sure we can do better than this *frightful* winecup ..."

'Good heavens,' thought Shutbridge, 'Perhaps he might even be human after all. There's simply no accounting for what membership of a successful team does to people.'

He himself was feeling good. More than good. He was feeling so good, in fact, that before the evening was out, at about the time when the stalwarts were beginning to stay and their wives were deciding it was time for them to go, Claire Marguerite Shutbridge would find her husband more than somewhat in his cups, slumped against the wall below a reproduction of 'Napoleon Inspecting The Royal Marines Guard Aboard HMS Bellerophon, July 1815,' his red mess-jacket having ridden up behind his head, lovingly clutching the Corps Gazette in which there appeared a significant promulgation;

'PROMOTIONS: TO BE ACTING CAPTAIN: LT R M SHUTBRIDGE, 26 1 77.'

With the promotion was a secondment to the Gulf state of Oman.

Smith left the ward at the end of visiting time and feeling like a million dollars, walked down the stairs of the maternity wing, smiling and nodding at the people he passed in a manner which, elsewhere, would have got him certified. He came to the front steps of the hospital and there stood for a moment or two, turning up his collar against the cold of another miserable British winter. Then with a bound that exuded all the joy of his safe return, to freedom and fatherhood, he leapt off the steps, ran to the gate, turned left and made his way through the streets.

The 'Gibraltar Bar' was packed. Shouldering his way in, he bought a pint of beer and a box of fifty cigars from George the landlord, looking about him and greeting people as he was being served. Along the bar a bit were parked a familiar pair of shoulders. Daffney's. He was talking to his old mate, Sergeant Dodge. Smith drained half his pint and began to circulate, handing the cigars around.

"Nah, I don't care what you say," Dodge was saying, "To me, a bloke who goes adrift is a mug. It's a sign he's yeller, it's a sign he's got no guts, it's a sign he can't *hack* it no more ..."

"Oh cheers, ops," spluttered Daffney, "That's what I like about you, Nudger, you're so fuckin' loyal."

"What, to the Corps?"

"No, to me!" retorted Daffney in an aggrieved tone of voice, "That was my best run-ashore since Sing-ers! Anyway," he added confidentially, "You weren't the only person I had to beat."

"No?" replied Dodge cynically, "Who then?"

"Remember 'Jumper' Collins? Our Sar'nt-Major in Aden. He stopped off in Aussie back in '59. Ended up manager of a goldmine 'fore he came back. But I beat him."

"How?"

"'Cos I didn't get the slammer when I came back!" grinned Daffney, "He did!"

"How you didn't, to my dying day, I shall *never* know," said Dodge, disgusted. "I dunno what this Corps's coming to."

"Mind you, he was a corporal when he went ... within three years of completion-of-sentence he was a company sergeant-major!"

"Well, you won't beat *that*," said Dodge emphatically.

"Won't I?" queried Daffney lightly, "I've put in for a commission ..."

Dodge spat beer.

"You?" he gurgled, "You'll get it an' all, *you* will ...!"

"I haven't exactly got the ideal record for it, have I?" howled Daffney, hanging on to the bar, convulsed.

A cigar box appeared over his shoulder.

"Cigar, Sergeant?"

It was Smith.

"Oh ta," said Daffney, calming down and taking one. Smith moved round and offered one to his companion who accepted it appreciatively.

"Nipper?" enquired Dodge.

"Boy," said Smith.

"Mother and son doing okay?"

"Best holiday they've had."

"Congratulations."

"Cheers."

"By the way," interjected Daffney, "D'you two know each other? This is Smudge, this is Nudger. Nudger's an old pal o' mine from Aden days. Well now," he said, offering flame as the other two shook, "Whatcha gonna call him, Smudge?"

"I'll call him Nudger, if that's okay with you ..." grinned Smith.

"Nah, ya berk ..." snorted Daffney, "Whatcha gonna call your nipper?"

"Neil," answered Smith.

"Kneel?" echoed Daffney, "You gonna get him a knighthood?"

"That'll be the first thing he gets", said Smith.

They were empty. Dodge waved his glass.

"My round?" asked Daffney, "What's yours, Smudge?"

"Brahn and bitter please, Sergeant," replied the bootneck.

"Same again, Nudger?"

"Same again, Pinks," said Dodge, putting his glass on the bar.

George served. One by one, in quick even succession as befitted service by an ex-drill instructor, three full ones arrived back on the bar top. Smith sipped, topped up and set down the bottle.

Dodge raised his glass.

"Well, here's to ya, Smudge. Here's to your nipper ..."

"Yeah", said Daffney, bending his elbow, "Here's to your little boy."

"Good health," said Smith, "May the winds stay light, the seas calm and the soles never drop off your feet."

He drank, then drew on his cigar millionaire-style and puffed out a series of near-perfect smoke rings, thinking it quite the best cigar he had ever smoked in his life.